D1577077

Kicking and Screaming

Kicking and Screaming

An Oral History of Football
in England

Rogan Taylor and Andrew Ward

By arrangement with BBC Enterprises Limited

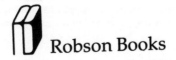 Robson Books

First published in Great Britain in 1995 by Robson Books Ltd,
Bolsover House, 5–6 Clipstone Street, London W1P 8LE

British Library Cataloguing in Publication Data
A catalogue record for this title is available from the British
Library

ISBN 0 86051 912 0

Photoset in North Wales by
Derek Doyle & Associates, Mold, Clwyd
Printed in Great Britain by
Butler & Tanner Ltd, Frome and London

To
Tom Finney, OBE

Contents

Authors' Acknowledgements

As George Hardwick, captain of England in the 1940s, reminds us in Chapter 8 of this book, 'Everything passing through the game of football was by word of mouth. The written word wasn't readily accepted, because football had existed for so many years without it.'

We have attempted to capture this oral tradition. What follows is football history told by those who were there. Our book concentrates on the events of this century, recalled by players, managers, officials and fans who witnessed them.

Our material has been drawn entirely from interviews conducted during 1993 and 1994 for the BBC television series *Kicking and Screaming*. In this book we have concentrated on providing an oral history of football in England, whereas the television series addresses a longer history and has a wider scope. We are deeply indebted to the series producer, Jean-Claude Bragard, executive producer, Tony Moss, and Alan Brown, who first proposed the idea. The interviews were conducted by Alan Brown, Harry Lansdown, Rogan Taylor and Shelley Webb. They were supported by an indefatigible team: Matthew Bowers, Barbara Brown, Will Bryant, Hilary Colter, Phil Crossley, Steve Haskett, Brenda Hollingworth, Gordon Howe, Pat Langan, Jim Nichols, Gina Seddon and Alex Thompson. We are also grateful to those who willingly gave their time to discuss particular issues. They include: David Barber, Bryon Butler, Eric Dunning, Simon Inglis, Tony Mason, Steve Wagg and John Williams.

We would also like to thank Klara Jamrich (interpreter) and Valeria Toth (translator) for help with the Hungarian material, and Penny Morgan and William Jones in Oxford.

Neither the television series nor the book would have been possible without the very generous co-operation of the interviewees. We are more than grateful to these men and women whose memories and recollections provide fascinating insights into the history of organized football in the country of its birth. Their words have been edited, and changes have been made to about 50 small details, such as names and numbers, to accord with other historical sources. The aim of this book, therefore, is to give a *feel* for the development of the professional game, and there are no better people to do that than those who were there.

1

'I used to play in the street'

Learning the Skills, Developing the Interest

Skills can be learned in the simplest of settings. Most professional footballers developed a tough, competitive nature in the streets and parks near their homes.

Pre-war Practice

Sir Stanley Matthews: In those days, every kid wanted to be a footballer, and he wanted to play for his local team, and when you were a young boy you wanted to be a dribbler. I used to practice with a little tennis ball – not a big ball because we couldn't afford a big ball in those days – and I think it improved my ball control. I used to hit it against the wall because the wall was like a partner. I didn't know at the time, of course, but this was very important and I think that's how it started.

Alice Barlow: I always seemed to be kicking, you see, because me father had the big yard down Water Lane

1

[Preston] and he had boys that came in with the horses and we were always kicking about with them. They used to make balls wi' twine and things like that. When I started work down at Dick Kerr's, we used to kick about in the back, and a gentleman saw me. I think he must have had something to do with Mr Franklin [manager of Dick Kerr's Ladies]. He saw me Dad and of course me Dad said, 'Yes' and took me up to see Mr Franklin and that's how I come to join Dick Kerr's Ladies.

Wilf Mannion: Where I come from, South Bank, we were playing across the street, with anything we could get hold of. If it wasn't a sixpenny ball it'd be a pig's bladder, anything at all. You got that morning, noon and night. You were mostly groomed for the shipyards, steelworks and blast-furnaces so if you did make the grade [at football] it would be a good way out of that circumstance. Oh, you played on any type of ground. It's a wonder you weren't a cripple. You were up and down. You were one leg shorter than the other, you know. You had to control a ball in some impossible cases. It was like playing on the waves, up and down, and you became a complete master of most situations by playing on such grounds. It was nothing else but ball, ball, ball. It was all football.

Ron Greenwood: I was brought up in the north and I used to wear clogs. You know what clogs are? Leather tops and wooden bottoms, and irons on the bottom. I used to play football all the time, in the streets, so much so that I was always in the cobblers getting new irons on my clogs because I was always wearing the irons off on the bottom. I used to go and watch Burnley play and then you'd think about things and do it. You'd just play, and sometimes you didn't have a football, you had a soft old thing that was made out of rags and things like that. There was no knowledge, like they've got now. They can look at television and they can relate to what different clubs are doing. We didn't have anything like that. We just played instinctively the way you think the ball should be played, and you scored goals or you stopped goals, and so in that respect playing in the streets taught you how to combat, how to fight for the ball, how to win the ball, what to do with the ball, how to dribble, how to shoot. It just came naturally. But now, of course, you don't see kids playing in the street, do you? You don't even see them playing with footballs in the park. It's very sad, really, because the natural progression of playing football is to do with a ball. That's all you need, a round ball.

Tom Finney: I lived on a corporation estate, and they had houses all round and a circular field and everything was played on there. It was football for virtually nine months and cricket for three months and that's where I spent most of my early days, all the time I could spare, or on the local park, and it was a question of not counting how many on each side. Many a time it was 20-a-side and you just chased after the ball and got a lot of enjoyment out of it. No goal-posts of course. You threw jackets down for goal-posts, and if it went over the jacket and you felt that it had gone in, you said, 'Well it's a goal and that's it and I'm sticking to it.' We didn't have football boots as such and when Christmas came along that was the one thing that you wanted, and you really treasured a proper pair of football boots and sat down and dubbined them and, in those days, soaked them in water till they fitted your feet; sat with a bucket and put your boot in until they really felt that they fitted you well. They were a treasured possession.

Nat Lofthouse: Oh, I used to play in the street, coats down for goals, five-a-side, and they were happy days, great days. You never thought about anything else, only having a game of football in the back street until the bobby came and shifted you. When the local bobby came, we would pick our coats up and get off the street, and if you didn't he would just give you a whack over the ear or something like that. If he missed you, he'd turn and say, 'I know your father, I'll tell him,' because he knew everybody and that's how it was done in those days.

Post-war Practice

Sir Bobby Charlton: I played every day with somebody. If you were lucky, you had a football. That was a big thing, because there weren't a lot of footballs around at that time. It was just after the war and football boots and footballs were very hard to come by and they had to last well because they were being used every day. After the war my father reared pigs. A lot of people reared pigs, so that they could give bacon to the rest of the street, and we used the pig's bladder to supplement the bladder of the football. It happened all the time. Somehow or other you had to find a football somewhere. We've been in a park, playing football on a Saturday, and had to wait until about 12 o'clock till everybody went round all the houses trying to find a football. And those matches lasted all day. You kicked off at about 10 o'clock and the teams could go up to anything like 20- or 30-a-side and people just left and joined as they needed to. At 12 o'clock there'd be a great exodus of players who went to the pub and then at about three o'clock they would all drift back again, or they went for their lunch or their tea. The only thing that stopped the game, really, was darkness. I've played there with our Jack on a Sunday. I quite often played there for seven or eight hours non-stop.

Alan Mullery: I was born in Notting Hill and when we had the six-week holiday Mum used to go to work at five o'clock in the morning and she'd come home about nine o'clock to make sure everything was okay and then she'd go out and do another job. As seven-year-olds, or eight-year-olds, we had to occupy ourselves and in those days there was no cars down the street. If a car came down the street, he was rich and if he parked the car in the street there was no wheels on the car when he left, you know, things like that. We just used to put two coats at each end of the street and just play football all day, with a tennis ball, and you'd play for five or six hours and it would end up about 103–102 in goals.

Dave Webb: I think, where I come from, you were one of three things: you either become a boxer or a footballer or a villain. I think the majority of them become villains, but I was fortunate, I had an aptitude for football, and I stuck with it. You're always taught about technical coaching and everything else, but, funnily enough, you learned your football by playing on cobblestones and putting a couple of house-bricks down as goals, and you started off with five-a-side and two hours later there's 15-a-side, and that's the way it attracted people, and that's where I'm sure a lot of the fellas in my area would have learned their way, just as a natural form of football.

Peter Marinello: I trained two nights a week at Easter Road [Edinburgh]. At that time there was a lot of semi-professional players, part-timers, who used to train Tuesday and Thursday night so they invited me to come along and join them. I was only 12 or 13 and I was really quite small, and Mr Stein thought, 'Well, this little kid can't run with these older kids' so he took me round to the back of the terrace and got the groundsman to paint imaginary goal-posts on a wall with white paint, and I just used to hammer a ball back and forth, like it was a one-two off the wall. Then he used to get me on the track and give me a ball and I just used to run round the track with a ball, and I did that two nights a week and he used to give me a little envelope in my hand. It was £4, which was an incredible lot of money. That was about 1962–63, and I did this for two or three years.

Ian Wright: I played in the street from really young, when I used to live in Brockley. Then, when we moved to the estate over in Honor Oak, there was a bit more space to play in the block. We weren't allowed to play in the block but we did and I used to play a lot of street football and then I got into a Sunday side when I was about 11, St Paul's in Deptford. Danny Wallace was there at the time and it was really good. Football was everything. Obviously there's a lot of distractions for kids now, computer games and everything – I'm even hooked on 'em so I can imagine what the kids are like – but at the time for me there was only football and cricket as recreation and everybody did it. In the summer holidays I played from as soon as the sun was up until my mum was calling me at nine at night. Without consciously knowing it, I think it might have developed my skills. I just loved playing, especially when we used to play a game called 'FA' where you'd score a goal and then you'd get through to the next round. Thinking back I got the same buzz then as I do playing an important game now. My partner was Conrad and we hardly lost. It was really good.

2

'There was only one match'

The Tradition of the Terraces

Why does football fascinate so many people? What attracts them in the first place? What was it like at the grounds during the first half of this century? Supporters' memories of those days remain vivid.

The First Time

Jack Curtis: I was a schoolboy, at a very small church school, when I saw my first game ever, and it occurred in 1925. Leicester were playing Newcastle in a Cup tie replay, and that morning the headmaster stood up after the assembly was over and said, 'Are there any boys here who would like to go to watch a football game this afternoon at Filbert Street?' and one or two of us bravely put our hands up. He said, 'If you go, I'll cane you three on each hand tomorrow morning, and I promise you that.' Well, playtime came and my pals and I had a little discussion at the back of the toilets and we decided to go. I remember the game was a good one, 1–0 to Leicester. We got in a bit late and I remember being passed down over the heads of all the popular side, as it was then, and I sat next to the pitch, almost touching the grass of this great holy of holies. Next morning at school the head had assembly and said, 'Come out here anybody who went to the match yesterday.' My colleagues and I went and we stood in front of him. 'What did I promise you?' he said. 'Right, go to my secretary, bring me Tom Tickler.' Tom Tickler was the red cane, about two feet long, and he duly flicked us three on each hand. At the end, when he'd caned the last boy, he patted us each on the head and said, 'Good game, lads, did you enjoy it?'

Maud Gascoyne: It was in 1904. I was five years old when my father took me down there [to watch Nottingham Forest] and it was such a big responsibility for him because he couldn't watch the match – I was running about all the while because I was bored. We went home and he never said anything all the way home and then he said, 'I'm not taking you any more until you get a big girl.' He didn't tell me until we got home but we tucked into our sausages and things and enjoyed those.

David Barr: There was a person who worked for us when we lived at Blewberry [in Oxfordshire] and she suddenly developed a passion for watching Reading play. She took me, with my mother's permission. She said, 'It's good for the boy to see the match.' She put me on the terraces at Elm Park and she disappeared. I watched the match with great pleasure and I never saw her, until I suddenly saw her behind the canteen, writhing, as I thought, with a man, and apparently she had a boyfriend that she could only meet at Elm Park and that's why she was so keen on taking me there to watch Reading. And that's how I started. I became bewitched by these wizards that play for Reading Football Club.

Ken Sheehan: My very first game, I think, was the fifth round of the Cup in 1937 when Millwall played Derby

County. I remember they beat Derby County 2–1 that day but I never saw the match. We got as far as the gates and there was such a crowd milling around that my father said, 'There's no way I'm taking you in there,' and we had to go home again.

Going to the Match

Jack Mellor: It was a case of getting a tram down into town [Bolton]. We used to walk from Great Moor Street which was always an enjoyment because the crowd were all surging along Manchester Road and they were absolutely solid and occasionally of course the players would be with you. I think the players used to get on the ground about three-quarters of an hour before the start and there's many a time I've walked down with team members, David Jack and Joe Smith and all that crowd. The players would always wave and have a chat while they were walking down to the ground. I always remember Joe Smith. I said to him, 'Well, how will they go on today?' 'Oh,' he said, 'I can tell you how they'll go on. I'll give you a correct score, too.' I said, 'Oh?' He said, 'Yes, none each. It's how they come off that makes the difference, but they always go on none each.' I always remember that, and I've told plenty of people since.

Alec Lodge: I lived in a village about four miles from Huddersfield, and of course in those days there were very little public transport, certainly no buses, and we had a tram service which were about two miles away and a train service about one and a half miles away. We walked to the railway station and then dismounted just up the road at a place called Deighton. I still remember the fare was tuppence, and then you came to the ground and there was hundreds of bicycles in those days. As years have gone by, Leeds Road has been widened and the gardens have got less and less, but in the old days the housekeepers could fit probably 30 or

40 bicycles in the gardens, and charge for them, which was quite a lucrative thing. And needless to say there was no danger of them being stolen. You went in and there were about four policemen outside and one at each corner of the field. And on the train we usually had a chap from the village who brought a basket containing four pigeons. He let one of the pigeons off at quarter-time with a little tag on the leg with the score, another at half-time, one at three-quarter-time and one at full-time. There was no wireless in the early 1920s and certainly no television.

Frank Leigh: They had a big wooden screen up for the scoreboard [at Blackburn]. When I got a little bit older, I used to be a runner to the Empire Pictures to telephone for the half-time scores. There were no other telephones, you see. I used to come back with the scores and they put them up on the scoreboard.

Rev Peter Smith: You liked to believe that everybody was interested, that they should be going to the match. The Match. There was only one match and that was it, and in those days people walked or went on the bus or trolley-bus and, in the olden days, the tram. They didn't all flock in cars and get in everybody's way and create parking problems. We marched shoulder to shoulder to and from, especially when it was a big crowd. It was a thing people did together.

Cyril Wilds: A man near us had a lorry and every Saturday when the Spurs were playing at home he used to put forms in the lorry and we used to go to the Spurs match. My father was a great football fan and he used to round up about 30 people for the lorry. I looked after the lorry, for which I got one shilling, which was quite a lot of money to me in those days. On the way back we always used to chalk the result of the match on the side of the lorry and everybody cheered. And near the Spurs ground was the church, right at the side, and there was always a bride, and of course there was a great shout out when the bride went past, as if to bring Spurs luck.

Harold Corns: We put our colours on and waved our flags, and we used to have rattles in those days. It was very exciting. If we won we were okay for that weekend but we'd go home and kick the cat if we lost, which we did a few times.

Rose Jales: I was born in 1916 and my father took me when I was nearly six. I had to go. The situation was that my mother worked very hard in those days, because my father didn't have a job, and she thought Saturdays should be hers to do as she wanted to. Having two girls, she said to my father, 'You take one, I take the other one. If you want to go to football, you take one of them.' He just looked at the two of us and he said, 'I'll have that one,' and that was me, because I was the noisiest. He took me and he drilled me all the way there. We used to walk from halfway down City Road, where we lived in Islington, to catch the number four bus. We used to get off at Highbury Barn and walk down, getting into the rhythm of everybody, all chanting, all singing, laughing, joking. It was one great big happy crowd walking down from Highbury Barn and all the time he'd talk about what we were gonna see, the positions of the men, giving me a little bit of an idea. I gradually began to know the players and the names. That meant I didn't need to be asked to go. I soon got interested and began to feel that I knew the players, that he should pass to him, that somebody should run down the wing with the ball, and it all clicked. I think I was born with a football brain.

Ken Sheehan: My father's side [of the family] all lived in Peckham. They were Millwall supporters and they never missed a match and very seldom missed a reserve game as well. They would mostly meet on a Friday night to talk about the match, and then they would all meet up at the same spot at the ground every week. After the match, they had a sequence, one uncle one week, another uncle another week. We would go back and have tea, which invariably was winkles and shrimps and some watercress sandwiches, and they would curse the team and swear and say they'd never go and see them again they were so bad, but the following Saturday they were there. They never missed.

Jack Curtis: It meant that on Saturday afternoon at three o'clock there was a venue. I knew it was going to be there every fortnight. I used to work in the morning, and when I was married I would do the shopping first and go down with two bags. Yes, of shopping. We all did. You went to the same spot on the terrace. You stood up. Had to do that. Couldn't afford to sit down, anyway, and you stood among people who were always standing in the same spot every week. I didn't know who they were, hadn't a clue where they lived, but at least you knew they were going to be there every week. Hello, hello, hello, hello and here we are again, sort of business. And that's what it meant. You identified with the players, like children do today. We had our champions out there. They were fighting for us and playing for us. Nowadays, of course, we encourage youngsters to buy a shirt and have the name of his champion put on the back of it. Good heavens, we couldn't even afford to buy a shirt to wear, never mind a special one with the football name on the back. Times were hard, but we were part of the team and it was somewhere to go. It was a way of life in which men found their niche because there weren't any women on the terraces in those days. It was a man's world.

Dr Sydney Woodhouse: We went in as boys around 1906 or 1907 and my recollection is that they were a pretty rough crowd at St Andrews [Birmingham] but they were an orderly crowd. They weren't a boozing, shouting crowd. They were mostly cloth cap and on the poorer side, I would say. Large crowds of working men. Of course they seemed old to us but I suppose they were mostly between the ages of about 20 and 40 then. And they went in in their thousands to Aston Villa, West Brom and St Andrews. When they got a local match they filled the ground.

Alec Lodge: In those days you came to the match and everybody had a cloth cap on. Everybody smoked, of course, and on the occasions my mother came – I came with my father – the big attraction for my mother was when it became dusk. There were no floodlights, of course, and it became dusk about four o'clock in the winter, and she used to watch all the men lighting their cigarettes and pipes. It was just like a monstrous Christmas tree, and it was so fascinating for her to watch all the lights on the other side of the field. There was also a local brass band from Mirfield. It used to walk round the field, play at each corner and at Christmas particularly it was really fascinating because they used to play carols and the people used to sing the carols. The mascot at that time was a fellow dressed like Charlie Chaplin and his main thing was that he had a bowler hat which he used to knock off. He used to go round the field, supposed to be picking this up, and his foot just caught it and kicked it a yard forward, and he'd go round the field to tremendous cheers. But people respected him and clapped him as he went past. Also, another thing, there was a little fellow who used to sell mints. I can remember him now shouting, 'Val Mints, a penny a packet,' and people used to throw pennies down from the top of the terraces and this chap would throw a packet of Val Mints back.

George Mansell: There was no place like the cowshed [at Wolverhampton]. You knew quite a lot of people there and the cowshed fellas with the cheering and the booing and telling the referee how to do it. The one main character was the herbal-cough man. He'd got a peg leg and he used to sell the old herbal cough [medicine] in there with his bowler hat on. We were playing Grimsby down there, teeming down with rain and he got the fishing rod out. They was doing all kinds of tricks in those days.

Harold Riley: The crowds actually looked very much more uniform. Men tended to dress in similar ways. You could smell body odours so much more in those crowds. You could smell tobacco and at half-time it was like looking at an illumination, all the cigarettes being lit up and smoke coming off the crowd, a scene I drew many times.

Rev Peter Smith: Well it's a religion, isn't it? I've sometimes said, rather light-heartedly, that to some extent we do the same thing. It's a drawing together of people with a common interest, a common devotion, you might say, a degree of commitment to something that people think is important. If you try to analyse it, you get in all sorts of tangles – why you're doing this and what you're really supporting – but, oh yes, it becomes quite an important part of life.

Special Occasions

John Lee: I went to the Cup Final in 1922 when they [Huddersfield Town] were at Stamford Bridge. I said to the lads, when we were going down by train, 'You won't believe me but I had a dream last night. I know you'll call me a bloody fool, but I dreamed that they shouldered Billy Smith and he went down and he rolled into the penalty area and we got a penalty.' And that is true. We put two shillings with a bookie, backed Town, and they won 1–0 by that penalty. We'd never been to London before so we had the morning just looking round, before the match, with our mouths open. We'd never seen anything like it before. Then we caught a tram up to the Stamford Bridge Ground. And we were amazed at the size of it. It was a real eye-opener.

Maud Gascoyne: When I was courting, me Dad said to

me, 'This lad that you've got, is he a Forest supporter?' And I said, 'Oh yes, he is.' So he said, 'Good, because you wouldn't have him in this house if he hadn't been.' I wanted to get married on Bank Holiday Monday, and we couldn't get married in the afternoon because my father wanted to go to the match and nothing was going to stop him going there. So I had to jiggle me plans about a bit and have it at half past ten in the morning rather than half past two in the afternoon.

Rose Jales: We only had two rooms upstairs so there weren't much room to bring any boyfriend home, but my father always used to say to me, 'You're getting on a bit now and I know you mix around with 'em. All right, you laugh and joke at the Arsenal but anybody you see outside, I wanna see 'em first, on the doorstep. Knock at the door, I'll come down and I'll have a look and I'll have a little chat and I'll find out who they support. But don't bring anybody near this door unless they support the Arsenal. They won't come over this doorstep unless they support the Arsenal.' But I met my husband on an excursion train that the railway used to run – supporters only.

Percy Harwood: I did see the Dick Kerr's Ladies game [at Goodison Park in 1920]. There was people turned away. Oh, aye, there was over 50,000 there. I don't like telling you this, but this Ladies centre-forward was nearly as good as Dixie Dean with her head. She could really head a ball. And this fella took his youngster to the match, and he's talking to the fella next to him. When the kid went home he said to his mother, 'Can you eat lady footballers, mother?' So the mother says, 'No, why?' He says, 'Well, I was at the match with me dad on Saturday and he said he wouldn't mind having a nibble at the centre-forward.'

David Barr: The sex symbol in those days [1936] was a lady called Margaret Lockwood. They ran a competition in one of the magazines for defining the word glamour, and I wrote a bogus article about Queen Mary being undoubtedly the most glamorous woman in England. I won it, of course, and the prize was lunch with Margaret Lockwood. We were meant to go down to the Gainsborough Studios and meet her at 12 o'clock. I calculated that if we met her at 12 o'clock, ate at half past 12, finished by one, I could get off to see Reading play Chester in the FA Cup round two. We went down to Gainsborough Studios and Margaret Lockwood hadn't even turned up. We hung around, and we finally met her at her flat in Dolphin Square. It was about 1.15, and it was getting a little tense. I said, 'Good afternoon, Miss Lockwood, erm, I'm so sorry that I can't stay because Reading are playing Chester,' and off I went, so I never had my lunch with Margaret Lockwood. A lot of people would blame me for being rather stupid.

3

'Billy was a grey horse'

The First Wembley Final

Wembley Stadium hosted its first FA Cup Final on 28 April 1923. The match, Bolton Wanderers against West Ham United, heralded football's arrival as a *national* game. The official attendance was 126,047 but some sources suggest that as many as 250,000 were there.

The New Ground

Harry Beattie: I was just turned 21 then and I wanted to see this marvellous new ground that would take everyone who wanted to see football into it quite comfortably, so my friend and I bought two tickets for the South Stand for this great match. I think they cost us about five shillings. The papers of course were giving it every inch of publicity they could and it was going to be an exciting day for us. In fact it was a birthday present because, in addition to the tickets for the match, we also had tickets to go to the theatre after the game.

Jack Mellor: West Ham, of course, were the local team, and it was the North versus London. Wembley had been boosted up to be the finest ground in the world and all this sort of thing and it was the first time that it had been played on. Everything pointed to a record crowd, of course, and it was.

Arriving

Dr Sydney Woodhouse: I think people got the impression that there'd be room for everybody, and it was a fine day and of course one of the clubs happened to be a London club with easy access to the ground. There were five stations around the ground, rail and underground, and between them they were pouring people in at a tremendous rate between two and three in the afternoon. So when we arrived at one of the Wembley stations we joined a solid mass of spectators moving towards the entrances. People were paying at that time. Those who had tickets were probably mostly in their seats, but thousands were arriving from the surrounds of Wembley between two and three.

Cyril Wilds: The public lavatories were about the size of a tennis-court and all those that wanted to get out were crashing with all those that wanted to get in. Then they'd run round the other side and the same would happen. Men were all over the place, to be perfectly frank, and it was very, very frightening. I was only a young boy, but I suppose it would be the same for most people. I don't remember many women being there. My father told me that when you get in the crowd you keep your hands at the side so you can protect your ribs, and always walk on your toes, otherwise you'd lose a shoe sometimes.

Frank Bishop: Being a West Hammer I was naturally delighted that they'd got in the Final and of course my mates were also naturally delighted. We hired a motor coach to get to Wembley to see the game. We got there early – I should say about two o'clock – and of course there was plenty of vacant places, but as time went on the places all got filled up. Eventually it looked as if we were chock-a-block full, then all of a sudden there was an onslaught at the back. Well, we guessed what had happened. It was evident that they must have swarmed through the gates in some way or other, climbed in or whatever, to get to see the game.

Harry Beattie: All of a sudden we saw people being rolled down over the heads of the crowd behind the goal. Youngsters mostly, I presume they were. They got put over the barrier at the bottom of the terraces. Well then, very soon, the crowd went over as well, on to the cinder track. In fact it was like waves of the sea coming in. Each wave went a little bit further. Then another wave would come and they'd go a bit further across the track and then they were right across the track. Then they were on to the green sward behind the goals.

Dr Sydney Woodhouse: A solid mass now was formed all around the stadium and we were moved towards the west end and impelled up the slope behind the west goal. We never saw the turnstiles. I think they had been quite incapable of dealing with paying spectators, and we entered the outer circuit of the ground through two large gates which were pushed inwards and would have admitted a large van. We were impelled up the west outside bank and through corridors on to the terraces, arriving perhaps two-thirds of the way up from the pitch, and now, at about quarter past two, the ground was completely filled and spectators were getting over the fence on to the pitch, earlycomers having been pushed down from above. So by three o'clock when the match should have started, the whole pitch and the surround were completely filled.

The Crowd on the Pitch

Harry Beattie: Before very long, the ground was one mass of heads. In the centre of them was a little ring – it looked a dot to us from the distance – which was the red coats of the military band. Well, the King was due to arrive before the match, and I think he arrived because the band played an anthem, and then they marched off and their place was immediately filled.

Cyril Wilds: It meant a lot to see the King and Queen because in those days the mystique was there; they didn't eat and drink, they were somehow different, and to see them go by and everybody taking their hat off. And with that great big old-fashioned Daimler with the top back. I remember thinking I could do with one of those cars in my business, because I used to do a lot of funeral work!

Harry Beattie: Although it took an hour to clear the ground enough to play the game, I think people thought, 'Well, here's the head of the country here, we must do something.' Gradually, there began to be a filter of people going out of the ground, and as we looked across, over to the North Stand, at the centre there, before long it was a flood of people going out. They were coming and going as if the sluice-gates had been opened. Well, I think the ground began to clear in the centre. I think it was due to the common sense of the people; they were there to see a football match, and they weren't going to see a match while they were on the ground, it was hallowed territory really, and I think a pressure must have built up from the centre of the ground outwards, and that increased the flood of people going out and gradually, after about an hour, they were right back to the touch-lines. In fact, it formed a human rectangle in which the play was to take place and the players came out and we got the game started. All this time, the flood of people going out was still continuing. It was that that saved it. One chap I spoke to afterwards said he'd got in for nothing, and he'd got caught up in the crowd and it rushed him into a guinea seat, one of the best seats. He thought, 'This is grand,' but within a few minutes another crowd rushed in, rushed him out and, before he knew where he was, he was outside the ground. And that sort of thing was happening to lots of people.

The White Horse

Jack Mellor: People were still pouring in and there were thousands still outside. They couldn't move one way or another, and then, of course, they brought the horses in. They started in the centre and gradually pushed and pushed until the people were right on the touch-line. They couldn't get them any further back.

Dr Sydney Woodhouse: A super on a white horse leading a posse of mounties emerged from the players' entrance, which was on the north side at the halfway point. They firmly and deliberately pushed the crowds towards the two goals and the side-lines. It took over half an hour. By about 3.40 the pitch was entirely clear but they were solid on the side-lines and behind each goal, and the match started. The match was already, of course, running three-quarters of an hour late.

Cyril Wilds: I was behind the goal. The West Ham goalkeeper was Hufton, and he was in the goal area whereas the rest of the players were cluttered in the centre of the pitch. Everybody was worried and there was one or two people he spoke to and I spoke to him. I said, 'I'm getting a bit worried with all this crowd and they're over the pitch.' He said, 'I'm worried about my' – I think he said his wife or his friends – 'that have come. I've looked up in the stand and I can't see them.' There must have been at least 5,000 people on the pitch, I should imagine, or more.

The Match

Harry Beattie: The match started, and there was a sensation after only about three or four minutes, when David Jack scored for Bolton. I think that shocked the crowd because there was no reaction other than the cheering from the Bolton people, but half an hour later, when John Smith scored for Bolton, he was given offside. That started it, because he was not offside, apparently. I couldn't tell from the distance I was at the back at the other end of ground, but all the pundits said that Smith was perfectly onside and it should have been a goal.

Jack Mellor: David Jack's father, Bob Jack, was manager of Plymouth and Bob Jack said to David, when they were stuck, when the crowd had invaded the pitch and they were waiting on it being cleared, 'Well, David, I hope that you're the first that ever gets a goal at Wembley.' He said, 'If I haven't scored in five minutes, I shall come off.' Anyhow, he scored in two minutes so it settled everybody's nerves again.

Harry Beattie: Of course, touch-lines were the human one. The ball bounced off them and went on. If it went over the top, it was a throw-in, but, otherwise, the referee got the game through. I think he did a good job under those circumstances, even if he was wrong by disallowing that goal.

Dr Sydney Woodhouse: Even corners, when taken, had to be accommodated by forming a small corridor for the kicker to take a run outside the pitch in order to swing the ball inwards.

Harry Beattie: John Smith scored in the second half and gave Bolton their win. During the game people were still going out of the ground because, after all, if you're stood on level ground you just cannot see a football pitch if there's about 10 people in front of you. They just got fed up and said, 'Well, let's go,' so they went out and that all helped to ease everything round the ground so that the presentation was able to take place, and away people went, including ourselves.

Dr Sydney Woodhouse: I never remember seeing an ambulance or seeing anybody pass out from the crowd, and the dispersal at the end of the game was quite quiet. Had there not been free access to the pitch from the bottom of the terraces, the casualties would have been colossal. I think the crowd safety was due to the behaviour of the crowd and the absence of any barrier preventing people getting on to the pitch because it was as easy to get on to the pitch as it could be today at a county cricket match, and that was the whole saving grace. Otherwise I think hundreds would have been crushed, literally hundreds.

Leaving

Cyril Wilds: I thought, 'Well, I better get back to the lorry,' but when I come outside all the roads were like Oxford Street or Piccadilly Circus. I couldn't find my way back for my life. For at least an hour I couldn't find my way back. Eventually I did, and I waited and waited and waited and nobody came. It was quite a good residential road, and a lady in the house came out and said, 'Would you like some lemonade?' This is nothing to do with football but I remember that she gave us lemonade with ice-cubes. Well, in those days to have a refrigerator ... and I can remember even to this day that I enjoyed the ice-cubes more than I enjoyed the lemonade!

Harry Beattie: When we got out, the place looked like a battlefield. Turnstiles were smashed. The entrances, which were only temporary – they hadn't finished them properly – were broken down. We wandered away quite easily, up Wembley Way to Wembley Park Station, where the police were cutting the crowd off at the base of the slope from the station. They were cutting them off in train loads, as it were, and we were lucky enough to be at the front of the queue when they were stopped, so when we got the right of way after about five minutes, up the slope we went, down on to the station, into the train and, with scarcely any waiting, we were whisked straight into London. We got to wash up and dress up and so on, and had tea, and then we went to the theatre and we enjoyed our evening there and it was the end of a perfect day really.

From the Horseman's Mouth

Glyn Lynch: When Maureen and I got married in 1957 we went to live in furnished rooms in Chislehurst, Kent, with a retired policeman who was nearly 80. Mr Palmer was the chap we lived with. And another elderly man used to come and visit. I met him once or twice and I didn't know who he was. After six or seven months I joined the police, went to training and came home one weekend after having seen an old film of a man on a white horse. I happened to mention this to Mr Palmer and he said, 'Oh yes, that's George Scorey, the old boy who comes to visit me.' Well, perhaps a week afterwards, who should be in the front garden talking to Mr Palmer but George Scorey. So of course I went to talk to him. I said, 'I understand that you worked in the Met as a policeman for years.' 'Oh yeah,' he said. 'And I understand you were at the Wembley Cup Final.' And Mr Palmer said, 'Tell him what happened that day, George.' And George laughed and said, 'Yes, it was quite comical really because I wasn't even supposed to have been there. I was walking round the West End on Billy and decided to pop into Rochester Row police station, which is not far from Scotland Yard, near Victoria, for a cup of tea, and this inspector came out and he said, "Scorey, we've got a job for you. Get up to Wembley. There's thousands of people up there watching the football game and they're becoming ugly. Get up there and sort them out." I said, "Where's Wembley, I don't even know how to get there?" So he said, "Straight up the Edgware Road for about four miles and turn left. Now get on." I said, "Well, Billy won't make it." "Get on, get up there." ' So George, who'd been looking forward to going off because he'd been on since six, was on his way to Wembley. He went up on Billy, got to the stadium and, the way he explained it to me, there were thousands of people outside the stadium that had come out. When they saw George, they shouted, 'You'd better get in there, mate, they're all over the pitch.' So that's precisely what George did. He walked through the tunnel on Billy into the crowd. And he went into the ground and started telling the people to move: 'Get over there, mate. Get back. Let these people carry on with their game. Get back.' And he just gently walked Billy into the crowds, very slowly with ever-increasing circles. Gradually the crowd drifted back towards the terraces and eventually the game started. George stayed in the ground for a time and decided after a while that as everything was now back to normal, he'd go back to where he was before, back on duty. And with that he and Billy went back to London. Now the day was very overcast, drizzly in places and really dark for photography. Even by modern standards it would have been very difficult. George didn't particularly notice that there was a cameraman there but what he did say was that when he saw the photograph, and the film later on, Billy was seen to be white. He wasn't. He was grey, and a dark grey, not a very nice colour grey. In order for Billy to be seen, the film had to be overexposed and that is why Billy became the white horse, and he wasn't white at all. Years afterwards, when I spoke to him, George Scorey still couldn't believe that it had happened to him. He wasn't remotely interested in football. And when people went to see Billy they were shocked. They didn't believe it was Billy because Billy wasn't white, Billy was a grey horse.

4

'No messing about'

The Men in Charge, 1920–46

Two of the best-known managers of the inter-war period were Herbert Chapman, who created triple-Championship-winning teams at Huddersfield Town and Arsenal, and Major Frank Buckley, who, between 1919 and 1955, managed seven Football League clubs, most notably Wolves.

Herbert Chapman of Huddersfield

Joe Walter: Three years with Bristol Rovers and then to Huddersfield Town, *the* greatest ever. What a football team! What a trainer! What a manager – Herbert Chapman. Nobody could touch us.

Alec Lodge: Well, they won the Cup, I think it was 1922, then they were Champions 1924, 1925 and 1926, then runners-up in the League 1927 and 1928 and then Cup Finalists again just after that. Well, it was fantastic. There's been nothing like it since that period of 10 years in the 1920s.

Joe Walter: Herbert Chapman was wonderful. I shall never forget him. And Jack Chaplin was a good trainer. We had a good trainer and a good manager and nothing whatever to grumble about. Herbert Chapman used to look after us, you know, tell us to behave ourselves. No messing about. No ladies! He used to tell us to cut the smoking out. He wouldn't allow us any cigarettes if he could help it, but we could have a drink at night. We always had a glass of sherry before we went to bed. Herbert Chapman had a lovely manner with him of getting you to play. You were just going out on the field and he always had a glycerine tablet to give you. I always remember that. First we put it in our mouth, get it on the field and throw it away. Going out on the field he'd just pat you on the back. He said, 'Best of luck, Joe, do your best.' He knew we knew what to do with the ball. He left it to us: 'Try to get the ball and always make use of it.' He used to say, 'Get up the wing and get the ball over, get it well over, out of the goalkeeper's reach.' I used to go up that wing and nobody could catch me. I could move then. I can't move now. Ha, ha.

Alec Lodge: Herbert Chapman brought Clem Stephenson from Aston Villa and Clem Stephenson was a schemer who could see what was going to happen before it happened. In my opinion Stephenson was one of the first to have a strategy of playing the game. He played to a system and the system was chiefly passing the ball on the turf.

Herbert Chapman of Arsenal

Jack Curtis: Arsenal came in with the idea of a stopper centre-half. Previously centre-halves were allowed to wander, and it now became a pendulum. The stopper centre-halves stayed there and then the two full-backs were like pendulums on a clock. If play was on one wing, one full-back went to take it and the other one came back to cover behind the centre-half. You had three forwards up front, two in the 'V' point of the 'W' with a lot of alternatives. One of those men had two men in front of him and one at the side. He'd got three alternatives with the ball.

George Male: If play was on my side [right-back] and I had to go forward to meet an oncoming winger or I had to come back with him, which meant that I had to be wide and therefore away from the goal area, that meant that Eddie Hapgood [left-back] would have to be covering. Mainly you'd find that Herbie Roberts [centre-half] might cover you. You might even get your wing-half, right-half in my case, come round behind me because I'd gone across towards the centre to cover the centre-half so you've got a diagonal kind of covering system. When you had contact, a lot of it went to Alex James [inside-left] and then he spread it out, but if I saw a big space and our winger going up there where their full-back wasn't covering properly, I would try and find a long ball. My favourite ball, more than playing short, was the long ball into an open space for, say, Cliff Bastin, or whoever was outside-left, or the centre-forward who'd gone away to get in front. If Jack Lambert [centre-forward] went over that way, then David Jack, inside-right, would be prepared to go into the middle and vice versa.

Denis Compton: Every position is important, but the two most important positions, I think, were what we called the two inside-forwards, inside-right and inside-left. Wingers were on the wing so that the inside-forwards had the space in which to move and we gave them the space to put it to us because we were away from them, we didn't congest the middle of the field. We didn't run at 100 miles an hour. None of that. It was 90 per cent skill.

Charles Reep: In 1933, the captain of the Arsenal came to

Royal Air Force Station, Henlow, to give a lecture. I was there, as a pilot officer, in the front row. Charles Jones was the Arsenal captain. He'd just had false teeth put in and, halfway through the lecture, he had to go behind the blackboard and put the teeth back in. I remember it now as though it was yesterday. He gave us diagrams on the board – how the long ball was used by Herbert Chapman with great purpose. In those days the ball was heavy and no player could hit it the length of the field as they can now.

Denis Compton: Herbert Chapman died very young but I remember he was a short, rotund man, a lovely man, a real gentleman but quite tough. He said, 'Always remember this is a skilful game. This is a game where you've got a football and it is that football you have got to master. You've got to be able to do everything. You can try and make the football talk.' And I've never forgotten that. The training we did was a few laps every day of the week, say, 10 laps round the ground. From there we would go on to the college, as we called it, where we used to practise and play a wonderful game, our favourite game, called head-tennis.

George Male: He had control of all the dressing-room staff, and as a manager he also had a lot to say about the box office. He would not spare himself in any way and I think this was the reason why he died as early as he did [in 1934]. I think as far as the playing side of it was concerned the directors didn't stand a chance – he was a governor. I don't know about the financial side of it, but on the playing side, he was the boss, and you knew it, even though his voice was so quiet. When he talked to you there was no bullying. He could persuade you in the quiet way he'd talk to you, and you went away and thought, 'Yeah, there's a lot in what he says.' He was keen that you got plenty of sleep, things like that. He'd take the team away for a couple of days to Brighton and you'd go in the swimming-pool and go round a golf-course. Obviously he wouldn't like you to go on Piccadilly and pick one or two floosies up!

Denis Compton: He was a very strong man but a gentleman from head to toe. I vividly remember, when I was on the groundstaff, the gloom of Highbury Stadium on the Monday after the Saturday's third-round FA Cup tie at Walsall when we lost 2–0. There was one player called Tommy Black, who, I think, Arsenal had brought from Hendon. He was brought into the side at Walsall because somebody was injured and in the second half there was a very nasty foul on one of the Walsall players. He reported to Highbury on the Monday to be told immediately, 'You're wanted by the manager.' He went up there and Herbert Chapman said to him, 'Tommy, you will never put an Arsenal shirt on ever again for what you did was disgraceful and I won't allow anything like that.'

Ted Drake: The Arsenal side was Moss, Male, Hapgood, Crayston, Roberts, Copping, Joe Hulme, David Jack, myself, James and Bastin. That wasn't a bad side, in fact it was a good side. Arsenal were the greatest club in the country, an example to everybody, right from Sir Samuel Hill-Wood, a wonderful old chap, a wonderful fella.

Peter Hill-Wood: My grandfather, Sir Samuel Hill-Wood, who was chairman from 1927 to 1949, had the highest regard for Herbert Chapman and thought he was the most outstanding man he'd met, and always said that if Herbert Chapman hadn't been a football manager he would have made an excellent Prime Minister, so I think that gives an indication of the calibre of the man. He persuaded the Underground, London Transport or whatever it was, to change the [tube station's] name from Gillespie Road to Arsenal. And I think he liked the name 'Arsenal' because it came top of the list. Arsenal was the first name when the scores were read, if we were at home, and he wanted

Arsenal to be in the forefront of everything.

Richard Chapman: I was really quite small. I would have been six at the end of the war and used to go to Arsenal, or *the* Arsenal, with my grandmother, who went there pretty well every week. We entered and saw the bust of my grandfather and, as a small child, you're slightly overawed by all of that and especially as I had to confess I was a Spurs supporter at the time. I loved the atmosphere of it. It was early post-war and it was always foggy and I can still smell the chestnuts that they used to roast outside. Now it's hot dogs and other things that don't smell as nice as chestnuts.

Major Buckley

Harold Corns: One particular time we [Wolves] were doing fairly badly. The crowd were very frustrated match after match. It came to the Chelsea match at the end of the season [1927–28] and we lost. The crowd got so frustrated that they invaded the pitch after the game, and pulled up the goal stumps at the South Bank end. I didn't participate in that activity but from then on Major Buckley must have got his finger out, and we sailed away and we didn't look back the following season.

Stan Cullis: I soon realized that Major Buckley was one out of the top drawer. He didn't suffer fools gladly, and he was a manager who knew exactly what he was doing, and where he was going. His style of managership in football was very similar to his attitude in the army because you didn't try any tricks on Major Buckley. He had a style of his own. Major Buckley implanted into my mind the direct method of playing which did away with close interpassing and square-ball play. If you didn't like his style you'd very soon be on your bicycle to another club. He didn't like defenders overelaborating in their defensive positions. Their job, he maintained, was to get the ball to the forwards as quickly as possible. Major Buckley also knew how to deal with the press. When it appeared in all the newspapers that the Wolves were using a monkey-gland treatment, you would have thought it was one of the most marvellous things that had appeared in professional football. It was purely Major Buckley's idea of getting the headlines. I think, on reflection afterwards, that we'd had an anti-flu injection and he'd managed to transfer it to the press as being 'the monkey-gland treatment', which was something that none of the other clubs had.

Tommy Lawton: Well, when we [Everton] went to Wolves [in the League] we knew they were on these pills, and when we went in I saw Stan Cullis. I'd met him through being in the England side. 'Hello, Stan,' I said, and he walked past me with glazed eyes. There's no question they were on these monkeys' pills, they definitely were, and after they'd licked us 7–0 I was sure they were. This was our Championship season. It was heavy going, and they came off the park and they hadn't raised a sweat. The only wet on the jerseys and on the shorts was from the rain, without any question at all. At half-time we were 5–0 down and Jock Thomson, who was our non-playing captain for Everton in those days, said, 'Never mind, lads. They've got five but they're playing with the wind.' So little Stevie [Alex Stevenson] said, 'Some wind!'

TG Jones: When we [Everton] played Wolves [in the FA Cup], it was beautiful end-of-the-season weather and you needed short studs because the old leather studs would break and come through your boots. Anyway, we went down by coach to Wolverhampton, from Harrogate, and when we got there the ground was a sea of mud. Well, there'd been no rain for ages but they'd flooded the ground until Saturday morning. We were on our bottoms more than we were on our feet, to be quite honest.

Stan Cullis: Major Buckley used to flood the pitch nearly every home game, because he was convinced that he had a team of players who could play better on a heavy pitch. Everton arrived at Wolverhampton and found water lying on top of the pitch and yet we hadn't seen any rain for over a week. On the morning of the match the Everton manager sent the trainer down to Molineux to have a look round and when he got down and walked out on to the pitch he was absolutely horrified. He hastily ran back to the hotel where the Everton team were staying to tell the Everton manager, so he was told to go back and find out where they changed the players' boots, because in those days the players would have a stud and then they would implement another stud on top if it was a heavy ground. The trainer was deputed to go down and put another piece of leather on the boots. But when he asked the secretary of the Wolves who had the key of the boot-room, the secretary said he didn't know. The trainer went to the groundsman, and he asked him where the key was. He didn't know. I don't know how many people he asked, until he finally ended up in Major Buckley's office. He asked Major Buckley for the key to the boot-room, and eventually Major Buckley gave him this key, after this fella had practically gone on his knees to ask for it. After that, Everton had the rule changed so that clubs would not be able to water the pitch during a period of the season.

Billy Wright: He was an army major and very disciplined. Don't forget I was only young at the time, 14 or 15, but I know that in the Waterloo Road stand at Molineux there was a passage, and the Major used to wear plus fours and brogue shoes, and I guarantee that if we heard him come down that passage with his brogue shoes, 90 per cent of the groundstaff ran. I went down in the dungeon, boiler-room or boot-room. He was a great disciplinarian. We played a match against Dewsbury in Yorkshire and they had one or two Man United players and we lost 6–1. The next day the Major got us all in the dressing-room, and went through each individual player, telling us what our good points were and what our bad points were. I was outside-right, and he came to me and said, 'Bill, change step for me.' I didn't know what the heck changing step was, because I hadn't been in the army, I was too young. And he showed me what to do, and of course I went for it and fell right on me face. 'Cor,' he said. 'No wonder you can't play football. Do you go dancing?' I was fifteen. 'No, Sir,' I said, 'I don't go dancing.' 'Tell you what,' he said. 'You start to go dancing. Go to the Civic in Wolverhampton, learn the waltz, do the foxtrot, so you learn to balance on your feet.' And he was absolutely right because when you learn to dance, you're on the balls of your feet and you keep your balance.

Jackie Sewell: Oh, Major Buckley was a great man. He was a very frightening man, his whole character. I've seen him make grown men have tears in their eyes. I was only 16½ myself at the time, and I always said to myself, 'If he ever talks like that to me, I'm going home, I'm not coming back.' If you played bad, he used to turn round and say, 'Go and get a job,' or 'Whatever job you're doing, forget about football, go back to it.' The first trial game I played [at Notts County], we were getting beat at Rolls Royce, about 3–0 at half-time. He changed the whole team round himself and we won 4–3 and I think it was because we were petrified what would happen if we got beat. But when you were doing the job for him, he'd give you the earth and he'd look after you very well.

John Charles: At that time, the manager was a manager, he wasn't a coach, and sometimes he used to sit in the stand and direct from the stand. I remember we [the Leeds United players] trained on the big ground one day and we were running round in twos and all of a sudden there's a big 'Stop!' and everybody stopped. He said, 'Now, face your partner.' I was with a little fella, Harold Williams, and Major Buckley said, 'Take your partner by the hand, put your other hand round his waist and now begin', and all of a sudden the music started playing, and he started saying, 'One, two, three, one, two, three.' Now, you can imagine me, I'm 6ft 2in and this fella is 5ft 2in, and we are dancing across the field and he's shouting like hell, 'You're not doing that right, it's just one two three, one two three.' It was to get rhythm, to get movement. He was amazing actually, the ideas that he used to have. I'll tell you the story of when we went to play Manchester United. It was a cold January day [27 January 1951] – we were in the Second Division then – and we got into the dressing-room and there were six bottles of whisky on the table, so we thought, 'Oh, we're going to have a party.' 'Right,' he said. 'Jump on the table.' He rubbed every player down with this whisky – he done it himself – and we got beat 4–0. And I remember coming in after the match and he's standing at the door and he said, 'What a waste of bloody whisky!'

5

'More or less like slaves'

The Player's Work, 1920–60

Until the 1960s, Football League rules stipulated a maximum wage and a one-year 'retain-and-transfer' system. Most players were grateful for better-than-average wages, but some of them wondered where all the gate money was going. In fact, some of a club's expenses were specific to the era – entertainment tax, the purchase of training grounds and club houses, and large playing staffs.

Wages

Len Shackleton: Dougie Wright, the wing-half-back, lived near us in Gosforth and we used to walk down to Newcastle every Saturday morning we had a home game. We'd go past St James's Park and they're queuing up at 10 o'clock in a morning. We're averaging about 56,000 and they're queuing up there and I said to Doug, 'It's not right, this, you know. There's people queuing up at 10 in the morning and they're paying us a tenner!' Money didn't motivate me, and it still doesn't, but it was absolutely wrong.

Tommy Lawton: Well, we accepted it. We had 'Yes, Sir,' 'No, Sir,' 'Three bags full.' It was good money in those days, when you think that pitmen were only getting 30 bob a week when they were working. My mother worked in the weaving sheds, working six looms for 30 bob a week. When you were getting £6 and £7 and £8 a week it was a fortune, and when you got £2 bonus on top of that it was nearly £10 a week. That was marvellous. Oh yes, we knew our status, so we kept it there.

Charlie Mitten: I walked off the field with Stan Matthews [after the 1948 Cup Final]. He said, 'Look at that, Charlie? A silver medal and we get no money.' But we never gave much thought to the money side. I said, 'Yes, I believe the band get more than us, Stan.' 'Yeah,' he said. 'Bloody disgrace, isn't it?' I said, 'They must have played better than us, that's why?' Anyway, it was all a bit of a joke and a laugh.

One-year Contracts

George Hardwick: At the end of every season it was the wail all round the dressing-room: 'I wonder what I'll get next season?' 'I wonder what they'll offer me for next season now?' 'Am I going to be retained or are they going to kick me out?' And especially with the young players. They used to suffer an awful lot with the worry of being kicked out and no future ahead for them. There wasn't anything you could do about it. You were truly slaves. At the end of every season, your contract was reviewed and if you hadn't had a very successful season it wasn't unusual for your salary to be reduced from £8 to £6 or from £12 to £10.

Norah Ball: You didn't know whether you were going to be signed on or not. It just depended on how well you'd played, you see. If you'd had an off-game or two, well, you were wondering whether you were going to be signed on again. The contracts were only for the season. It was very insecure.

Sir Stanley Matthews: Before the war, and also just after the war, you would get a letter saying 'Stoke City', and addressed to you: 'Dear Mr Matthews, we've decided to retain you for the following year, your wage is so-and-so.' Or they say, 'We are sorry you are on offer for a free transfer.' We had no say. We were more or less like slaves in those days. I asked for a transfer one year before the war. I was turned down, so the club held you. You were tied. You couldn't do anything about it.

Tom Finney: The retained players were called in one by one and it would be something on the lines of 'Well, you've had a good season and we're offering you the same terms as last season, sign here,' and he would sign a blank form and they would fill the terms in after.

Johnny Haynes: I went to see Frank Osborne, the manager, in 1959, and he said, 'Fine, John, you're obviously on £20 in the winter and £17 in the summer.' My mate Maurice Cook, our centre-forward, goes in, and Frank says to him, 'You've had a good season, we'll give you £18 in the season and £15 in the summer.' He said, 'I'm not happy about that, Frank. Johnny's just been in, and he's on 20 and 17.' Frank said, 'Yeah, but he's captain of the team and an England international and, to be honest, he's a better player than you.' So Maurice says, 'Not in the summer, he's not.'

Looking for a Transfer

TG Jones: Well I had no situation at all. I know that Matt Busby wanted me at Manchester United. I know that Tom Whittaker wanted me at the Arsenal. I'd been told this from good sources and one of them – I won't mention who it was

– came to me and said, 'Tom, you're wasting your time. You're on the transfer list but they won't transfer you. They've put you on the transfer list to make you happy, and that's where you're going to stay.' I asked to see the board of directors and I met them. I explained the position to them. I was 30 or 31 then and I couldn't afford to be playing in the reserve side. In fact on some Saturdays I played for Hawarden Grammar School Old Boys. And I was captain of Wales. Incredible but true. They never missed me at Everton. They didn't even ask where I'd gone. I said, 'Well, if you won't let me go, I'm afraid that I will walk out and play non-League football,' because I'd already had a business offer from the men who ran the Pwllheli Football Club, an ambitious little club. It was not what I wanted, but it's what I was forced to accept. Their attitude was 'No one leaves Everton.' And I did. I walked out. It cost them a lot of money. I like to think it cost them a place in the First Division the next season [1950–51].

Tommy Lawton: I'd got into the England side as a young lad and I saw the lights of London and heard what the other lads had said about what it was like in London. You listen to the other players about clubs like Arsenal. 'Oh, that sounds all right to me.' So when I went back after an international I gave it a couple of days, then I said to Harry Cooke, the trainer, 'Could I see the governor, Harry?' 'What for?' he said, because you'd got to make an appointment to see the boss. Theo Kelly was the secretary-manager. I said, 'You know, it's personal really.' So he got on the phone. Theo was upstairs and even in those days we had a lift from the dressing-rooms up to the office. Harry gets on the phone: 'Lawton wants to see you, Mr Kelly.' 'What's he want?' 'I don't know, he just says he wants to see you.' 'Right, send him up in 10 minutes, and make sure it is 10 minutes, Harry.' Ten minutes, on the dot, I knocked on the door, opened the door and walked in. 'STOP.' I'd just got inside the door. 'STOP.' I looked round the door and there's Theo.

A big long room and he's right at the bottom sat behind his desk with his papers. 'Go back outside, close the door and when you knock you will hear "Come in" and when you come in stand on that mat and wait until you're told to come in front of me.' I said, 'Right, yes, yes,' closed the door, knocked on the door. 'Come in.' Stood on the mat. 'Come forward.' I closed the door and went up. 'What do you want?' I said, 'Er, well, Mr Kelly, I've come, you know … I want a transfer, to be honest. I want to get out.' He puts his glasses on and looks at me. He says, 'You what? You want a transfer? I've been trying to give you away for these last four months. You want a transfer? I know where you've come from. There's the door, open it, close it quietly, press the bell, get into the lift, go downstairs, go and do your training this morning, come back this afternoon and do your training this afternoon, and do the same the rest of the week. Don't waste my time.' I felt that big. Taught me a lesson. I thought, 'Well, how lucky I am.' That was it.

Transferred

Jackie Sewell: I was picked to go on tour [with England] to Australia, and in the process of that I was transferred from Notts County for a world record transfer over to Sheffield Wednesday [in March 1951]. Now that was a frightening thing because I couldn't find Tommy Lawton to talk to. When you're a young bloke you don't know anything about this, and you get directors hammering at you. I think I went to the Victoria Hotel in Nottingham about midday on a Thursday with Eric Taylor from Sheffield Wednesday, and I told the directors, 'I'm not going, I don't want to, I'm going home, I don't want to know.' 'Oh, you must, you must go and talk to him.' It finished up eight o'clock at night before I signed on. It was a deadline for transfers, and they'd sent Eric Houghton, my manager, over to Stoke with the third team, got him out of the way, and they're on to me: 'Do the club a good turn, it's better for yourself,' and they hammered at me. And I said,

'Right, if you don't want me, I might as well leave you', and just as I'd done that, walking down the stairs at this hotel, here's Eric dashing in. I said, 'You've just missed me, missed it by five minutes, I've just been signed off.' I hadn't got a clue, I didn't know that some of the directors were in trouble and needed money. I got my signing-on fee and I think it was about 20 quid at that time, but they didn't tell me it was a record transfer fee. My landlady shouted at me the next morning, 'What have you done?' and here I was, headlines all over all the daily press as a record transfer fee, and I thought, 'Oh, I feel sick.' I went down to Meadow Lane, and they were all looking at me. I said, 'What's going off?' and then I went and found Tommy, and at lunch-time I think it was the first time I got tiddly. He was giving me cherry brandy to keep me calm, and he told me, 'Look, kid, they've spent all this money because of what you can do on the football field. Don't worry about it, just go out and carry on as you have been.'

John Charles: We went up into the room [at the Queen's Hotel] to meet Mr Umberto Agnelli, the chairman of Juventus, and we talked and the deal was done [April 1957]. He put the cheque on the table and when he turned back the cheque had gone and the two [Leeds United] directors had disappeared! With the cheque! They didn't even say goodbye to me. At the time I thought it was funny, but it wasn't really. I went to Italy for the money. That was the sole reason. But I liked Italy. I thought it was great and the people were wonderful and I had an enjoyable six years at Juventus. Well, the thing is that the signing-on fee at that time was, I think, £10,000 for two years. The wages were only £18 a week actually, but the bonuses could have been £200, £300, £400, up to £1,000. It all depended on which team you played against. The players here were getting £18 a week, and over there I was getting £18 a week but I was getting bonuses and a signing-on fee.

Derek Dougan: We played against Newcastle and I was called into the manager's office, a manager called Freddie Cox. He said, 'The football club [Portsmouth] is really struggling for money and you're the only one we can sell', because all of the other guys were all ageing footballers who'd been part of the double Championship-winning team in '47–48 and '48–49. I did feel like I was a prize animal. Here we are, we're struggling for money and it's a bit like: 'What assets can we sell? Let's go and get Dougan and go to Blackburn Rovers.'

Training and Coaching

Nat Lofthouse: Years ago, the ball never played a part as far as training was concerned. It was just lapping round the ground for about half an hour, three-quarters. You'd do, I don't know, 30 or 40 laps, then you'd come and do bodywork with heavy medicine-balls and weights, then limbering exercises.

George Hardwick: [Middlesbrough trainer] Charlie Cole's argument was that come Saturday you'd be busting your sides to get at the ball. That was his theory. Naturally, as a footballer, you want to be playing with a football. That was our theory. Old Coley used to go mad if we pinched a ball and went out on the pitch. He was running around from one to another. We kept the ball flowing, you see, and he was trying to get this ball back. We'd keep it rolling until he was shattered and gave in and left us.

Sir Stanley Matthews: They used to say, 'Well, if you have too much ball, you're gonna be tired on the Saturday.' Of course you had those leather balls. Mud and water put an extra 3½ or 3 lbs on the ball. If it was a very sludgy, muddy ground, they'd play with a Tugite ball because it wouldn't gather the mud. And of course we had those very big toe-capped boots. They used to last you for two years.

TG Jones: We had no coaches or anything like that. We had a wonderful old chap as a trainer, a fella named Harry Cooke, but he never discussed football very much with us. He was simply a man who looked after the gear and saw everything was all right. As regards coaching, it was done from player to player. The young players took notice of what the old players had to say, and I still believe that's the best way of learning about the game. We had no manager as such. The so-called manager, a man named Theo Kelly, was really a secretary and not a manager. The players used to manage themselves. I mean, Dixie Dean was still at the club, a fearsome man to we young people, and Charlie Gee, England international centre-half, and Tommy White, another England international centre-half. Players like that. Whenever we called a meeting – we didn't have them very often, to be quite honest – it was all discussed then, or if you were on the ball they'd be telling you what to do. It was the players who coached each other, as I remember it, and throughout the ages I haven't seen anything to beat that system.

Sir Stanley Matthews: When I was with Blackpool, Joe Smith was our manager. He was very clever. He used to say to us, 'I can't tell you what happens when you go on the field, it's entirely left with you lot. What I want to tell you, you've got to work hard and give everything on that field.' He'd come in the dressing-room and say, 'Oh, boys, get two goals before half-time so I can enjoy my cigar.'

Tommy Lawton: Oh, team talks? They just said, 'Well, you know what to do, don't ya?' You'd say, 'Yeah.' 'Well, don't forget now, you've got the same shirt, you've got the same shorts and you've got the same stockings. Pass the ball to them. That's all you've got to do.' That was the team talk. And off we went.

On the Groundstaff

Alan Mullery: The general manager of Fulham was a guy called Frank Osborne, who was a lovely man, and he said to me, 'Do you wanna join the groundstaff or do you want to go to the city and work for two years and study something and then come back and be a professional footballer if you're good enough?' I didn't have a clue what you did as a groundstaff boy. I looked at my dad and I said, 'I want to be around the players and learn the game, so I wanna be a groundstaff boy.' He [Frank Osborne] said, 'Fine. Great. Go outside, see the groundsman and he'll give you some kit.' The old man walked up Finlay Street and off he went and I had become a groundstaff boy. It was a Thursday. I walked out on to the pitch and the players were playing a five-a-side over the far side from Fulham, over by the river, and the groundsman was cutting the grass for the Saturday match. It was a guy called Albert Purdy. I always remember him. I walked over and I said, 'I'm a new groundstaff boy, what do I do?' I got some kit, got some old rags on, a torn tracksuit, whatever, and he said, 'Find yourself a cardboard box and pick up all this paper that I haven't picked up so that I can cut the grass.' All the other part of the ground, other than one quarter, had paper blowing off the Thames and off the terraces on to the pitch, so I went picking up crisp paper and putting it in the box. We had a big South African goalkeeper called Ken Hewkins. He was about 6ft 4in, a real wild man (as I found out in years to come), and as I walked into the middle of this five-a-side, picking up the paper, he said, 'Son, get off the pitch, we're playing,' so I went and walked over to the side. As the groundsman came down cutting that bit of the pitch, he said, 'What are you doing?' I said, 'Well, that chap over there has just told me to get off.' He said, 'Get back in there and get the paper,' so I went back in and big Hewkins came and said, 'Son, get off this pitch, we're playing, wait till we've finished.' I said, 'Well, the groundsman's telling me.' He said, 'Who?' I said, 'The groundsman.' So as the groundsman came back again he walked straight up to the groundsman and hit him straight on the chin! And he knocked the groundsman out and the mower was going all over the pitch and I chased after this mower. I'd never seen a mower in my life – we never had any grass where we lived, it was only concrete – and I was sort of cutting the ground in a zigzag formation as the old groundsman was laying on the floor. That was the first 15 minutes I was at Fulham. I thought, 'Dad, I want you to come back, I don't want to stay.' The second day was even more exciting. I was given another job. I worked with a little guy. I remember his name – Jack Gordon. I can see him now, he was about 5ft 2in, had a cigarette in the side of his mouth, peak cap. I said, 'I've been assigned to you.' He said, 'Fine. Let's get underneath the stand.' So we went underneath the stand with a wheelbarrow and two shovels and a tin. I didn't know what was in the tin. He said, 'Right, if you see any buns, pick up these buns,' so I said, 'Okay.' I picked up these buns, and he got an old knife and he spread something like mustard on this bun, you see, and he put it down by the little kiosk there and said, 'Right, we're gonna have a cup of tea now', so we went into the shed, had a cup of tea and I said, 'Excuse me, what are we doing?' 'Oh,' he said, 'You'll see before long.' We went out and there was all these rats waddling around as if they were drunk. He picked up a spade and he smashed this spade on this rat and squashed it. He shovelled it up, put it in the wheelbarrow. He said, 'Right, it's your turn now,' and that was my second day at Fulham, the start of a great time.

Restrictions

Reg Smith: When I was at Millwall there were certain regulations which everybody had to follow. One of them was that you must never be late for training, and the book had to be signed at 10 o'clock in the morning. Another was that you had to be in bed by 10 o'clock every Friday night. They used to send the trainer or the assistant trainer round. Two or three times in that period there was a knock on the door. 'Mr Smith in?' 'Oh, yes, he's in bed.' 'Oh, well, we'd like to see him.' The trainer would come in, have a look, say, 'Hello, Reg,' and be quite satisfied.

Anne Savage: They couldn't move a finger without the club had to know where they were and what they were doing. When they signed a player, I think they thought he played better if he went to bed and if he didn't associate with women, and didn't drink, didn't smoke. Ted didn't smoke and he didn't drink. Very, very strict. They had them like boys, little tiny boys. They lived in Arkles Road, Liverpool, and there was three first-team players in the one little terrace house. You can't believe it, can you? And they paid 30 shillings a week, full board, and she was quite a nice lady. We used to go up on a Sunday to tea and they'd got a billiard table and they played billiards. It was all clean fun.

Injuries

Zilwood March: I'm 101 in October [1992], and I played for Brighton for about four years and Portsmouth one. My worst memory? Well, getting knocked out and going completely blank. I woke up in the dressing-room, dressed and ready to go home. We were playing Plymouth Argyle in the League, and we were the top two, you see. And either one or the other had to win to win the League, and Moses Russell, I don't care if he's alive and hears me, he butted me in the mouth, that's the whole rubber. Next thing I was in the dressing-room, dressed up to me waistcoat. (We wore waistcoats in those days.) Well, it was the end of my career. It was in 1922, and I would be 30 then so I was getting on. I thought to myself, 'I can earn my living better than this.'

Tom Finney: I think it happened a lot in my day that

outstanding players were asked to play when they weren't fit and I suppose really the decision should rest entirely with the player. I've got to confess that I fell for that on several occasions, had injections, and probably didn't do myself any good by playing before I was 100 per cent fit. The trainer would watch you run round and say, 'Well, you're going fairly well, it doesn't look as though there's anything wrong.' I said, 'Yeah, but I can feel that if I want to go that extra yard it's gonna go.' I got through a game but I wasn't doing the injury any good and consequently it put you back another two or three weeks.

Anne Savage: He [Ted Savage] was the type of man, and there were quite a few men like that, they don't want to know they're injured. They won't accept it, so he didn't apply for any pension or anything like that, but he finished his career as a footballer. He couldn't run any more and he was told he'd have arthritis in that leg as long as he lived, and that leg used to go black up to the knee and he had very bad sleepless nights with it. But he never complained. He did try to get work and no one offered him a job, and I was very, very angry about that because quite a few of the men came back, the footballers of the day, and they were in the same position.

Norah Ball: When he [Jack Ball] finished at Luton, he injured his foot and couldn't play properly any more and they didn't give a damn. If you finished football, you finished, and that was it. He was very bitter, but he never used to say a lot. He was a mild-tempered bloke. He just said, 'Well, you've got to make the best of it, lass.' That was him. When they had a post-mortem on his body (because he dropped dead), every part of his body was worn out through football. It just shows what a toll it takes on people, doesn't it?

Out of Hours

Nat Lofthouse: A paint company asked me if I would go round selling paint brushes. We used to train from 10 o'clock in the morning till 12.30 or one o'clock and I'd got the afternoon spare so this gentleman, a paint manufacturer, and I used to go round selling paint. I'd no idea about it, but the guy must have thought, 'Nat Lofthouse selling my product, all right, it will sell.' Sometimes it did.

Tom Finney: It was a very short career and the bulk of the players in those days finished up as either publicans or in a sports shop or of course stayed in the game as trainers, so it was looked upon as not a very good career to go into. When I came out of the forces in '46 I was 24 years of age so I'd really lost six years of my playing career. Prior to coming out I was in Italy and I corresponded with my brother Joe, who was in Burma, and we decided that we were going to have a crack at going into business together as plumbers and electricians. My brother was a qualified electrician and we started up in 1946. I did my training with Preston North End in the morning but, before coming to training at 10, I went to the workshop and did a little bit down at the office. In those days you'd finished training by one o'clock and of course invariably I went back and worked as a plumber in the afternoon. All the spare time I had away from football was spent mainly going down to the workshop in the afternoons and continuing in the plumbing business. I do remember when Alan Hardaker had just been appointed as assistant secretary to Mr Howarth at the Football League, and I think his place was at Longton, just outside Preston. To me it was just a Mr Hardaker ringing up to say he had an emergency and I think he wanted a new sink unit fitting in or something, and it happened this time that I turned out and actually fitted it, as well as giving an estimate, and I think that's why he was quite surprised.

Eric Houghton: Pongo Waring [of Aston Villa] was a very good player, a natural, but he was unpredictable. He came from Tranmere Rovers, and the club wanted to make him feel at home. They got him a nice little house near the ground. The secretary thought he'd go round – we didn't have a manager in those days – a day or two later to see how things were going, and he knocked at the door and Pongo asked him in, and he went into what he thought was the front room. Pongo had got some chickens in a chicken coop. He'd got no furniture in the front room. He'd got a couple of chairs and a table in the back room and in the front room he'd got a chicken coop. He was unpredictable was old Pongo, but he could play, he could play.

George Hardwick: As a little source of income we used to organize local dances and sell tickets for them. They were very popular with the local girls, particularly, and it was one little source of revenue which we couldn't possibly have via the football club, and it was legal. The Football League or Football Association couldn't jump down our throats and say, 'That's it, you're suspended for life,' or whatever. It was a little bit of enterprise on our part, and it worked very well.

Commercial Deals

Denis Compton: I was approached [about Brylcreem] in 1947 by Beecham's and I must say I had a wonderfully close relationship with them. It was marvellous. I never regretted it. I used it and it was on the posters and in the tubes and buses and all that sort of thing. The wind used to blow my hair all over the place and I didn't mind and of course because of that and because I always had an unruly head of hair, the crowd would say, 'Compo, where's your Brylcreem?' and that was a big asset to the advertisement of the product. I had fun though, and I never got embarrassed about it and even today I hear it from a few of the old boys:

'Oh, you're the chap who used to use Brylcreem, aren't you, the old Brylcreem ads?' I say, 'That's right.'

Ray Daniel: When I went in the second team at Highbury, which again I thought was the height of my career, the first-team dressing-room was just down the passageway and all the big wheels were there. But the biggest wheel was Denis Compton because when you went in the first-team dressing-room you had these boxes of Brylcreem, and everybody would be plastering themselves with Brylcreem. They sent a few bottles to the second-team dressing-room to keep us happy, but he was a fascinating character. He was good-looking, he was handsome, he was debonair, he was everything. I remember coming back to London from a third-team game at Newcastle, and in those days it used to take about six or seven hours, and every station you pulled in there were these immense advertisements of the Brylcreem Boy. It didn't say his name but we used to nudge each other and say, 'We've seen him before somewhere, you know,' and this was marvellous. He was a great asset to Arsenal, a great asset to Middlesex obviously, and somebody I've admired all my life.

Billy Wright: I think the only advert that I did was Quaker Oats. We were playing at Charlton and in those days we used to get the train in the morning to Paddington, have lunch and bus to the ground at Charlton. We were 2–0 down after 25 minutes, so I went to get the ball for a throw-in, as I was playing wing-half, and this lad in the crowd says, 'Hey, Wrighty, I can see you've had no bleeding Quaker Oats for your breakfast this morning.'

Tom Finney: There was nowhere near the commercial market that there is today for players. I got one with Shredded Wheat Nabisco, and I had a boot on the market and shin-guards and I had a football and those were all added income which was very, very nice and made your wage quite a reasonable amount of money.

6

'England went sport mad
after the war'

A Nation Affected by War, 1938–53

During the Second World War, football was pressed into service, as were many of the game's professional players. The years following 1945 saw a boom period but also saw the Bolton Disaster. Football continued to attract huge crowds, until a serious decline began around 1953, the year of the so-called 'Matthews Final', when 38-year-old Stan Matthews dramatically won a Cup winners' medal after two runners-up medals in the previous five years.

In Germany – May 1938

Stan Cullis: We could see that it [Germany v England] was a game that had been fashioned with propaganda intentions right at the start. We went to the stadium in Berlin to get ready for the international match, and a horde of German soldiers put themselves in a certain position in the ground as if they were part of the organization. We were informed by a representative of the FA that we should go on to the field with the German players and after the national anthems we were to give the Nazi salute. I, along with other England players, objected to giving the Nazi salute, despite the Football Association informing us that it was only courteous to salute the German people. But at the same time we were informed in a nice diplomatic way that if we didn't give the Nazi salute we wouldn't be selected for any future England games.

Sir Stanley Matthews: The British Ambassador, Sir Nevile Henderson, talked to us and then decided we'd do the Nazi salute, and that was the time when the FA secretary, Sir Stanley Rous, said, 'Win today, there'll be a case of cutlery for you.' That was the first time they ever gave us a bonus. We got a case of cutlery for winning against Germany.

Eric Houghton: When we played the next day – we were Aston Villa against Löwenberg or somebody like that – they treated it more or less as an international match. Our manager, Jimmy Hogan, said, 'They'll expect you to give the Nazi salute.' The FA fella in charge of the England team had come to our manager and said, 'We've had a chat about it and we think it would be better if your players gave the Nazi salute to be really friendly.' We had a meeting about this, and George Cummings and Alec Massie and the Scots lads said, 'There's no way we're giving the Nazi salute,' so we didn't give the Nazi salute. Our argument was that we were a club side and not an international side. Anyway, they treated us very well, but it did leave a bit of a bad taste, us refusing to give the Nazi salute. The next time they said we'd got to give the Nazi salute, you see, so we had a meeting and said that, for peace and quietness, we'd give the Nazi salute. At the next place – I think it was Stuttgart – both teams give the Nazi salute, so we went to the centre of the field and gave them the two-finger salute and they cheered like mad. They thought it was all right. They didn't know what the two fingers meant. But we've been several times since to Germany and they've treated us very well.

Under Fire

Eric Houghton: The funniest penalty I ever took was in Germany. We played there just before the war and I think we were playing in Hamburg. We were drawing about three all and about five minutes to go and so I thought, 'I've got to get this in, to win,' and of course Billy Walker had always told me never to get flurried when you're taking a penalty. I was taking me time and I was putting this ball on the spot and the German goalkeeper came off his line. He said, 'You Engleesh pig, you Engleesh pig.' He was trying to put me off, you see. I said, 'All right, mate, you keep calm.' I said, 'You get back on your line and I'll endeavour to knock your square head into a round un.' And it just missed his head going in, hit the stanchion, just missed his head coming out, and he was on the floor. I was in the Royal Air Force in the war and I was stationed at Croydon, and one day my pal and I were having a nice meal in the NAAFI hut and the sirens went. We were on duty so we'd got to go, and we got halfway across this big flying field and we heard something coming down. We threw ourselves on the floor and there's a big piece of shrapnel about from your elbow to your wrist. It dropped about two or three feet in front of us. If it had hit us it would have killed us. I said to Smithy, 'I wouldn't be surprised if that weren't that bloody goalkeeper from Hamburg.'

George Hardwick: There was a great deal of fear which was inevitable in a war. The people involved in the war, either in the forces or making bombs or making aircraft or making tanks or whatever, had so little entertainment, and of course there was no lighting anywhere. Everything was pitch dark throughout the week, and it was a very dull life for everyone. Being able to get to a football stadium to see top-class players was a great attraction. It was something we lived for and we could offer a degree of entertainment. There was a particular incident at Stamford Bridge. It was at the time the V2 rocket had just appeared on the scene. We were playing away merrily and I think we got a goal and were winning 1–0, and then suddenly there was this almighty crash, then everything shook and I automatically went down on the deck. The ground vibrated and I started to lift my head and every single person was flat on their bellies with their head in their hands. A V2 had landed just over the river.

Russian Tourists: Moscow Dynamo, 1945

Frank Butler: The Russians flew into Croydon in two aeroplanes, and the idea was 'We've got to be kind to the Russians.' They'd helped us beat the Germans and they were our great allies, but they were very secretive days. They arrived with a lady interpreter. Her name was Anna and I, as a young reporter, spoke to her and asked her questions: 'Could you help me to interview the players.' And every time I spoke to her she more or less ran away, so I christened her Alexandra the Silent Interpreter. We were a bit caught with our pants down, our soccer pants down, because we were so sympathetic to the Russians. We thought we mustn't treat them too badly, we've got to be kind to them, and at Stamford Bridge they drew 3–3 with Chelsea and played some brilliant football.

Ken Sheehan: I was still at school and we'd heard all about this great Russian team and we thought that if we went to school in the morning and broke away after lunch it would be all right. By the time we got to Stamford Bridge you couldn't get near the ground. Thousands were milling around and by the time we did get to the turnstiles they were closed, so we climbed over the walls with a lot of other people. I said to the lads I was with, 'We're never gonna get up on to the top to see the game,' but people started to push and push and push and at the finish I was actually sitting on the back of the net, and people were sitting all the way around the touch-line. I've never had a view of anything quite like it.

Brian Mears: The first game I went to was the Moscow Dynamo game when the war had just finished, and it was extraordinary really. I don't think anybody had seen a Russian in the flesh and they came out with bouquets of flowers, presenting them to our players, who didn't quite know what to do with them, but somebody came on to the pitch and took them. There were 100,000 people in the ground, spilling on to the pitch, up on the roof. I must have been 13 or 14, something like that. I looked at my dad and said, 'Is it like this every week at Stamford Bridge?' And he said, 'Shut up and get on with your ice-cream.' So, of course, it wasn't, but the crowds were enormous then.

Frank Butler: Then Moscow Dynamo went down to Cardiff and beat Cardiff City 10–1, and then they had a match with Glasgow Rangers, a bit dirty that one. The big centre-half, Semichastny, got his nose broken, a black eye, and all sorts of threats from Moscow and that, but the funniest game of all was at the Arsenal. Well, it was played at Tottenham because Highbury was used for war purposes, and it was played in a thick fog. The Russians had persuaded us to use two referees, one on the line, and Stanley Matthews was in that Arsenal team. The Russians beat us that day and I couldn't get the result because you couldn't see. I never saw any of the goals. We had to go down and find out the result. I said to Stanley Matthews, 'What happened, Stanley?' He said, 'Well, every time I dribbled past a man they pulled my shirt, pulled me back.'

So, in the interview through Alexandra the Silent, I managed to say, 'Stanley Matthews said your players pulled him by the shirt every time.' The answer came back: 'Ah, in Russia we do pull a few shirts but we don't break legs like they do in English football.'

FA Cup Sixth Round: the Bolton Disaster

Bert Gregory: We don't like to talk about it much but it's as well not to forget it because it's a reminder of what can happen if you don't take precautions. They were starved of football during the war and this were directly after the war. This was March 1946. And Stoke City had Stanley Matthews, who was a great attraction. He pulled crowds all over the country, a great player. Wanderers were well known for Wembley visits and you're getting ideas that you're going to go to Wembley.

Audrey Nicholls: I got a good place, about a third of the way up from the front and to the right of the goal, so I had quite a good view, and it got very, very, very crowded and it began to be very uncomfortable. My recollection is that the players came out, the match actually started and then for some reason that wasn't apparent at the time they went off. There was still people coming in and I think they were climbing over a very low wall that had a gate, and that was over to my right. The wall was not much higher than the gate, and spectators who couldn't get in through the turnstile climbed over the wall so there was a lot of pressure from that side and a lot of pressure from the back. I was beginning to be so uncomfortable that I realized I would have to get out somehow and there was no point in going towards the gate because that was where the pressure was coming from.

Bert Gregory: That end, when it was full, would hold

28,000. It was mucky, it was messy. It had been done years beforehand and they used to put any old flags they could get, like kerbs, for steps, but in between the kerbs it were dirt, where people stood. The water come off the banking and it didn't bother them. They'd get on the ground and they'd stand in the water, anything. It wasn't quite full that day but they'd congregated at one end and that's where the trouble was.

Shirley Pilkington: I was at the far end, the Great Lever End, and all I could see was people spilling on to the pitch, and the pressure of people coming down from the back of the embankment and we could obviously tell that there were problems but we didn't know the extent of the problems.

Harold Riley: The people at the back were trying to get in so you felt this surge, and it was the first time in my life that I had felt the power of a crowd. It was like the waves of the sea, like when you are swimming sometimes and you feel the suction. I remember thinking that it was incredibly powerful, but I was young and I was excited about the game. My uncle said, 'We'd better get you to the front.' I was passed over to the front and then the disaster happened where people fell and the barriers went down. It was like a release of a tidal force.

Bert Gregory: We got into the stand, about three rows from the front. We had a good view of what were going on, but little did we realize that it was so serious. The wife was getting a bit excited and I said, 'Oh, it's all right, it's only a crowd, they'll sort it out, there's room over there.' You see, they were only war conditions and they hadn't got the staff for marshalling the crowds. They were climbing on the railway, walking along the back of the ground, and climbing over and it caused a lot of pressure on this end. I said to my wife, 'Oh, don't worry, they'll be all right.' She said, 'Some of them people are injured.' 'Oh, no, they're feeling a bit distressed, they'll be all right.' They brought a lady on and laid her down at the back of the goals, on the grass verge, and she said, 'That woman's dead.' 'How do you know from here?' 'I can tell, woman's instinct.' Somebody puts a cover over her face. Well, my missus's head is shaking. I said, 'Why are you getting excited about it, it's all right, she'll be all right.' 'No, she's dead.'

Harold Riley: There was a lot of crying and shouting, and suddenly I was looking at the crowd from the pitch as opposed to being in the crowd looking at the pitch. I remember a policeman on a horse. I remember the people at the top of the banking jumping up and down to see what was going on. There were people in a daze – I'd never seen people in shock before – and there were people who didn't know what to do about the people who were injured. The dead people were covered up and left like bags on the ground. I'd seen dead people because of the bombing, but you didn't expect it in a football crowd.

Audrey Nicholls: I remember that I asked the men in front of me if I could pass them and come down because I wanted to get on to the track, where I think a few people had climbed over the fence. These men said, 'There's no way you can get down there.' The next thing I knew they'd lifted me up above the heads. It was really marvellous of them and I was passed over the heads, down on to the track. Not very dignified but I was very glad to get out of it. When I got on to the track, there were a number of bodies on the pitch in that corner, maybe eight or 10, lying on the ground. I'd been frightened already, being in this crowd, but I was really terrified when I saw dead people there. They were a ghastly colour, a colour that I'd never seen on a living person.

Nat Lofthouse: I could see bodies being put out at the Bolton end, near the corner-flag, and I thought they were fainting cases because you could see there was a bit of a commotion on the terraces. A policeman ran on and said to the ref, 'Will you stop the game, please, those people are dead.' The referee stopped the game and we came into the dressing-room and they brought some of the bodies through the dressing-room because you had to come through our dressing-room to get to the treatment-room, the St John's room.

Bert Gregory: While the players were off they were bringing the dead out from underneath the crowd there, putting 'em outside of the goals. I started getting a bit apprehensive. I thought, 'Aye, she's right. How's it she can tell better than me? I think she's right. I think some of them might be dead.' When they were carrying one off on a stretcher right in front of us, they tipped the stretcher and he rolled off into the track. I said, 'Aye, I'm sure.' The police broke the fencing down to relieve the pressure and, when they got it settled, we watched the match. It wasn't a good match. There was like a feeling over the match, you know. It were an awful feeling.

Sir Stanley Matthews: The referee came in the changing-room and said, 'Well, we better finish this match.' He didn't say there was any disasters or anything like that, so we knew nothing about it. It was only after the match when we knew what really happened.

Audrey Nicholls: My parents were very surprised to see me because it would only be, what, half past three, maybe, when I got home. I told my father that there'd been some trouble, and that there were some dead bodies lying on the pitch, and he couldn't accept that. He said, 'Oh, surely they've just fainted.' I said, 'No, no, they're dead.' I'd got a lot of mud on my shoes and they were absolutely ruined, and my mother decided that she'd take me into town to buy me some new shoes because I think they were my school shoes, so off we went. She wasn't very pleased. When we got back home, of course, my father had heard the announcement of the disaster on the radio. I think I had a pretty narrow escape and it was because of the kindness of those men. That was typical of the spirit of the times that they were concerned for me, a girl, and they just lifted me up and off I went down. They were marvellous.

Bert Gregory: I was working at the ground, and on the Monday morning the manager sent for me. He said, 'Find a rope, Bert, will you, and see the police. They'll tell you where to go. Rope that portion off.' When I went there, there were belts and raincoats and hats and scarves, what a sight, so I roped it off. Later on, I was detailed to pick up these two barriers. They were flattened to the floor and I was instructed to pick them up, take them away so that people wouldn't keep coming asking questions, put them out of the way. I know where I put them, they're gone now. Later on we renewed them. We borrowed a joiner from the local colliery, and he came to help me to put these barriers up again.

Post-war Crowds

Geoff Kingscott: I was nine years old when I went to the Cup Final in 1946. Derby County had appeared in a Cup Final before, but not for 40 years, and they had never won the Cup. Just remember that it was the first Cup Final after the war and I believe in social history everyone records that England went sport mad after the war so the excitement was tremendous. At the end of the game, when Derby County had at last won after extra-time, there was a man near me with tears streaming down his face, saying, 'I've waited 40 years for this,' and I remember us being absolutely amazed. I'd never seen an adult weeping before. It was almost unseemly. I saw caps being thrown very high in the air as if they would never find them again and this worried me as a young boy. Later in life you realize why there could be this depth of emotion but as a nine-year-old I was puzzled, almost embarrassed.

Peter Blake: I'd leave quite early and then walk towards the game and probably get there an hour before the game started. And a terrific tension would build up, and probably there'd be a kind of damp smell in the air. There was an atmosphere. These were golden years with Charlton, when they were in the Cup Final two years running and won it one of those years, and there would be crowds of 60,000 every week and I'd stand on the terraces and sometimes you'd be passed down to the front or you'd work your way down to the front. And I suppose to a 14-year-old boy it was just enormous excitement. I mean, you knew every player and you supported them deeply and it was an extra-ordinarily exciting thing to be happening.

Eddie Baily: If you went to Newcastle you couldn't get in. There was so many arenas like that, so many. You've got to realize there was no television. In those days, people used to say, 'When do they come and play us?' 'When do we play Manchester United?' 'When do we play the Arsenal?' They'd wait four months and say, 'When they come we'll all go and see that.' You waited to see a star player, and the waiting to see a good team was always exciting.

Charlie Mitten: We didn't play at Old Trafford, we played at Maine Road. We had 83,000 against Arsenal [January 1948]. We had 80-odd thousand against Yeovil in the fifth round of the Cup [1949] and we beat them 8–0. I walked on the field with the right-back and I said, 'Oh, we'll have a good game today.' He looked round, and he says, 'It's a fine piece of pasture.' He was a farmer!

George Petherbridge: We arranged our wedding for the day of the local derby, City and Rovers, so that we'd be in

Bristol. And you can imagine, any local derby in those days was the high point of the season, wasn't it? I mean, we were averaging about 27,000. It was great. A lot of the City players wished us both all the best, and I led the team out. They let me lead the team out because it was me wedding day. We beat the City 2–1.

Rita Petherbridge: And George scored, so that was a good day all round, wasn't it? We got married at 11 o'clock on the Saturday morning. The car was late – they said the car had broken down, had a puncture – and once we got round the church we couldn't get through. The crowds! I didn't know till after but the vicar had to clear three or four rows because all the youngsters were in the first three or four rows, in the pews, and the relations couldn't get in to see the wedding. Everybody was stood up, and loads outside.

George Petherbridge: The vicar said, 'It was a full house today, I wish we could have one every Sunday.'

Bert Trautmann: German Goalkeeper

Bert Trautmann: I was captured in Germany in 1945. It didn't take the English long to bring me over to London, on to Northwich and I finished up in Camp 50 at Ashton-in-Makerfield between Liverpool and Manchester. We got to know the humour of the people. You had to understand that first and foremost. Before you understood the language actually. And the saying was that if you have five spectators on a football ground they would be two trainers and three scouts, and I suppose even in those days they watched players, and I came to the notice, even as a POW, of some of the professional clubs. Eventually I signed for Man City and I stayed with the club for near enough 15 years. And of course there were apprehensions in the supporters of Man City, signing a German. The papers were not too kind to me. I still remember *News of the World* about 'Jerry the German', and on the other hand there were marches with banners, saying to City, 'If you sign this German we are going to boycott the matches' and so on. Some of my best friends, actually, were Jewish people, and it was the Rabbi of Manchester, Dr Altmann, who said, 'You are silly people. You can't blame a single German for what happened during the war, so let him show us that he is a good player or that he is a sportsman and then we'll see.'

Trevor Ford: Let's face it, I was in the war and I disliked him because he was a German. Now, I'd never met the guy in my life and every time we played them I thought, 'Well, now is my chance to have a go at a German.' I must admit I was definitely wrong. It took me 20 years to find out, but he was a great guy, a great character, a wonderful goalkeeper, and I did him an injustice.

Bert Trautmann: Having taken part in two Cup Finals and so on, I think the most moving moment in my life was in the early fifties, when I played my first game down south against Fulham, when Arthur Rowley and Stevens played, and the papers said we should have lost 7–0, 8–0 or 9–0, and we lost 1–0. They said I had a marvellous game and I was at the Thames end in the second half, and when the game had finished the crowd stood up and applauded me, and, something I've never seen since, both sets of players, Fulham and City players, lined the entrance for me to go back into the dressing-room. I think that was the most moving aspect of my footballing life.

'Stan Mortensen's Match': the 1953 Cup Final

Nat Lofthouse: I think Bolton Wanderers have been in two Cup Finals which affected the rest of the country. The '53 one we're talking about now, I think everyone in Britain, apart from Bolton people, wanted Stan Matthews to win a Cup Final medal, because he'd won every other honour and he'd never won a Cup winners' medal. In the 1958 Final, everyone was so tragically sorry that Man United had lost their team at Munich, and everyone apart from Bolton people wanted Man United to win at Wembley, so we had two Cup Finals where Bolton were the underdogs.

Sir Stanley Matthews: We did a bit of practice on the Tuesday in Blackpool, Stanley Park, where the turf was green and grassy because we wanted to get the conditions and I pulled a bit of a muscle. I was a bit scared of it, and I wasn't sure of myself. Anyway, we go down to London and we stay at Elstree, I think, and the doctor was there and he injected me on the Saturday morning. I felt a lot better, but I still had doubts in my mind going on to the pitch. After I'd kicked in, I knew it would be okay.

Nat Lofthouse: It was electric because obviously there were two Lancashire clubs in the Cup Final, 35 miles away from one another. There was a comradeship about it, I think, and obviously it was a good-humoured Final.

Bert Gregory: We had a player who'd had one of these knee injuries. He played and he'd only been playing 10 minutes when it's gone, so he's hopping about till half-time and then he come on again after half-time and he scored a goal, hopping on one leg. He bobbed it in, you see, and that was 3–1 [to Bolton], but we started flagging. The wing-half was injured, hopping about on the wing, the winger had to come inside and the inside-left had to come to half-back and then we were being overrun. In the last quarter of an hour Blackpool overrun us. When the final whistle went, I looked at my missus and she's crying. There were a lot crying after t'match because we had been winning.

Nat Lofthouse: What I remember mostly about it is

winning 3–1 and 17 minutes to go and I thought – not that it made any difference, what I thought, eh? – 'We're going to win here.' Three–one and suddenly Matthews came into the act and they won in the last seconds, 4–3, but it was one hell of a Final. Really great Final.

Sir Stanley Matthews: Yeah, 3–3. They say that I always wanted the ball to my feet. Yeah I did, because I was so closely marked and there's no use staying too far upfront. I always went further back so I could get the ball, and if I was closely marked I'd play a lot in midfield. Anyway, it was a beautiful ball by Ernie Taylor, and now I can see everything in front of me in the goalmouth. There's only one move, my favourite move, I'm going to do – I've got to beat him on his left side – and if I can beat him on his left side I'm in the penalty box where the danger is. Now, Stan Mortensen and I have a very good understanding. If I beat him on the left side, I have three moves. The first move is a cutback and he's not offside. If that's not on, I centre the ball to the farthest point because the goalkeeper's the nearest, he's panicking. If that's not on, I hit the ball in the goalmouth and see what happens. Now, I was too much in a hurry and I beat him just to the right, instead of going forward, and as I beat him, I'm looking for Stan Mortensen and I see him running to the nearest post, you know, but as I see him, there's a big gap and Bill Perry. It was such a simple pass anybody could do it. It wasn't a devastating pass and all credit must go to him [Bill Perry] because he hit this first time and it went into the back of the net, in the far corner. Anyway, I said to Stan after the match, in the bathroom, 'I was looking for you.' He says, 'Well, I was closely marked and as I knew what you were doing I shouted to Bill Perry, "Bill fill the gap".' And he took his centre-half with him, and he left Bill Perry that gap. That was clever thinking. It should have been 'Stan Mortensen's match' really. He scored three goals and made the fourth.

7

'Made in England'

England's Post-war International Team

England's wartime team was one of the world's finest ever. After the war, a team captained by George Hardwick virtually named itself. England lost only one of their first 18 post-war internationals.

The First England Manager – Walter Winterbottom

Sir Walter Winterbottom: At the end of the war I was at the Air Ministry, having helped to run the big coaching course at Carnegie College where I was lecturing. Sir Stanley Rous [FA secretary] wanted us to run a course and we ran a course for directors, which is unusual, managers, secretaries, coaches, fitness trainers and so on, and out of all this we began running different courses for different people. That was just before the war, and at the end of the war Sir Stanley asked me to run another course at Dagenham when I used professional players like Raich Carter, Tommy Lawton and co. to coach some youngsters, and because of this I went up to Scotland to organize a coaching course up there for their senior players. Sir Stanley then felt, 'Well, it's time we had a man in charge of coaching at the FA,' and I was invited to take this job – Director of Coaching. It also had a sideline to it – manager of the England teams (amateur and professional).

Tom Finney: I found that Walter Winterbottom was a very good tactician and a very good coach, and he was recognized the world over, very well respected by quite a number of the continental clubs that we came in contact with. In the early days, when I went in the England side, we had the great names like Tommy Lawton, Frank Swift in goal, George Hardwick and Wilf Mannion, Raich Carter, Neil Franklin, Billy Wright. I think Walter felt that – and he used to say so in the talks – it was no good him trying to tell us how to play the game. We had been selected for our country and in his opinion we were good enough to go out and express ourselves on the field of play, and that was generally what we were allowed to do. He would generally go through the tactical side of opponents rather than talk about how we were going to play.

Billy Elliott: He was a good talker was Walter but he talked sense. You had specific jobs to do against continental teams, and you used to try to fulfil what he wanted. I mean, imagine giving tactics and trying to tell Tom Finney how to play. Nobody could do that to a world-class player like him, but he used to listen to Walter and he used to try and fit into what Walter had to say, along with the rest of the players.

Tommy Lawton: Ah, well, when Winterbottom took over as England manager the first thing he did, he looked round the room and there were people like Matthews and Mannion and myself, big Swifty, Laurie Scott, Neil Franklin, and he said, 'The first thing we'll do, chaps, we will meet in about half an hour. I've arranged a blackboard and we'll discuss tactics.' So I looked at him and I said, 'We'll discuss what? Are you trying to tell me that you have got a blackboard downstairs and you want us to be there at one o'clock and you're going to tell Swifty how to play goal? You're going to tell Laurie Scott and George Hardwick how to play full-back? You're going to tell Neil Franklin how to play centre-half? And, God forbid, you're going to tell Stan Matthews how to play outside-right? And me, you're going to tell me how to score goals? You've got another think coming. You've got about as much chance of getting any of this lot down there as I have of flying. Goodnight.' So very soon after that Lawton was out of the England side. My days were numbered then.

Billy Elliott: Walter was an amateur who played for Manchester United. He was never like a big player, and I think this is why they used to knock him down a bit. You don't necessarily have to be a star to be a good manager. I mean, there's many who had been ordinary players, no international caps, won nothing, but they became good managers.

Sir Walter Winterbottom: I wouldn't have pushed tactics as far as they do today. The only game plan I would have is: 'You know the way we can play football. We've got Stanley Matthews here and he's going to go down the wing and he's going to be crossing over. How do we time our moves to give him service and how do we time our moves to come in on the right timing when he's making his crosses?' You know, it's as basic as that. But you would talk to them about the way the other team played, because you were probably the only one who'd seen them and you knew the kind of strengths they had and so on. Therefore you had to say to players, 'You have to look out for this, that and the other. What do we do about it?' Coaching is bringing about team understanding, and team understanding comes from the players themselves, and player power is far stronger than coaching power. In my playing days it was all player power. Little was done by managers. Managers used to sit in their offices when we were practising on the field. The older players would say, 'Come on, we've got to do this and that and the other. Don't you go wandering up there, Winterbottom, leaving a big gap down here.' You know, this sort of thing.

A Great Team – 1946–48

George Hardwick: I don't think there could ever have been a team in the history of football that entertained so much because that's what we set out to do: 'Now, all these people have paid all this money, let's show them, let's give 'em a show, let's do it.' If we scored one I'm screaming at them, 'Now two, two, two, come on, let's go, let's go.' When we got two I was screaming for three, and I was screaming for four, and I was screaming for five, and the only time I got a little bit upset with myself was when we were beating Holland 8–0 and we got a penalty and hadn't the guts to score with it. I just knocked it at the goalkeeper. I thought, 'Oh no, no, no, we've got eight,' and I hadn't the heart to go for nine.

Billy Wright: George was very suave and handsome. We used to say that all the girls were after George. But he was a very good skipper, he was not a demonstrative skipper. I learned a lot from George. He would quietly tell you what to do. He wouldn't remonstrate and tell you off. He and Laurie Scott were two classy full-backs. They weren't the hard tacklers. They were getting the ball clean in tackles and using it. And what I learned from George was a lot about being captain of a side.

George Hardwick: Walter [Winterbottom] brought dignity to the game, to the players. He rose above all the horrible things that were said about him in the press. It was very difficult for them [the press] then because we were winning all the games but nevertheless we were criticized when we went to Switzerland. They scored in the early stages of the game. I was captain of the team and I didn't spot what was happening in the Swiss team, because it was the first time we had ever seen a deep-lying number nine, who was pulling away, and number 10 was coming steaming through in an attacking role. I should have seen this and I didn't. I should have told Neilie [Franklin], 'Neilie, forget that guy down there, this is your man,' and I didn't. They scored very early, and for the remainder of the game we kicked in. Even Stan Matthews hit the post and fancy Stan having a shot at goal; I mean, it was against his religion. But they beat us 1–0. It was unbelievable and the press crucified us and crucified Walter. We went straight from there to play Portugal in Portugal, and they were one of the top teams in Europe. I said to the lads, 'Now we're gonna show these people what we can do, we're going to make them eat every word they've printed. We're going to go out there and we're going to crucify this lot. They'll never see the way we go, so let's go.' We were four up in 10 minutes. We finished up 10–0 and I think we quietened the press, and we gave Walter back his hours of glory. We would play for Walter. He was a gentleman, one of the nicest men I have ever known.

Billy Wright: We went to Portugal, to Lisbon, and it was an absolutely magnificent stadium and the pitch was second to none. Our trainer was Wilf Copping, the old Arsenal wing-half, and he said, 'If you don't beat this lot today, you should be hung,' because the pitch was absolutely superb. Our side was Frank Swift, Laurie Scott, George Hardwick, myself, Neil Franklin, Eddie Lowe, and then it was Matthews, Mortensen, Lawton, Mannion and Finney.

Sir Walter Winterbottom: The claim in Portugal was that their goalkeeper was the best goalkeeper in the world, or certainly the best in Europe, and he took the field with a personal bow. He came on after all the other players, to applause and accolades and so on, and he let five goals in in the first half so he was changed at half-time and they brought the reserve goalkeeper on. They wanted to change him, too.

Tom Finney: The greatest England side I played in was probably the one that beat Italy 4–0 in Turin. Italy were then the World Cup holders – they won it in '38, of course, and it hadn't been played for since. That was probably the greatest win away from home that England had, against an extremely good Italian side and a very partisan crowd as well.

Billy Wright: We won 4–0 against Italy and Italy had not been beaten for a couple of years. For the first 20 minutes, we struggled. If it hadn't been for Frank Swift in goal, we would have been two or three down. I think it was midway through the first half when dear Stan Mortensen picked this ball up and ran half the length of the field and hit a shot. I thought, 'Oh, he's centring the ball,' and it went between the goalkeeper and the near post and hit the far side netting. Until he died, Stan would always tell you, 'I shot.' The last one, the fourth, it went from Frank Swift to Laurie Scott, our right-full-back, who passed it to me. I passed it to Matthews, Matthews passed it to Mannion, Mannion passed it to Finney, Finney beat the full-back, drew the goalkeeper and put the ball in the back of the net. We went from our goal to their goal and no Italian touched the ball. That is a goal in a million, isn't it? Tommy Finney got two for us that day, and we won very well. In one of the big shops in the centre of Turin, on the Monday morning, there was a 10ft by 8ft picture of the England side and underneath it had 'Made in England'. That was some sight, I tell you, that was some sight.

Sir Stanley Matthews: Oh, Turin, yeah, that was a most

beautiful victory, the best England team I've played with and Italy had the best team I've ever played against. The night before the match a swarm of supporters came in for autographs and we found out they came from Malta. Anyway, years later I go to live in Malta, and one of the ministers wanted to see me – this is an unbelievable story – and I go, and he says 'Oh, how nice to meet you, I was one of the supporters who came in 1947.' 'That's very nice, Mr Minister.' He says, 'But you're not known for your dribbling, you're known as the man who took a comb out of your pocket and combed your hair while you were playing.' 'Well, Mr Minister,' I said, 'that's not true.' He says, 'It is true,' so I said, 'Okay.' Well, years later, I'm coaching in South Africa – I lived there for three years – and I'm invited to a golf-club, and a beautiful buffet, and I'm speaking to the manager and he shakes hands with me and he says, 'I would like you to meet two chefs.' One of them was a black man, and the other was a South African and he says, 'I'm from Italy, I've been here four years, I saw England play, in Turin.' He spoke English, of course, and he said, 'You took a comb out of your pocket.' I said, 'Yes.' I had to say 'Yes'. Isn't it funny, I must have done. I know it was a very hot and sticky day.

George Hardwick: It was certainly the most confident team in the world because we never ever dreamed of losing. We used to sing wherever we went. All sorts of things, like 'My Name is McNamara, I'm the Leader of the Band,' that sort of thing. We weren't worried about it. We didn't think, 'Oh, God, we're going to Wembley' or 'We're going to Hampden Park.' Nothing upset us. The only one that used to be a little bit chicken was Stan [Matthews]. We were good mates. He used to sit by me a lot and we used to run together. We'd get in the coach and he was always a bit sour-faced. We'd all start singing and say, 'Come on, Stan, come on.' 'Oh, it's all right for you, it doesn't bother you, you don't suffer with nerves like I do.' I'd say, 'Oh, Christ, Stan, you're going to do what you love doing. What are you nervous about?' But once he crossed that line, that white line, he was dynamite. No nerves then. He used to crucify 'em and particularly the Scots.

Tom Finney: I think at that particular time, probably '47–48, I would have said that that was the best England side I played with, but unfortunately we hadn't the opportunity to play in the World Cup. We didn't play in the World Cup till 1950, some two years after, by when, of course, a lot of the great names had fallen by the wayside and were no longer playing international football. Had we had a World Cup in '47–48 we would certainly have been there or thereabouts.

Expenses

Stan Cullis: When we played international matches, you got there the best way you could. In other words it was left to you to decide how you would get to Wembley. Some players were lucky – they had friends who had a car to take them. Others got on the train to take them to Wembley.

Tom Finney: Of course you travelled third class. You were going down midweek so it wasn't too bad, but coming back after the game the train was absolutely heaving and there's many an occasion when you had to stand up all the way to Preston, and of course these others that were travelling with us, like Stanley Mortensen and Stan Matthews, would have to stand up. It was a regular occurrence which was taken as part and parcel of the job.

Sir Stanley Matthews: When we arrived they [the FA officials] called you 'Matthews' and 'Lawton' and 'Mannion' and 'Carter'. After breakfast we go in a special room in the hotel. The secretary in those days was Stanley Rous and they had a gentleman named Mr Huband, the treasurer, who always had his bowler hat on – I can never remember him taking it off – and he was the one to look after the expenses. They give you a little card and it says, 'from Stoke to London'. Well, we had to put this down and Tommy Lawton put an extra sixpence on his travel fare, you see, and Mr Huband also had the prices and he said, 'Lawton, you've overcharged,' so he crossed the sixpence out.

Tom Finney: Yes, I had quite an experience with my first game, at Belfast against Northern Ireland. I went by train to Liverpool and then we went across by boat. Frank Swift was then a seasoned international player, and I well remember him saying to me, as a newcomer, 'I'll show you how to make your expense sheet out.' He showed me and added a few bob here and a few bob there and sent it off to the FA. I got a very curt note back: 'Dear Finney, we're returning your expense sheet. Herewith enclosed a new one to make out and for your information the third-class fare from Preston to Liverpool is x shillings and you didn't have any meal because you only travelled from Liverpool to us.' Frank Swift had told me to put a couple of bob down for a meal or something. I had to resubmit an expense sheet, which was rather an embarrassment really!

Stan Cullis: We were in a queue leading up to the underground railway at Wembley and I can recall standing in the queue, which was about a mile long from Wembley Stadium. The spectators who recognized us were nudging each other and informing their friends that so-and-so who'd been playing that day for England was having to take his turn in the queue. You waited the same as anybody else. It was pointed out that it was our responsibility to get to the ground and away from the ground and I wasn't conscious of any England player being very upset about having to stand in a queue to get back to London, for instance.

Billy Elliott: I was picked for the Football League to play Scotland at Ibrox, and this was a time I was playing at

Burnley. Just as I was coming out of the house, the bus went away from the bus stop. The next bus wasn't for 20 minutes. Well, I'd got to get a connection, I had to get myself to Manchester, so I rang for a taxi. A taxi came and I told him to get in front of that bus going to Manchester, drop me off and I could get on the bus. The taxi-driver did this. After five or six minutes I paid the taxi, flagged the bus down, got on the bus to Manchester. Okay, we arrived in Manchester and then I teamed up with Nat Lofthouse and Tom Finney and the rest of the northern players. Just before the game at Ibrox we were called for expenses. It was my turn and Sir Stanley Rous and Alan Hardaker says, 'Expenses, Elliott?' I says, 'Well, from Burnley I had to get a taxi,' and I gave him the tale about being late out of the house, blah blah blah, so he turned round to me and he says, 'Well, it's your fault you missed the bus.' I said, 'Well, I accept that.' 'Well,' he says, 'you're only getting your bus fare, you're not getting a taxi.' I think the taxi come to about three and ninepence, but I didn't get it. 'Next time,' he says, 'you'll be out of your house a little bit earlier.'

Stan Cullis: Oh, no, no, no, you certainly weren't allowed a taxi. I can remember one player – as a matter of fact it was Denis Compton – who went in to present his expenses, and one portion of his expenses was classified as 'Miscellaneous' and this FA official, looking at the paper that Compton was presenting, said, 'Not only do you not know how to spell miscellaneous but you are not getting anything like an expense that is known as miscellaneous, so I'm going to scrub that out.' So Denis Compton didn't get his miscellaneous expense.

The Selectors

Tom Finney: As a player, you'd no idea how the selection went. They had a selection committee, and they had Walter Winterbottom as the manager and all you were concerned about was whether you were selected or not. You weren't really bothered about how the selection took place and I don't know to this day how the selection really did take place, whether Walter selected the team or went in to the selection committee with a proposed team and that was it or they argued and said somebody else should be in. You were invariably informed by the press, who would ring you up and say, 'They've just selected the team and you're in.'

Sir Walter Winterbottom: I didn't have the full responsibility of picking my own teams, and I shall never forget the first meeting of a selection committee. We met in the Victoria Hotel, Sheffield, and we had eight selectors plus a chairman. The way things were done was 'Nominations for goalkeeper?' and we had five goalkeepers nominated and then, through a process of reducing that number, we gradually got down to the last two and it was a vote then amongst nine people and if it was four and four then the chairman would decide which goalkeeper it was. Remember, in those days selecting a national team was really a means of giving recognition for high skill. It wasn't really looking at building a team to play on and win anything. It wasn't that at all. We were selecting players for that match, a friendly match against a country, and there was a reward in this: so-and-so has been a great player, it's time we recognized his great ability and let him be in the next England team. There was a different slant on it. It's only when we got into World Cup football that people began to realize we had to produce a team that might have a chance of winning the World Cup, and that meant playing the same players together as often as you possibly could.

Len Shackleton: I did the book with David Jack, and I did a page about the selectors. There was Harold Shentall, chairman at Chesterfield. He was one of the top bods in the Football Association, and he's a guy who picks the team with Walter Winterbottom and all things that go with it. At the end of my book it says what a shambles it is when he was a greengrocer and he knows as much about picking cabbages as what he knows about picking goalkeepers.

Sir Walter Winterbottom: They were largely people of great interest who had played the game and who knew a good deal about it because they were always talking with their own managers. Let's be fair, they knew a fair amount, and very often they would come to a selection committee carrying the opinion of their manager about players. It wasn't necessarily their own thinking, you know. The managers would say, 'Well, this player's far better than that player, he ought to be in the side,' and they would come with that knowledge. And whilst it was like that at first, ultimately we began to send them out to watch players.

Dora Cobbin: My father was Bob Cobbin. He was elected to the [Nottingham Forest] committee in 1912, I think, and he was on the committee for 44 years, 28 of them as chairman. Eventually he was elected to the Football Association Council. He was on that for 33 years. He was made a life member and then in 1946 he was made an honorary life vice-president as a reward for his long service, and of course he took part in everything. They didn't have a manager in those days so the FA International committee used to pick the team but I remember my father saying more than once that they really ought to have a manager who could devote his time to watching players, because it took up a lot of time for the councillors to go watching players. As far as I know, my father hadn't played football. He knew a lot about it but not from a playing point of view. The FA would probably tell him which match to cover and other councillors on the International committee would be given matches and then they'd all have to meet together in London to discuss these players and eventually pick a team, which sounds a bit haphazard these days. Still, they coped.

George Hardwick: In general I don't think footballers were regarded in any considerable esteem by the directors of clubs. This pattern was set by the Football Association because when you were picked to play for England you would receive a notification from the Football Association: 'Dear Hardwick, you have been selected to play for England against Scotland at Hampden Park on (such-and-such a date). You will report to (this hotel) in Glasgow, bringing with you your boots, etc, and a bar of soap, and you will report at (this time). In the event that you should be later you will notify the Football Association immediately. Signed Sir Stanley Rous.' Now you didn't feel very big after you got that, you know. You were delighted to play for your country, you were honoured to play for your country, but, God in Heaven, they might have been a bit more friendly about it.

8

'We were so insular'

The Need for Change, 1950

England's failure in the 1950 World Cup Finals speeded up the process of self-examination. How do we best prepare for the future? How do we emulate the continentals and South Americans? Formal coaching courses were already established, and this gave rise to a contentious issue: how do youngsters best learn skills and tactics?

The Exodus to Bogotá, Colombia

Neil Franklin: When he was at Cambridge Robledo became a big Arsenal fan. He goes back to Bogotá and there's lots of trouble, so he becomes a local diplomat, and he thinks of organizing football on English lines. He thought, 'If I can get this sort of football here, it would take their minds off fighting each other' and all the rest of it, so he got in touch with me and he organized things and we went out there. At the time, we weren't getting much pay in England. It was definitely cash that I went for. I just went. I played the last game of the season on the Saturday against the Arsenal, down at Stoke, and on the Sunday I went to South America, flying via Miami and all the rest. Colombia wanted to get organized and be in FIFA eventually. I got out there and I realized that from the football point of view it was a bit of a wild place. They weren't organized at all and training wasn't right. I used to enjoy my game – it was played on Sundays out there – but I was glad to get back. I was back again for the start of the season and I got suspended for six months.

Charlie Mitten: We were on tour at the end of the season in the States with [Manchester] United and of course it had broken in the press about a week before that Neil Franklin and George Mountford and Bobby Flavell and those had gone to Colombia. So I was in my room in a Times Square hotel and the phone rang and it was Mr Robledo (nothing to do with the Robledo brothers). He was a millionaire cattle baron and the president of Santa Fe and beside him was George and Neil, and we had a chat on the phone. He said, 'The boys say you're the one they want,' and I said, 'Well, I'll come and have a look if it's all right with you.' He said, 'Yes, there'll be a ticket in the foyer for you tomorrow.' I told the boss [Matt Busby] and he was upset. But I said, 'I'm going to have a look anyway, Boss, because I'm 29 now, and I've got £300 in the bank and I'm living in a club house and I'm supposed to be one of the best wingers in the game. And we're playing against teams here who're getting four and five hundred quid a match and we're murdering them. There's something wrong in England about the finances.' 'I know, laddie,' he said, 'but there's nothing I can do about it.' I said, 'Well, my contract's expired, Boss. I feel free to go and have a look and come back to you. I promise you I'll come and talk to you after I've had a look.' There was a ticket downstairs and I went to Bogotá. The boys went back on the *Queen Mary*, and Stan Pearson took my baggage home. I got to Colombia and there's about four or five thousand people at the airport, and the pilot said to me, 'They've come to welcome you.' I went down and met them and had a press conference and talked and went to the stadium and then they said, 'Would you do some training?' I did a couple of laps and I found out that the altitude there was 8,500ft and I was breathing a bit deeper and a bit more often. He said, 'Now, don't worry about the breathing. There's nothing wrong with you. Everybody does this when they first come to Colombia. A week and you'll be all right.' He said, 'Well, Charles, there's a lovely house there for you, with a maid and a chauffeur and a car. It's yours, free, and I'm paying you £5,000 a year signing-on fee and £5,000 salary, plus bonuses at £35 for a win.' So I thought, 'Well, that's 10 times more than I'm getting at United and it looks a piece of cake.' I said, 'What sort of players am I playing with?' 'Oh,' he said, 'you'll play with Hector Rial and Alfredo di Stefano.' International players, you see. I thought, 'Oh, I'm in good company then.' So I said, 'I'm interested, Mr Robledo, but I promised Matt I'd go home and talk to my wife and family before I give you the answer.' So that's quite all right. 'Oh, by the way,' he said. 'If you want to come, your wife and children's passage is free, no problem.' I went home and had a chat with my wife and decided that, at the age I was, it was time to do something about getting financially sound. So I rang up Mr Robledo and I said, 'Yes, okay, I'll have a go,' and of course the boys were delighted. I went to see the boss and we had a chat and I said, 'Well, listen, Boss, we've won the Cup and we've won the League three times for you, we've won everything except the Boat Race for you and we've got nothing.' He said, 'I understand, laddie, but that's the rules.' I said, 'Well, the rules are wrong, they should be changed, so I'm just going to take a little bit into my own hands and look after myself. I've done my bit for you.' 'I understand, laddie,' he said. I told him what I was getting – £5,000 salary and £5,000 signing-on fee. He said, 'Good God, do they want a manager?' So we started laughing. I said, 'I don't think you'd stand the altitude, Boss.' Anyway, we left the best of friends. I went to Colombia with the family and I was more-or-less an instant success. I must have scored about 24 or 25 goals that season. After about six months we were second top, and Millionarios were top, and I started to consider the class I was playing in. Colombia weren't in FIFA and they could pinch the best players all over the world for no transfer fees. All they had to do was give the players a good salary, which was the right way, instead of giving the clubs the money. So the players were earning a good living, and we had players from all over South America. Uruguay had just won the World Cup and we played them three weeks afterwards with a selection of Colombia and I played with them, and di Stefano played centre-forward and Rial played inside-left and we beat them 3–1. This is the world champions and we beat them 3–1. I mean, the blood was flying down the ankles a little bit, they were getting stuck in, and I thought, 'Well, we can't be so bloody bad, can we?' Just then Colombia were thinking of joining FIFA, which meant we all had to go back to our parent clubs or be transferred to another club. Mr Bernabéu [president of Real Madrid] came over to Colombia to have a word with di Stefano and Rial and they said to him, 'What about Mitten?' So we had a dinner party together, the four of us, and we talked business and Real Madrid wanted di Stefano, Hector Rial and myself to go and play for them. I said, 'Well, I know the salary's all right, and it's for three years.' Mr Bernabéu says, 'Well, Charles, it's up to you.' I said, 'Well, I'll go home and have a chat with my wife first.' So I went home and I came back. She was homesick, wanting to go back home. The children were speaking Spanish instead of English, or a little bit of both, so I decided to go home and that was the mistake I made in football, because I could have had European Cup medals as well because they went on to win it five times, with di Stefano and Rial as players. I would have rivalled Gento for position, of course.

The World Cup

Sir Walter Winterbottom: The World Cup started with Jules Rimet, the French president of FIFA [Fédération Internationale de Football Association]. Only 13 countries took part in the first one [in 1930], won by Uruguay. We didn't want to play in this for the reason that we felt there wasn't really an agreement to form a truly international body. [All four home countries withdrew from FIFA in 1928.] But FIFA gradually grew in strength and then more and more countries wanted to participate and therefore it became truly international. So the insularity was born of the fact that we had invented the game, we'd brought the game about. Even so, we were out of the leadership part of FIFA at that stage [the 1930s] because it all surrounded itself in this World Cup competition, and therefore after the war we decided we must get back in, and our first World Cup, of course, was in Brazil in 1950.

Tom Finney: Well of course the team had changed considerably. Neil Franklin had left the country and gone to Bogotá, and he was an outstanding player. He had played 27 consecutive games for England as centre-half when he went off, suddenly, and was never to play again for England, which I felt was a travesty of justice because in my opinion he was a great player and would have been in any era. When I think back now to the World Cup, we had a three- or four-day get-together in London after a hard season, and hard grounds at that time of year, and we went off then and stopped in Rio right on the Copacabana beach, in a hotel where you were very fortunate to get any sleep with the noise that was going on. It was early hours and there were car horns blazing away and of course you went from a temperature here of some 60 degrees into something like 90 degrees and bone-hard grounds.

Wilf Mannion: You got out there into a climate where you needed to be a few weeks, after having a hard season, just walking about maybe, but he had you training in the heat and things like that. It was all against us. It proved it when you played your first game. We played it in the big stadium. We played Chile and we won 2–0 but it was as if you had weights on you, and there was oxygen ready for you to have at half-time.

Sir Stanley Matthews: I remember the food wasn't good at all. Tommy Finney and Wilf Mannion and I shared our rooms and we were eating bananas mostly. There was no preparation as there is today.

Sir Walter Winterbottom: It was a new experience for us, and it was end-of-season. You see, South American teams are in mid-season when they play this World Cup. They're all fresh. We're at the end of a season exhausted all the time, and the club managers used to say, 'Walter, you ought not to be taking so-and-so, he's completely run out of form, you know. He's tired, he wants a rest.' And refereeing wasn't as good as it is today. It wasn't universally consistent. They had different attitudes in South America to the way players could handle you and push you off the ball with impunity, but if you brought them down by tackling their feet then they used to get furious. I used to think this was really difficult. Our game was based on fierce tackling for the ball, and that used to get all the spectators up in arms out in South America. So there was the contrast between the two.

Frank Butler: I remember going out. We flew out to Rio. It took hours and hours. We stopped at all stations, Paris, Lisbon, Dakar, all the way there, and we had a party of 17 players and eight journalists. Only eight sports writers! Two other players, Matthews of Stoke and Jim Taylor, were playing for the FA in Canada and they were going to join us in Rio, and Jack Aston and Harry Cockburn of Manchester United

The wasteground where Tom Finney learned his football. *(Tom Finney)*

Arsenal fans congregate near Gillespie Road underground station.
(London Transport Museum)

King George V surveys the scene at the first Wembley FA Cup Final, April 1923. *(Hulton Deutsch)*

Huddersfield Town, League Champions 1924-25. Herbert Chapman is on the extreme left of the back row. *(Colorsport)*

George Male, Arsenal and England
(Colorsport)

Queen's Park Rangers players enjoy training with a ball, February 1939.
(Hulton Deutsch)

BRYLCREEM
your hair

Keeps hair in top form

Denis Compton, the original
Brylcreem Boy. *(Playfair Annual)*

Major Frank Buckley. *(Colorsport)*

Tom Finney and his son, Brian, appear in a television advertisement for
Shredded Wheat. *(Tom Finney)*

England players give the Nazi salute before the game against Germany in Berlin, May 1938. *(Associated Press)*

Stan Matthews, playing for the Royal Air Force, March 1943. *(Hulton Deutsch)*

Chelsea vs Moscow Dynamo, Stamford Bridge, 1945. *(Albert Sewell)*

The Bolton Disaster, March 1946. *(Hulton Deutsch)*

England, 1946. *Back row:* Scott, Franklin, Swift, Wright, Cockburn.
Front row: Finney, Carter, Hardwick, Mannion, Lawton, Langton.
(George Hardwick)

Young Brazilian boys learning basic skills on Copacabana Beach,
Rio de Janeiro, 1950. *(Hulton Deutsch)*

England vs Hungary, Wembley, November 1953. Ferenc Puskás and
Billy Wright lead out the teams. *(Hulton Deutsch)*

England goalkeeper Merrick and centre-half Johnston scramble the ball away
from Hidegkúti of Hungary. *(Popperfoto)*

were playing in America and they were going to join us, so we had 21, but we did miss Franklin very much. We started off and all the Brazilians were giving us headlines – 'the real masters of football are here' – but we beat Chile in the first match, which was quite easy, and then of course the dreadful thing that happened was we flew up to Belo Horizonte from Rio to play the United States of America. Now they were great baseball players and great footballers but not soccer players, and that team of America had nine part-time players and they were on about $10. I remember their coach was born in Scotland, a fella called Bill Jeffrey, and I flew up with him and he said to me, 'I don't want to pump you too much, I'm not trying to get information, but is it true they're not playing Stanley Matthews against us? The greatest footballer in the world. Surely they've got a trick, they're going to bring him on?' And I said, 'No,' and Stanley sat next to me in the tiny little ground at Belo Horizonte and we played like chumps, not like champs.

Wilf Mannion: Against the States, you know, that was the biggest shock of all. They took you from the big stadium and they put you on a field. It was like a YMCA football pitch. Everyone was crowded together. There wasn't much room to work in, and although it was unbelievable, like shooting-in practice, we got beat 1–0. The new players coming in, the likes of Watson and Bentley, hadn't had time to be together.

Frank Butler: One of the papers put a black border round the front page and said, 'The impossible result, United States 1 England 0.' It was incredible. That day Walter Winterbottom got the blame for it but he didn't pick the team in those days. He was just the manager and he carried the can. We had about 23 selectors, capable of going into a geriatric ward, and they used to pick teams but on that occasion it was left to one man, Arthur Drewry, who was the President of the Football League, and he chose the team and he did his best but that was a dreadful result.

Sir Walter Winterbottom: America, let's be fair, had held Switzerland to a 2–2 draw. Remember America wasn't just a team from America. It was a team of Europeans, too, who'd only been over there for three months and were allowed to play. It was a game in which we dominated. They scored one by a deflection which went in, and from then on, of course, everything was done to stop us playing, but you can't blame it. We missed our own chances and we should have taken them. Someone of the press was doing some statistics of the game and said we hit the woodwork 11 times. I remember we hit the woodwork a lot but I didn't know it was 11 times. But that's ridiculous, you know, by any standards!

Tom Finney: We had probably 85 per cent of the play. I hit the woodwork on several occasions and it just wouldn't go in and they got two chances and put one in the back of the net and we lost the game. It was like when North Korea beat Italy in a later World Cup because they were just a nonentity. It's just one of those things that happens in football. You could have played them again another 100 times and beaten them. It was a poor pitch for an international, but it was the same for both sides and we had no excuses whatsoever really other than we should have beaten them comfortably.

Billy Wright: That's one match I'm never allowed to forget. People say, 'Well, you played badly.' We didn't play brilliantly, we didn't play badly, but we couldn't hit the target. When we lost to the United States of America, we just wanted the ground to open up and us to go in, because it was a disaster. I think that's the worst result I ever had when I played for England.

Sir Stanley Matthews: Oh, I didn't play. I think the players who didn't play were lucky. The ground was bumpy, lumpy and the Americans were tackling hard, hustling them and charging and what-have-you. I think if we'd played for 24 hours we'd have never scored. It was one of those days, and then of course we played Spain a few days later, and we lost 1–0.

Skill on the Beach

Tom Finney: There was hundreds, literally hundreds, of kids playing on the beach, and not with footballs. Some of them had little rubber balls, but some of them just had brown-paper parcels which were tied together with string. One youngster came along and we said, 'Now, come on, let's see how often you can keep it up,' and he went 100 times with this brown-paper parcel tied with string with both feet. He could keep it up 100 times. We said, 'There you are, there's your answer, this is where they learn all their skills.' I'm a big believer in that. Look at the number of players from the poorer countries, like your Pelés, and the great players that have come from very, very humble beginnings and very, very poor homes and gone right to the top in the professional ranking.

Billy Wright: You saw them practising all over the place. In fact, they used to beg for money and go and buy an orange. They'd bite a little hole in the orange, suck the juice out, and the orange then became a ball. And in fact Tom Finney tried to emulate this little boy. And the boy I think got about 76 touches of that orange, keeping it up in the air without touching the ground, great skill. I think Tom was the most successful – he got 38. And that's how you learned, and you saw what they were capable of. We saw the opening game in the World Cup in Brazil. It was Brazil and Mexico, and we saw people bending balls, which is now part of the scene, like a banana, both ways, with the outside of the foot and the inside of the foot, skills that we'd not seen before. And that was eye-opening, the bending of the ball, the skilful use of the ball and how they could bring the ball down. We learned a lot from that '50 World Cup.

The Need for Coaching

Sir Walter Winterbottom: Manchester United spotted me, as it were, and I went to join them. But in those days you could play professional football and still keep another job, and therefore I was still maintaining my teaching whilst I was playing. I got to know the system of training of Manchester United, because during my holidays, especially at the beginning of the season, I could go and train with the players. And it wasn't long before I left teaching and went to Carnegie College to take the diploma in physical education, and then I became a lecturer at Carnegie College and this meant I was able to look at the science of training and the way to develop fitness, which were not methods used by the football club. The football club had a very simple routine which was passed on from generations. You had to walk round the pitch six times and then you had to run round the pitch six times and that was your stamina training, and then a few physical jerks and a little ball-practice. In fact the use of the ball for training during the week, apart from the game itself, was very limited. You'd only have one practice game during the week and it was always done half-speed. There was no tactical awareness, you just played football, and people didn't have much knowledge of how to help each other, how to build a system. In my playing days I used to ask Billy McKay, a Scottish international wing-half, how it was he could pass through to the wing man, as he used to do, always get it there, and he told me his little trick but he said, 'Keep it to yourself.' And people used to hide from passing on information. They felt it wasn't the thing to do. There was a horror about letting other people know things instead of accumulating information, using it for the benefit of the whole team. Well, of course, having been to Carnegie and seeing sports science and knowing how football was not aware of things they could do to improve, one had to feel that this was the way we should go, and when I was appointed as Director of Coaching the one thing we started to do was have instructional courses of all kinds. I remember asking 60 trainers out of 90 clubs, 'How many have read *The Referee's Chart*, the laws of the game?' And out of those 60 trainers only five of them knew anything about it. How did they know the laws of the game? Only by the way they played it and what people had told them, but they hadn't read them. Nowadays, players and trainers not only know the laws of the game but they're looking for ways of getting round them. The lack of knowledge was abysmal really within the game, and the idea of coaching was to bring along players with more knowledge of how to keep fit, how to train, how to use tactics, the various skills, the variation of skill. You'd speak to famous players like David Jack, who was a great player with Alex James at Arsenal, and David would say the only way to pass a ball is to hit it with the inside of your foot. And we used to say to him, 'What about the outside of your foot?' 'Oh no, no, no, that's not on.' In other words they locked themselves into the process of playing that they'd been brought up to believe in and one had to change this. When I said to them, 'Look, the continentals are trapping the ball with their knee.' 'That's rubbish,' he would say. We were so insular that we wouldn't believe that other methods could be used for doing things, other ways of playing the game could be better than ours, and that had to change, of course.

Director of Coaching

Sir Walter Winterbottom: Managers in my day were all people with cheque-books who would go round and buy players. The famous Chapman of Arsenal used to use a cheque-book: £10,000 for Alex James, £10,000 for David Jack. Before you knew it, he'd bought himself a great side of top-class players, and this is going on today, of course. But we had to decide what to do about developing coaching here and, because so many of the players and managers didn't really know what coaching was, we had to introduce them to it, and the best way to do this, it seemed to us, was by encouraging older professional players to attend coaching courses and then somehow get practising coaching. Therefore we evolved this scheme of letting these coaches go into schools, not only to coach the boys but to coach the masters too. So many coaches were going through our schemes. We had 300 in 1947 taking our full coaching award, which was a big number, and there was a change in the attitude because they went back to the clubs, and stereotyped methods of training were being pushed on one side and new methods were coming in. And this ultimately meant that these players, instead of becoming trainers running around with a sponge, were now becoming coaches who knew how to coach the game. Gradually they got into full management. Ron Greenwood went to the Arsenal first of all, as an assistant, as a coach there, and then moved as a manager to West Ham.

Ron Greenwood: If you went on a course with Walter you came away thinking that he was a Messiah because he'd open your eyes and give you great insight into everything that was going on. He felt that he could either have a circus of people going around spreading the gospel – half-a-dozen or a dozen leading coaches going round – or he could have courses with these people in charge spreading the gospel further, so that instead of having 12 he had about 112 people going around spreading the gospel, and this is what he did. He set up these courses and got leading players like Alan Brown, who was a big centre-half at Burnley, George Smith, who was at Charlton, George Curtis, Bill Nicholson, great names who were leaders, and we used to go on courses and listen to these people, and basically what they did was give you an insight in how to teach, because coaching's teaching really. People deride coaching and say, 'Oh, it's a nasty word is coaching.' Christ, we all go to school and get taught! It wasn't coaching, it was teaching. So what we had to do, we had to be taught how to teach. We could all play but we didn't know how to present it. It's quite common knowledge, you know, that some of the famous players were hopeless at teaching, or coaching if you like to call it that. I mean, they used to stand there and say, 'Well, it's simple, why can't you do it?' It's simple to them, but the basis of teaching and coaching was breaking it down and analysing it so that everybody could understand it.

George Hardwick: Everything passing through the game of football was by word of mouth. The written word wasn't readily accepted, because football had existed for so many years without it. It was: 'You do this,' or 'You can do that,' or 'We'll show you how to do this.' But it had never been put in a book of words, and a lot of people for some reason didn't like the idea, and quite a few of the lads that played with me didn't like the idea and thought Walter was a bit of a clown because he took the trouble to do this. I felt, on the contrary, 'If he can take all the trouble in the world to put this to people and hope that it's going to achieve an improvement in the standard of football at junior level and schools level, at whatever level, then why shouldn't he do it, and why shouldn't we accept it, and why the devil shouldn't we learn from it?'

Bobby Robson: Very instructive, very informative, he was a wonderful man, a great director of coaching. He knew the game from A to Z, and furthermore could impart it, a great speaker. I learned a lot from Walter. I liked him immensely, because he really understood football. He was not a great player, had not had a great career, had not played for a very long time, but he was a prophet. He convinced me when I was an England player that I should continue in the game as a coach. He was my motivator in terms of staying in football, and passing on the knowledge.

Tom Saunders: Yes, I joined in. There was an exodus of schoolmasters who felt that it was very desirable to have these coaching badges. Many of them, sadly, thought that they were perhaps a way to get rapid promotion rather than to carry on in football and spread the message. Yes, I got one. I remember going back to the school – I was teaching at Olive Mount Secondary Modern School [Liverpool] – and my wife had sewn the badge on the tracksuit and I was the bee's knees, and I had all these youngsters round me before the start of the games lesson, giving them chapter and verse, and one young man very politely tapped me under the elbow and said, 'Excuse me, Sir, when are we going to play the proper game?' And that taught me a very sharp lesson very early on after getting that coaching badge – that the young people wanted to play the game and they didn't want to be dictated to too much.

Nat Lofthouse: I used to go to Lilleshall and Walter would bring coaches from countries like Italy, Spain, Germany, France, Holland, Belgium, and we used to listen to these coaches and they had diagrams and things like that and it was interesting. He said, 'Form your own opinion, use your own discretion, what do you think?' He used to put a little onus on you. I mean, a coach can only go so far. If the guy doesn't take it in or he can't do it, it's not much use the coach talking about it.

Brian Glanville: Walter was a very endearing figure but a very curious one because he had these two jobs. He was the first-ever full-time English manager, appointed in 1946, but he always used to say, when I talked to him in those days, being a young journalist in the fifties, that he felt that being Director of Coaching was a more important part of his job. I think what it bred was an orthodoxy with terminology, all these words and phrases borrowed from Hungary, like 'environmental awareness' and 'peripheral vision' and all the rest, and Walter found it very hard to get through to the troops. I remember being told once that Bobby Charlton had said that they were briefed: 'Walter gave us a lovely talk, a lovely talk.' 'What did he say?' 'I don't know.' And Len Shackleton, the so-called Clown Prince, a great maverick, a fine inside-forward, very seldom capped for that reason, sitting on the ground at Roehampton, where England were training. The story goes that Walter said, 'I just want you five boys going down the field, interpassing, no one in the goal, and then when you get to the penalty area put the ball into the goal.' And Shack looking up very wearily and saying, 'Which side of the goal, Mr Winterbottom?'

TG Jones: A great crowd of us all decided to become pukka soccer coaches, you see, and we were all given a badge and out we went. I was appointed as chief coach to the Liverpool County FA, which I think was the biggest County FA in England at that time, and at times I had about 30 professional players working for me, going around the schools and it was a good scheme. The children used to look forward to seeing their idols coming to the school and showing them how to play football. But after a few years it changed. I saw professional players leaving the course, not developing anything. I saw Walter Winterbottom bringing in more schoolteachers. Now, I've nothing against school-teachers, but this was a professional game and lots of these schoolteachers had never played. If they had played, it was only at an amateur level, and they were ousting the professionals. I mean, if a schoolteacher got a badge, which theoretically anybody could get, then that made him a coach for that school. Children were being taught theoretical football as against practical, professional football, and in my opinion that's what's wrong with football today, because the professional coach eventually died out and it's been taken over by the schools.

9

'This is where Hungary defeated England'

England v Hungary, 1953

On 25 November 1953, England lost 6–3 to Hungary at Wembley. It was England's first-ever home defeat to continental opposition. Hungary won the return in Budapest 7–1, and the men of English football started to do their homework.

Politics

Sandor Barcs: At the beginning of the fifties we lived in a historical period in Hungary which was called the Stalinist Era. Everything was very strongly centralized, so, for instance, if we got a letter from an Association, it was sent directly to the Sport Ministry and they translated it and told us what to answer. I became president of the Hungarian FA in 1950, and I had no power and my executive committee had no power. This is why I always used to say, 'To win at Wembley was not as difficult as to reach Wembley.' I met Sir Stanley Rous in Helsinki in 1952 during the Olympic Games, and we watched the Hungary–Sweden [semi-final] game together. It was, I think, the best game I've ever seen in my life. We won 6–0 and it was an excellent Swedish team, and after the match Stanley came to me and said, 'Sandor you are invited to England. We play a game at Wembley. Shake hands.' 'Well,' I said, 'I have an executive committee at home.' I did not dare to tell him what the situation was. I immediately reported to the sport minister, who was present at the Olympic Games, and Mr Sebes, the coach of the Hungarian team, and they were very enthusiastic, and when we returned home we made a report about it to the Party. Nothing happened for some months, and then one of the secretaries of the central committee rang up the sport minister and asked, 'Do you guarantee that we will win the game if you get the permission to play in England?' And of course he answered, 'In football anything can happen, nobody can guarantee such a thing.' Again two or three weeks passed by, and the same secretary rang up Mr Sebes. The same question, the same answer. Sebes informed me about that and I expected to be the next one rung up by the secretary, and it happened six weeks after that, and I told him, 'Of course, I cannot guarantee that we are going to win the game, but one thing I can guarantee, we will play a very, very good game and it will be a world sensation.' We got the permission. I phoned Stanley immediately and we agreed on the date.

Hungarian Tactics

Sandor Barcs: My club, MTK, which was the best club in Hungary in those days, had always had an English coach. During the First World War Mr Jimmy Hogan came to my club. He was one of the most successful coaches in Hungary.

Nándor Hidegkúti: The deep-lying centre-forward tactic was first played by my club team, MTK. There was a very adventurous centre-forward who always went ahead and attacked. This player left us to play in Belgium, so our coach had to develop a new strategy to make up for his loss. We had a player, Palotás, who played this [deep-lying] position. Then the national team tried this strategy with Palotás, but he was an older player and did not last a match all the way through. So in a match in Switzerland the trainer decided to put me to this deep-lying centre-forward position.

Jenö Buzánszky: When the Swiss team was leading 2–0, Péter Palotás, the centre-forward, was replaced by Hidegkúti. Hidegkúti was told to stay back and disturb and neutralize the centre-back. The result was that we came from 2–0 down to 4–2 and beat the Swiss. We played that game in September 1952.

Nándor Hidegkúti: From then on this was how we played and we followed this strategy until 1956. Playing this way, none of the other teams could prepare against us. We attacked with six people and they all were strikers, so this way we could score goals all the time. We kept telling our defenders, 'Do not worry, if they get a goal we score two.'

Towards Wembley

Jenö Buzánszky: We only knew Wembley from hearsay. Gusztáv Sebes tried to gather some information. He found out the width and the length of the pitch. As a preparation we widened one of our pitches at home because Wembley was wider. Then Gusztáv Sebes had five balls imported from England because English balls were different – ours were softer and therefore more sensitive. When we first kicked the English ball it felt like kicking a wooden ball. Also the players we played against the most in those days, the Austrians, told us that the grass at Wembley was like a sponge. The grass was soggy and more dense, so it requires more energy to lift your foot away from the ground. One gets tired quickly, so this is where we had an idea. We thought of the ball as the fastest player on the pitch, therefore we had to make the ball do the running. In football you have to be prepared for everything and we had prepared ourselves for it. We also had this saying, 'You can dodge one, you can dodge two, but you must never dodge a third.' So we had to pass the ball.

Georges Szepesi: Ten days before the London match, Sweden played Hungary in Budapest and it was a 2–2 draw. After the match I met the Hungarian correspondent of the *News Chronicle* who said, 'This Hungarian team is not the slightest little bit better than the one which was beaten 6–2 in 1936 in London.' Well, I was convinced that the Hungarian team was 100 per cent better and that we would win. At the time I was Head of the Sports Department on the radio and I was so convinced of our impending victory that I scheduled to broadcast the Wembley match twice on the same day, once live in the afternoon and then a recorded repeat at twenty past eight in the evening.

Gyula Grosics: We played very badly [against Sweden], and the 2–2 result was favourable for us, not for the Swedes. Since the Hungarian public by that time had been used to our successes, they reacted to the result and to our play with loud discontent. This probably had a positive effect on the match 10 days later, because one could almost feel the fear, the worries and the expectations we had before the meeting with the English.

Nándor Hidegkúti: We went to Paris to play a friendly game against the team of the Renault factory. That was a very easy team and we won 16–1 or so, which made us a little happier. That was how we went to London, where none of us had been before. We were very excited. We went by ship and when we glimpsed the white cliffs of Dover, which one could see in films, we felt very excited.

Sir Walter Winterbottom: Because Hungary was a Communist state, they would order things to be done. They would set aside club football purely for international football, and players would be moved into teams to strengthen that team with a view to that forward-line being probably the forward-line that might play for the national side. And players of the national team would all be centred in Budapest so that they could have training days each week as a team for the national side, and this made a world of difference. We used to get our players and we had no chance of having any training at all, and our worst problem was that our international match was usually on a Wednesday. We picked the team the previous Wednesday. If they played on the Saturday, which they would for their clubs, if there was any injury then we'd have a different team coming together on the Wednesday for the match. We always picked a reserve player for each position, and that reserve player had to go in the team. When Tommy Finney was injured for the match against Hungary at Wembley, George Robb, an amateur playing for Tottenham, had to come in and he'd never played in a professional national team before.

Tom Finney: I was injured at Chelsea on the Saturday and was unable to play, and if my memory serves me right I think we had Gil Merrick in goal, Alf Ramsey, Bill Eckersley, Billy Wright, Harry Johnston, Jimmy Dickinson and then it was Stanley Matthews, little Ernie Taylor, Stanley Mortensen, Jackie Sewell and George Robb, which was a very good England side.

Jackie Sewell: We went down to London and everybody there knew each other. There was Stan Matthews with Harry Johnston and his pals. It were a happy lot, we went training at Chelsea, tipping it around, and there was no problem, and there wasn't a thing in our minds coming close to what was going to happen to us. I used to go over to Stanley Matthews and say, 'Come on, Stanley, let's do some training.' He says, 'No, go away, Jack, and leave me alone', because he used to concentrate on his own little bits, and my God, he was good at it. We used to leave him alone until it come to the sprinting time, so then I used to chase him and sprint with him, thinking I could catch up with him, but I could never catch him. We just played around, relaxed, and what was missing was that we didn't know a thing about them.

Sir Walter Winterbottom: Well, I'd followed them. I saw them win the Olympic Games in Finland, almost the same team that came to play in England. They were kept together and they developed together so that they were strong, and in the preparation for coming to us they had a fortnight away from their clubs for special training. They'd played Sweden in Hungary and several of the press and myself were there, and because they only managed to draw 2-2 against Sweden it was 'a pushover for England at Wembley', and I was very cross about this because I thought Hungary were a great side and had got some great players. But, you see, that was an occasion when we had to make so many changes to our side. We had a team with two new players. It wasn't on to expect us to jell together in one match without any preparation at all.

Georges Szepesi: Three weeks before the match the [Rest of Europe] team had played England at Wembley and it was a 4–4 draw. Ramsey scored the equalizer in the 92nd minute from a penalty. So England was unbeaten [at home to foreign teams] for 90 years. I think it actually was the *News Chronicle* which ran the headline 'Match of the Century' and for a radio commentator to report on the match of the century is an unforgettable experience.

Sandor Barcs: I was present at the pre-match tactical discussion at the Cumberland Hotel which was held by Sebes. It lasted three hours, and I must tell you that I did my very best but I couldn't understand a single word of what he said. He was so excited, he couldn't express himself. When he'd finished, Puskás said to me, 'President, did you understand what he said?' 'No, I didn't.' 'Neither do I.'

Jenö Buzánszky: We went to Wembley by coach and someone sang the national anthem. Others occupied themselves in other ways but no one chatted and there was incredible tension. Everybody tried to relax somehow. We sang Hungarian folk songs and tried all sorts of things.

Georges Szepesi: Before the match all the players behaved in a very relaxed, easy-going manner. Kocsis, for example, said to Puskás, 'Let's make a bet. I bet I can keep this ball in the air for 100 kicks,' and then, when he was up to 98, Czibor snatched the ball off him so he could not reach 100, and they fell about in laughter. They were in a really good mood.

Malcolm Allison: Jimmy Andrews and I went to the game. We went round the outside of the stadium and there was a space where all the Hungarian team were warming up, just knocking the ball about and flicking the ball up. Jimmy said to me, 'Cor, look at their gear, the shirts are terrible.' I said, 'Well, it's an Iron Curtain country, they haven't got good gear.' He said, 'We'll beat these easy.' I said, 'Why's that, Jim?' He said, 'Look at that little fat fellow over there, he's a stone overweight.' That was Puskas, the number ten. And they came out and warmed up, and Puskas and Bozsik warmed up together. They volleyed the ball to each other over about 25 yards. They caught it on the instep and flicked it up and volleyed it eight times without the ball touching the ground. I said, 'I tell you what, Jim, these are not bad.'

Nándor Hidegkúti: The stadium was marvellous. I think it is the dream of every player to be able to play there once in his life. That is a soccer sanctuary. When we went on to the pitch it was a fantastic sight. A hundred thousand fans were there, and that is something. We examined the grass thoroughly. Well, the Austrians were right. The grass was fantastic – it was so thick you actually could not see the earth itself.

Tom Finney: In those days, as a player, you were not allowed to make any comments about the England side, and I was invited by the *Daily Express* to go into the press-box and comment about the Hungarian side. We saw them come out at Wembley about 10 or 15 minutes before the game with a ball each, and doing all sorts of juggling acts with the ball, and it was something entirely new to English players and to the spectators as well, and I heard one sly remark at the back of me, from one of the press men: 'Ah, they might be able to do that now but they'll not be able to do that when the game starts.'

The Match

Nándor Hidegkúti: I got the ball from Bozsik in the 45th second and around the 18-yard line I made a dribble. Johnston turned away, but I did not hit it straight away. I carried it a little further and when I struck the ball it went to the opposite upper corner. In the 45th second. That was very important psychologically for the team because we could relax a little. Now two goals are needed for the opponents to win. So we started to play, but we also lost a goal, so it was 1–1. Then Puskás passed me a ball, and I scored again, so we led 2–1. After that we were not so afraid of the English.

Georges Szepesi: All the foreign radio commentators and reporters were situated in the front row of the terrace, in the same row as the Royal Box. I was given the number-16 microphone box. Reporting that match will always remain a wonderful experience to me, and when Hidegkúti scored that unforgettable goal in the first minute I started to shout: 'Hidegkúti shoots, shoots, goal, goal, GOAL!' and I knew that the whole country experienced it with me, and then all of a sudden I felt a tap on my back. It was one of the English supporters and he offered me a small glass of whisky. I drank it and after that I carried on commentating in even higher spirits. I must add that it was an incredibly fair crowd all the way through. They cheered and applauded the Hungarian goals the same way as if England would have scored them.

Tom Finney: They gave an absolutely wonderful exhibition and I consider it a privilege to have been there to see it. The deep-lying centre-forward was an unknown quantity to us. We'd never seen this type of play, where Hidegkúti played very, very deep. Harry Johnston, who was a very good player, played centre-half, and was at a loss as to know what to do. He'd never seen a centre-forward go back into his own half of the field and get the ball, and they had Puskás and the other inside-forward, Kocsis, who again was an outstanding player, and England were 4–1 down at half-time.

Georges Szepesi: I was in ecstasy after every single goal but I think the most beautiful goal of my life was that third one Puskás scored and I shouted, 'This is a world sensation. Puskás pulls it back, with his sole.'

Kenneth Wolstenholme: That Puskás goal was perhaps one of the most incredible things I've ever seen. I can see it now. Merrick was in a perfect position by his left-hand post, so Puskás had no chance of beating him, and the ball was on one side of the goal. Billy Wright was coming in to cover and Puskás pulled it back with the sole of his left boot, turned on his right and hit it with his left foot and the ball's in the back of the net. All in about one-tenth of the time it's taken me to tell you that. Geoffrey Green, who wrote in *The Times*, described it beautifully. He said, 'Billy Wright rushed into the tackle like a fireman racing to the wrong fire.'

George Robb: That was quite remarkable because I don't

think at that time we had seen that kind of confident action. Stanley Matthews was a wizard with the ball but Stanley would not have dropped the ball, pulled it back with the sole of the foot and virtually in the same instant hit an unstoppable shot in.

Ferenc Puskás: It was a simple trick, the kind of thing I used to do when I was a boy. Perhaps it was a crazy thing to attempt in a big match, but it came out right in the end.

Georges Szepesi: In my opinion the all-time greatest Hungarian player was Puskás. I loved Hidegkúti, I loved Bozsik and Kocsis, they were all world-class players in their own field. But Puskás had three unique talents or skills. For one he was born a genius. Secondly, he was a natural captain, a general who always sensed what was the best thing to do in any given situation because he prepared for every match very thoroughly. And thirdly, he was such an adorable rascal, a real urchin from the outskirts of Budapest.

Billy Wright: Everybody talks about Ferenc and myself, and he was the great player, but it wasn't Ferenc Puskás that did us, it was Nándor Hidegkúti. The reason was that he was a deep-lying centre-forward and we didn't pick him up as well as we should have done. And Nándor was the creative man, he made space. I'm not saying that Puskás wasn't a great player – he was – but it was the system of playing Nándor deep that pulled us about in that particular game. It was between either Jim Dickinson or Harry Johnston who would pick up, it was always the closest to him would pick him up. Well, because of their great skill and because of that system, they created more space than we thought. On the day they were the better side. But one doesn't forget that we did score three goals against them.

Jenö Buzánszky: After about 10 or 15 minutes we figured out which flank of an opposition team was the stronger, which side we should attack on, where the vulnerable points in their defence were, and this information was then very quickly processed by our 'computers', by Puskás, Bozsik, Hidegkúti and so on, and they quickly reorganized the original tactics which we had discussed in the dressing-room. And straight away everybody changed their game and played differently. We didn't stick rigidly to our initial plan. The greatness of the players of the past lies in the fact that they used their brains a lot more, they did a lot of thinking on the pitch, and that was true of a lot of teams at the time, not only us Hungarians. We used to have a coach, Dr Károly Lakat, who was called 'The Professor' and he used to say, 'The game is played with your head, it's only the ball you kick with your foot.' So you need your head, that's what directs you, and England couldn't really change their tactics during the match.

Tom Finney: I was under the opinion that they would probably turn it round in the second half because they would obviously have sorted out this problem with the deep-lying centre-forward and Puskás, but it didn't work out that way. We did pull back to 4–2, and then it went to 5–2, and then 5–3 and then 6–3 and that was the first time I think we'd been beaten on our own soil by a foreign side, so it was a wonderful win for Hungary and really a lesson for English professional football players.

Jenö Buzánszky: It was another great facet of the Hungarian team that we didn't nurse the ball, we could get it under control at once and pass it immediately. There are two types of speed in sport. One is the running speed and the other is the thinking speed. If you look at Hidegkúti's first goal you can see that he did one manoeuvre and scored from 20 metres. Merrick was obviously not prepared for that. Or if you look at Hidegkúti's, the sixth goal, or the one which Puskás volleyed in an off-hand manner, or the one when Bozsik got the ball back and he turned immediately and scored into the upper corner from 20 metres. For someone to take such risks you have to handle the ball very confidently and have to be very fast. Hungary was ahead regarding this and of course I don't want to flatter the team too much as it would be self-flattery, but we were ahead of the world in a number of fields.

Gyula Grosics: In my youth, when I played in Dorog, there was a famous Hungarian coach, Péter Szabo, who taught me, as a goalkeeper, that in this position one needs as much self-education and innovation as possible. He inspired me to solve my tasks independently, and I have to say I learned a lot from the game itself. Just to name a few: the running out, the starting by hand, which is very important for a goalkeeper because a quick and precise hand-thrown ball can gain time and space from the opponent. This was not really widespread at that time, but I thought it was safer than kicking the ball, which might or might not reach its aim. I would add that my teammates had to adapt to my style, to the quick hand starts. Those who got near the goal were told to move in such a way so that I could easily throw them the ball. Puskás and Hidegkúti very often came back, approaching our goal to 20–25 metres, so the possibility to throw to them was very obvious.

Jackie Sewell: I said to someone during or after the game, 'Do you know, I'm very tired.' I don't think I've run about so much in my life as chasing them around, and that was that when this triangle business came into the football. They worked triangles all over the field, and this was just clockwork with them, and they didn't even have to look, and that was intriguing me half the time when I was there playing. Puskás would get a ball, inside-left position, and he wouldn't look, they'd do this triangle movement and push it back and forward and he would let this left clog of his go and you'd see somebody flying on the inside-right position or the right wing and he was dropping it straight at them, and they're hitting it before the ball hit the ground, and this was something that we weren't told about. It was fantastic to be on the field playing with them.

Jenö Buzánszky: There's another thing which was quite interesting about Hungarian football. If you watch the match you notice how much our forwards ran, how often they ran back to help, and we used to have another saying which is obvious in football today. I think that with this we were a bit ahead of our time. It was, 'If the opponents attack then as many players should come back as possible.' Puskás, Hidegkúti, Czibor and Budai, they used to help out in defence a great deal and they very often tackled around the 18-yard line, and when we would launch a counterattack all the half-backs would run up, Bozsik and myself as well. We all tried to help the attack. So we were also a bit ahead with this, and in the amount we ran and moved around during the match.

Nándor Hidegkúti: Hungary won at Wembley because on that day the team was in better condition, there were more talented players in our team than in the English one, and by that time this team had played together more than three years. We knew each other's dreams, every movement. The more unified a team is, the more chances it has to win. If I went forward, Puskás immediately came into my place. If Kocsis went to the side then Bozsik went to the centre. We always found a way to have an empty space in the field to where we can pass the ball. Buzánszky ran forward all the time – this was the first time in the world that a right-back overlapped the winger. It was a tactical move. When Budai ran inside, then Buzánszky immediately had to advance up the right so that we could give him the ball. Nobody knew that the right-back would go forward and might score a goal. This way we always had 'free' players to whom one could pass the ball. We did not play individually but in a team. We all had one aim, and everybody knew it. When we led by two goals then people could show their little individual tricks. Until then everybody played for the team.

Sir Walter Winterbottom: Hidegkúti was creating the

problem because he was the centre-forward, so called, and came 20 yards further back, drawing the centre-half (if the centre-half was going with him) out of position so that people could slot into the gap. Does the centre-half follow him to create the space and someone else fill in? Or does the centre-half stay back and let Hidegkúti be a free man working as a midfield player? You have a choice in these things, and usually you leave it to the player concerned. We had a meeting of all the managers in the First Division at the Café Royal to discuss all this, and Stanley Cullis made the point that he thought that centre-halves should stay with the centre-forward wherever he went, but we would argue against that on the grounds that the way they were playing in continental football they'd put the centre-forward's jersey on the left-full-back. And the way the game's played now, of course, is the best system of all, the sweeper system, and this means that there's one man at the back who's there to block the holes that appear. He can take anybody coming through and then he's a free man for attacks going forward as well, if he's a skilled player.

After the Match

Georges Szepesi: After the match I burst into the dressing-room and shouted, 'This was a miracle, boys. We have beaten England!' but they were sitting there in silence. There was no champagne, no celebration, almost as if they could not yet take in what had happened. Then I walked out to the stadium again and walked up to that point between the 18- and the six-yard line from where Puskás scored that unforgettable third goal – incidentally, it is still very often played on Hungarian television – which decided the outcome of the match, because at 2–1 England looked as though they might have been able to turn around the score. So as I stood there I was thinking that they normally erect a memorial at the place where great historical battles took place. They should put a small memorial on that spot in Wembley, from where Puskás scored that goal: 'This is where Hungary defeated England.'

Sandor Barcs: I needed 20, 25 minutes to reach the dressing-room as I lost my way. I had to go through the English team's bathroom, and at once Billy Wright jumped out from his bath, came to me with wet hands, shook my hand and said, 'This was a wonderful game, I enjoyed it very much. I congratulate you, Mr President. You have a wonderful team,' and really I was moved. It can only happen in England. Fantastic.

Nándor Hidegkúti: Yes, they were very friendly afterwards. There was the English–Hungarian table-tennis match in Wembley and we went there because there was the reception after the match anyway. We talked, with the help of interpreters. They came and congratulated us. It was very hard to imagine that after a lost match they come and congratulate you. But we learned that this was the English way to do it. We were totally surprised. At the reception we got very close to each other. We talked a lot and then went to see the table-tennis match.

Georges Szepesi: The following morning, Stanley Rous came to visit the Hungarian team. He congratulated them again. I accompanied Gusztáv Sebes to the inner reception hall where we sat down with a cup of coffee. There was a rather large case beside Rous. They were chatting about this and that, about the timing of the return match, when all of a sudden the head of the English Football Association opened his case and it was full of money, English pounds. Then he looked at Sebes and said, 'Mr Sebes, I did not only come to discuss the match but I would also like to pay you for the wonderful game. How much of this money would you like?' Sebes looked at him in astonishment and said he didn't want any money. 'But let me reiterate, gentlemen, I brought you money,' said Rous, 'I brought you pounds sterling.' But Sebes just repeated, 'Thank you very much, but we do not wish to receive any payment. We are pleased that England can come to play in Budapest, but I can't take home a single pound after this match.'

Sandor Barcs: After the game Stanley Rous came to the Cumberland Hotel with a suitcase and said, 'I brought you some money.' I told him, 'Please, Stanley. Save my soul. I cannot accept any money. We are amateurs.' And he said to me, 'This is unbelievable. This is the first time in my life that somebody does not accept money.' 'But I cannot accept money,' I told him.

The Return Game

Jenö Buzánszky: The return match took place on 23 May 1954 in Budapest. To try to describe how interested people were, I should tell you that about a million people applied for tickets! In the end they managed to squeeze 104,000 people into the stadium. We were slightly apprehensive before this match too, but at least we knew the English players so we were not as anxious as we had been before Wembley. Also, we played on our home ground in front of a home crowd and we played against a team which we had previously beaten 6–3. We always respected the opponents and we used to say, 'We must not relax until we are in the lead at least 2–0.' Things clicked together rather well on the return match, too. For example Mihály Lantos's free-kick at 20 metres right at the beginning of the match. Although it did not happen in the 45th second, it was in the eighth or ninth minute. So we had a good start and we played well. England had not yet succeeded in changing their game. I think they were a bit confused at the time as they tried to play a game somewhere in between the old and the new system. Of course we played our own game. We had prepared much more calmly and it was wonderful. As I always say, England arrived for *egy hét* [one week] and left with *hét egy* [7–1].

Gyula Grosics: For me the most remarkable characteristic of the English is their utmost respect of tradition, in many fields of life – and why should sport be an exception? The best proof of this is that a few months later an almost identically composed English team arrived and they played the same style as at Wembley, and this faithfulness to tradition showed in the result. We could surprise the English team even in Budapest, though we played the same style as in London. I feel that the English were very reluctant to give up a tradition which was actually their invention and which had brought them so much success.

Kenneth Wolstenholme: We changed the team a bit and Beddy Jezzard of Fulham was centre-forward. Now I'll never forget the *Daily Express* headline the morning of the match – 'Jezzard will blast the Magyars.' We lost 7–1. I thought then that we hadn't learned.

Syd Owen: The Nep Stadium in Budapest was probably the most luxurious dressing-room I've ever changed in to play a match. There were easy chairs all around and individual cupboards for players' clothes, and to sit down in an easy chair is not the preparation for an international match. I had great admiration for the way the Hungarians had developed their team-work to produce such exhilarating football. They were oozing with confidence and that is always a great thing in professional sport. It was difficult to keep in contact with Hidegkúti because he was withdrawing to deeper positions and getting balls from midfield players and defenders, and, by the time you've gone forward to intercept or compete for the ball, other people have joined the attack. That was the time that England suffered their heaviest international defeat.

Malcolm Allison: I remember talking to Syd Owen. We played Luton the Saturday after England had lost 7–1 and I went up and shook hands with Syd before the game. I said, 'How was it over there, Syd, playing against the Hungarians?' He said, 'Malcolm, it was like playing people from outer space.'

The Repercussions

Gyula Grosics: If we can say that the English gave the world the WM system, then we can say we gave the world this totally new system which we practised for years and which, four years later, was named by the Brazilians as 4-2-4. This was a typical Hungarian system and it became typical Brazilian.

Tom Finney: I think that this was the first time that it was brought home to the English people that we were no longer the so-called best side in the world and hadn't been for some time. I think we'd had a tendency to rest on past laurels and these teams were prepared to learn more about the game than what we as professional players were prepared to. It really showed the English game up and it was like carthorses playing racehorses, and when you think we had people like Stan Matthews and Stanley Mortensen and little Ernie Taylor, but we were just torn asunder. That was a start of English football looking at itself and saying, 'Well, where have we gone wrong?'

Ron Greenwood: I made sure that I went to Wembley to see the famous Hungarians play and a new light came into my eyes. I was watching a team playing the way I felt football should be played, and to me it was a revelation and it made a great impression on me. I felt there and then that if I ever became in charge of a team, that's near enough the way I'd want to play. At that time we were playing a lot of football in this country where it was a long ball up to the big centre-forward and knock back and what-have-you, and Hungary's passing angles were unbelievable. They would bring so many people into the play by knocking it up, getting it back, knocking it wide and moving again, and the movement was complete. In other words the man on the ball had about three alternatives. Consequently the angles and the movement caused catastrophic disaster in the English defence. They were chasing shadows half the time.

Sandor Barcs: British football was isolated. They didn't like the continental football. They felt themselves as the aristocrats of this game, and this is why they were isolated. I spoke about this problem with Jimmy Hogan, when he was in Budapest, and he told me that all the British coaches who worked on the continent spoke about the same thing when they came back to England: 'We are not aristocrats, we are not the best.' I will be impolite telling this, but we always differentiated between British and Hungarian football – what you played was industry and what we played was art.

10

'Revolutionary ideas'

Tactical Awareness in the Early 1950s

The 1950s brought more choice of what system to play. Tottenham's Champions of 1950–51 played 'push and run'. Wolves were three times Champions in the 1950s with their so-called 'long-ball game'. The West Ham academy were discussing tactics and laying the foundations for later success. Manchester City's innovative 'Revie Plan' mimicked the Hungarian deep-lying centre-forward and took City to two Cup Finals.

Tottenham Hotspur: 'Push and Run'

Eddie Baily: When Arthur Rowe came to this club as manager [May 1949], he came to a unit of players who were all natural passing players. He had come from Hungary, having been a coach there for about three years, and he had this belief about the game, that it's a lovely passing game, 'push and run'. Arthur Rowe used to have little sayings like 'Make it simple, make it quick' and 'He who holds the ball is lost.'

George Robb: Arthur was a very shrewd man and it might well be that, going over there and watching them play, he might have seen something that was different from our own game which has always has been 'strong tackling, move the ball, get it up into the box and the big centre-forwards, your Lawtons and your Lofthouses'. What impressed me at Tottenham when I went down there was that after they'd done their track work they used what was then the car-park for six-a-side and that was absolutely marvellous. The blokes loved it.

Eddie Baily: If you made a pass, the object of the exercise was to get somewhere quickly and get the return. We used to work in triangles and squares. You pushed it and you moved. It was a simple basic principle which we used to do all over the field.

Sir Walter Winterbottom: Tottenham were playing some beautiful football in those days. Mostly on the ground, but there were chip passes. I mean, Alf Ramsey, who played in that team, was a man for judging a chip pass just over the head of a player into the direction of an on-running forward, and so on. Well, that was Arthur's great contribution, welding a team who could play this style of football which was so attractive to watch. It was like silky stuff, and everybody seemed to have plenty of time with the ball and yet they were running into space. This work off the ball is absolutely essential if you're going to play a good game of football.

Bill Nicholson: Alf Ramsey joined us from Southampton and when he came into Tottenham's side and started playing he was a cool, calm and collected type of fella. And they nicknamed him 'The General', because he seemed to have everything under control. He was a good passer of the ball and he had very good control of the ball, too. If he had a weakness it was his lack of pace, but he was a good player. I would feel that if Ronnie Burgess hadn't been with the club, as he had been since well before the war as a youngster, Alf would probably have been the captain of the side, but Ronnie remained captain. Alf Ramsey became Arthur Rowe's favourite player really, but Arthur had a good liking for the majority of the players because in fairness they were all very good and they were all able to do what he wanted us to do, which was slightly different from what we'd been doing previously, particularly in Ronnie Burgess's case. Ronnie was a very good player but he used to run a lot with the ball, and Arthur's style was not to run with the ball but to run *off* the ball and to pass the ball when you were in possession of it, and of course you could do that best if the players off the ball were moving into position and showing you where they wanted the ball to be played. Anyhow, we had the push and run – make it simple, make it accurate, make it quick. On one occasion we were playing at Leicester and they said, after the match, 'We hate playing against you because it's like trying to catch pigeons.' We did have one or two players who could occasionally work the ball themselves. One was Les Bennett. He was good at pushing the ball and running, but he could also work the ball himself and Eddie Baily could sometimes do that, but Eddie Baily, in my opinion, was the best first-time passer of the ball at that particular time in football.

Wolves: 'The Long-ball Game'

Stan Cullis: Ever since I joined the Wolves, and right up to when I departed from the Wolves, we used wingers. Major Buckley considered wingers were essential, and when I took over as manager I saw no reason why I should not be privy to using wingers. When you consider, we had two international wingers on our books, Jimmy Mullen and Johnny Hancocks, who were both very effective players. I wouldn't be certain but I think we won the Football League three times and the FA Cup twice, but there again my memory is not as good as it was. Briefly, the basis of the style was to make certain that if you were going to play close, interpassing football, you would do it in your opponents' half of the field rather than in yours. In other words, the duty of the defensive players was to get the ball up to the forwards with accuracy so that they were relieved of any tension as far as the defence was concerned. But also they were happy to release the ball to the forwards so that we could be on the attack rather than be on the defensive, because I think to me it seems quite easy to reconcile the fact that transferring the ball to the forwards was a better way than transferring the ball via the defence.

Sir Walter Winterbottom: Stanley Cullis, of course, picked up on the ideas of Wing Commander Reep, who had worked out that the more you passed the ball the more the ball was going to go to the opposition without you getting near scoring, whereas if you put the ball into the penalty area or thereabouts as quickly as you can and your players work for it, you've more chance to score. Cullis wanted his wingers to fly, he wanted crosses to come over early and his players had to be quick in picking up the loose ball and crashing it into goal and so on.

Stan Cullis: Well, I met Wing Commander Reep when he wrote to me and said that he'd seen a few matches of the Wolves and he would like to discuss with me certain things that had happened. He came to see me and I suppose spent at least two hours informing me of how he was able to log every move that happened in a game. Most of the goals that were scored were attributable not to any great interpassing but very often were from one, two, three, four passes. I knew exactly what I was doing, I was conscious of how a certain type of play was able to produce the goals that were scored, and this is why I had every sympathy. He came to the Wolves purely as a spectator, he was never paid, but he did work for other clubs apart from the Wolves.

Charles Reep: It started in 1950 when I went to Swindon Town's ground and made a note on a piece of paper of the number of times Swindon had possession of the ball. And at the end of the match, it was about 270 times. The shorthand code developed itself and in the first two months, back in 1950–51, I discovered some things which even now are not known to some of the best managers in the world. One thing is that as the number of passes is increased in play, that the chance of a goal being scored is less, other things being equal. It depends upon the skill of the team, but if two teams with equal skills played together over a whole season, and one team kept its passing down to three, and the other team used unlimited passing then the team with only three passes would be at the top. Out of all the goals scored, one half precisely come from none to one passes, and 80 per cent come from not more than three passes. And that's been the same from 1950. Brentford were in the Second Division then, and they were facing relegation. The manager was Jackie Gibbons, and he was told, 'Up at RAF Bushey, they've got an RAF officer who stands on the touch-line writing things down and they've been scoring goals at a phenomenal rate,' and he was desperate, clutching at straws, and he sent a message through to me. Right away, I was lifted up from ordinary RAF football into the Second Division. Brentford had 14 matches left to play and in those 14 matches, the team rose to ninth place. The team contained Jimmy Hill and Ron Greenwood, and those two were stumbling blocks who wanted to play their own style of play. I was posted to RAF Bridgnorth, 14 miles away from Wolverhampton, and, when I got there, I discovered that the officer who ran soccer on the station was a friend of Stan Cullis. He told Stan Cullis that Charles Reep had come up and he'd been the man who had designed the system of play which had seen Brentford rocket up from bottom to top in a short time. At the time I arrived, the directors of Wolves had been trying to persuade their manager, Stan Cullis, to go in for 'push and run' and he said, 'Oh, I have no intention of doing so.' Stan said afterwards, 'Charles, that was a turning point, if you hadn't come, perhaps I might have had to give in.' And for three and a half years I was with Wolves as his guest, in a free seat, and I could go with the team for away matches if I wanted to.

Billy Wright: We were successful because Stan knew which side he wanted to have. He got Johnny Hancocks, the outside-right, and Bert Williams from Walsall. The rest were ordinary Wolves players who'd come from the groundstaff, and he knew which style he wanted them to play. We produced three League Championships, but the funny part about it is that the newspapers – because television wasn't so much around in those days – didn't like our style. They thought we played too much of the long ball. In the fifties they wanted to see us play like Tottenham would play, or some other team were playing, but Stan said, 'No, I know which way I want to play and I've got statistics.' We played to our strengths. Jimmy Mullen and Johnny Hancocks hit crossfield balls to each other and then they crossed the ball in a normal wing way. So we got the defences moving the opposite way to which they were used to. That was the style Stan produced, and he produced some great players. Not only Mullen and Hancocks, you had Peter Broadbent, Dennis Wilshaw, Roy Swinbourne, and in the half-back-line you had Eddie Clamp, Ron Flowers, Bill Slater, and these were international players. In one season we'd got seven who played for England. And so therefore he wasn't producing rubbish, he was producing players who were capable of playing for England and on more than one occasion the England half-back-line consisted of three Wolves players.

Stan Cullis: I would say that Billy Wright was the best example of a professional player that I'd seen, with his attitude on and off the field. I used to rely upon Billy Wright to implement what I had tried to implement off the field and

Billy Wright used to make certain, as far he was capable of doing, that the players behaved themselves on the pitch, and I think it's true to say that in the 16 years that I was manager at the Wolves we didn't have one player sent off.

Against the Continentals

Stan Cullis: These were matches at the Wolves under floodlights against Moscow Spartak, Moscow Dynamo and Honved of Hungary. Wolves were one of the first to step into the limelight for floodlit matches against continental opponents. Well, the Honved team that played the Wolves at Molineux, there were five players, I think, that had played against England and beaten England at Wembley, and Honved were two goals up at half-time. I pointed out to the players that they had played quite well and I was quite happy with the way they'd played and to go out and to play the same as they played in the first half. They went out and they scored three goals and we won 3–2, which convinced me that rather than bother about how continental teams played against us, we would use our own methods and be quite happy using them. It was one of the most auspicious occasions that the Wolves ever had to cope with because Honved was one of the great teams at that particular time.

Percy Young: One felt that it was a national triumph. We were, I suppose in football terms, rather intolerant nationalists. It wasn't that Wolves at that time were a better team [than Honved], it was that they had more determination jointly. It's not always the better team that wins a game, and the reason is something which is emotional and difficult to translate into instructions, or words.

Stan Cullis: Our play was designed to hit continental teams with passes that they weren't used to. In other words, we used to try and hit long balls over their heads for forwards to run on to, and we weren't happy interpassing. But to say, as some newspapers have said, that Wolves used 'the long ball' as if that was the only pass that they used, this was quite wrong. I got quite miffed, I suppose, at having our play described as 'long ball' when the long ball was only part of the game that we used.

David Miller: Wolves steam-rollered people, physically, temperamentally, and the manager, Stan Cullis, personified the same spirit and had been like that as a player when captaining England – you went through people as much as you went round them. That's how Wolves played when beating Honved and Spartak in those early floodlit friendlies at Molineux, and then suddenly we got European football and [in 1960] Wolves were left beating the air against Barcelona, totally lost. They spent the whole match within three yards of the ball and never touched it because Barcelona ran rings around them, by using the ball and movement off the ball, so Wolves were totally exposed as the personification of the English game by this advent of European teams and European football.

The West Ham Academy

Noel Cantwell: When I first came to West Ham in 1952, the training was stereotyped. There was a lot of running around the track and up and down steps and five-a-side football, but there was nobody teaching anybody how to play the game of football. Malcolm Allison was really the guy who went to Lilleshall first of all and learned from people like Herrera [later coach of Barcelona, Inter-Milan and Roma] who came over and gave their time to teach. So Malcolm came back with revolutionary ideas of what should happen to a football club. I think it would have been about 1954 that Malcolm's influence in the dressing-room and in the club became very apparent. He wasn't popular with everybody. As you know, a lot of people don't like change and he did lots of things that were unpopular with the manager. But fortunately he influenced John Bond, Dave Sexton, me, and Jimmy Andrews, people who became interested in the game. I've got a picture of a West Ham team and in the back row it has got John Bond, Dave Sexton, Malcolm Allison, Noel Cantwell and Frank O'Farrell. The one exception in that back row is Ernie Gregory. He's the only one who didn't manage in the First Division. If I can give you some of Malcolm's ideas. We were getting away from the big hobnailed, toe-capped dubbined boot and soon we were playing in lightweight boots and the day had gone when we had big shin-pads. If we'd been jockeys we would have been a stone overweight when we started. Our new shirts got presented to us on a very, very hot day at the start of a season and Malcolm thought, 'I don't like these long-sleeved shirts,' so he asked the trainer for scissors and cut the sleeves off the shirts! After training, we'd come to the café, Cassettari's, and we would sit upstairs and argue, and we'd have as many as 10 round the tables because we didn't have anything else to do. At football clubs then there were snooker rooms so you either became a very good snooker player or else you decided to put something in and try and become a better footballer, and of course the enthusiasm of Malcolm would rub off, and we'd finish our lunch and then walk back to the ground and we would practise for hours.

Philip Cassettari: My Dad, Phil Cassettari, has been running this café for 53 years and we've seen lots of players come and go. At the time I didn't realize how important it was. They were just footballers that came into the shop and in those days footballers didn't earn fantastic livings and they were quite glad to come and eat in the café and have somewhere to stay, and a lot of them were living in digs. Later there was Bobby Moore, Martin Peters, Geoff Hurst, Peter Brabrook, and I remember some of the older players like Dave Sexton and Noel Cantwell.

Malcolm Allison: When we first used to come to this café after training, when I first came to West Ham, we'd sit down and talk about football, about the game on Saturday, about next week's game, and I said to 'em, 'You know, we're not enthusiastic enough, we don't work hard enough.' They said, 'Yes, yes, yes.' When I said to them, 'Let's go back and train this afternoon,' they said, 'Well, I've got to go here' and 'I've got to go there.' Then maybe Noel would come back with me, and maybe Bondie would come back with me and maybe Dave Sexton, maybe, and then Malcolm Musgrove would join in and then Jimmy Andrews would come and then occasionally we would get Harry Hooper and then all of them. And then we got to moving all the salt cellars and doing this talking about tactics and became more and more involved. Then, after the shock of the Hungary game, it made us realize how much we had to improve, and they never argued about the situation. We just used to practise and talk about it, and sometimes train too hard. I brought in weight-training, heavy weight-training. Bill Nicholson said it was wrong and Ted Fenton didn't want to do it, and everybody said it was wrong. But I found that our jumping became better. We became stronger and quicker.

Noel Cantwell: And also warming up. Do you remember? Teams didn't warm up before games – they got stripped five minutes before they went out and embarrassingly kicked the ball around – but we would go in the gym at quarter past two and have a fairly good work-out and come back out and then get prepared. The weight-training gave you tremendous confidence. You felt stronger and you felt good. How one looks and how one appears is always very important. I think it helped when we got away from the old baggy shorts and all had good gear.

Manchester City: 'The Revie Plan'

Bert Trautmann: Of course we watched the England game against Hungary and, Hidegkúti, the centre-forward, was lying behind. And at City Johnny Williamson tried to play this game, lying deep, in the Reserves, and then we took it over and of course it was in all the papers: Man City's Hidegkúti, deep-lying centre-forward. We went to Preston North End and we got beat 5–1! But we persevered with it. Everybody was involved, goalkeeper, full-backs, because ideas had to come from the middle and we were looking for people like Roy Paul, Don Revie, or whoever ran. I probably played a big part in it because, after having saved balls, having caught a ball, the ball was already on the way. This was my handball experience. People were running into space and I delivered the ball with my hand, eliminating three, four or five opponents. We were like a military machine. Unfortunately, later on, when a lot of players had left us, City persevered with the so-called Revie plan and we struggled, because we didn't have the players. That proved to me that you had to have good players, intelligent players, to play anything.

11

'An internationalist outlook'

Into Europe and Becoming World Class

At Manchester United, manager Matt Busby and his assistant, Jimmy Murphy, created a youth policy which heralded the Busby Babes, Champions in successive seasons (1955–56 and 1956–57). Tragically, the team was devastated by the 1958 Munich Air Disaster in which 23 people died, including eight United players. The early 1960s saw two new Championship-winning teams – Bill Nicholson's Tottenham and Alf Ramsey's Ipswich. Meanwhile, Ron Greenwood built on his inheritance as manager of West Ham United.

Sir Matt Busby ...

Denis Law: There have been some great managers in the game – you think of Bill Shankly, Bill Nicholson at Spurs, the great double team, Jock Stein, of course, at Celtic – but Matt Busby would probably be the greatest one of all. He built a team after the war, the '48 side. He built the '58 team, and

125

unfortunately half were killed in the Munich Air Disaster, and he built the '68 side. So he built three great teams. Busby's philosophy on football was basically 'Go out and enjoy the game, try to entertain the people.' If at the end of 90 minutes you've lost or whatever, it doesn't really make any difference as long as you've tried your best. And when you think of the great players in the '48 side and the '58 team and also in the sixties when you'd the great George Best and Bobby Charlton, and Busby was the orchestrator. He would buy a player and slot them in. He had the youth policy and he could man-manage people, which not many people can do.

Charlie Mitten: Sir Matt was the best man-manager that I've ever come across, even to this day, and I've been round the world. He knew all his players inside out and he knew what to say at the right time and in the right place. He'd go to the lads and he'd say, 'Now, come on, wake yourself up.' Or he would put his arm round the old boys, and say, 'Come on, you can do better than that' or 'Well done, son, come on, now.' And it would make all the difference in the world.

Pat Crerand: He would go round and speak to us all individually. He would never at any time embarrass anybody in front of anybody. He would go round and talk to everybody about how he expected us to play and about his great philosophy of the game, that the ball was ours and you don't give the ball away and you pass it to the nearest red jersey. He made it very, very simple.

John Giles: I think Matt Busby became what's known now as a tracksuit manager, but that was before the Munich Air Disaster, when he was younger, when he was out with the young players, along with Jimmy Murphy, and he would mix with the players on the field. In his time it wasn't so accepted. He also had a good knowledge of the game because of his playing experience with Manchester City and Liverpool, and he was a cultured player who encouraged cultured play and the right principles of attractive play. Manchester United were always a very attractive side to watch.

George Best: I think if he'd gone into business, he'd have been successful, because to handle so many different characters takes something a little bit special. He remembered little things that we might not think are important but he knew were important. He remembered your name, where you came from, your wife's name. I remember the first time my father went to Old Trafford and I introduced him, and he came back about a year later and he said, 'How are you, Dickie?' He remembered my dad's nickname – he's Richard – my mom's name, the kids, what my dad drank, where he ate. That takes a special kind of man, and also he had a presence that very few people have. He walked in a room and the whole room went quiet. He had that special quality that not many people have. To be able to handle all us nutters – and we had a few, apart from me, I mean, Denis and Nobby Stiles and Paddy Crerand – took something a little bit special, and he had it.

Bill Foulkes: He was more like a father figure than a manager. He was quite ruthless at times, but he always made you feel as if you were the best. I think his biggest talent was putting a team together. He seemed to have an instinct for blending players together. Types, characters, abilities. He was a very charming, family man. He always gave you the impression that he was caring, that he was on your side in everything, and particularly if you were going for a rise. I went to him occasionally for a rise and I always came out thanking him, you know, for not giving me a rise because I never got one. Matt was a great manager, a great motivator, a wonderful man, but he wasn't particularly generous to his players. There's one story in particular. He said, 'Son, if the team do well and we are successful, the money will come' – but I'm still waiting!

... and Jimmy Murphy

Sir Bobby Charlton: Jimmy Murphy turned me from an amateur schoolboy player into a professional player, and it took about two years. Whenever he got the opportunity he used to pull me to one side and try to teach me the folly of trying to make impossible passes, when there was something more realistic that you can do, more beneficial to the team. He made me think more as a team player rather than as an individual, but nevertheless always encouraged me to make the best of the assets that I had.

Bill Foulkes: It was Jimmy Murphy who signed me as a part-time player. He was a great motivator. He could certainly get you fired up. I remember playing in a match in South Wales, in 1951. It was the Festival of Britain, and we took a young side from United down to play this exhibition match. Of course, he's Welsh and I remember the last thing he said before we went out: 'I want you to beat these Welsh bastards.' Yeah, he was a motivator more than anything and a good judge of talent. He was a great help to me.

The European Cup

Brian Mears: Chelsea won the Championship in 1955 and by doing that they became eligible to go into Europe in the European Cup, but unfortunately the powers that be, the Football League management committee, didn't seem to want Chelsea, or any club that had won that year, to go into Europe. My father was chairman of Chelsea at that time and was also on the Football League management committee and on the FA Council, and I have a feeling that the Football Association didn't object to it too much. It might have been one of the meetings where he was representing both the Football League and the FA Council when he stood up and said, 'I propose the motion,' and then stood up five minutes later and said to them, 'I'm sorry, but I must object to the motion.' At the same meeting, with two different hats. I think Manchester United were far more vigorous about going into Europe. They were welcomed by the European Federation, and the Football League said, 'Yes, you're absolutely right.' I don't think Chelsea pursued their right to go into Europe after they won the Championship, and I think that was a shame. Who knows what might have happened?

Brian Glanville: The secretary of the Football League, Alan Hardaker, was a very powerful figure, a dyed-in-the-wool northerner who once actually said to me that he didn't like getting involved with football on the continent, and he actually gave a little grin and said, 'Too many wogs and dagos.' In 1955 Chelsea were Champions for the only time in their history and, unfortunately for them, their chairman, Joe Mears, was a leading light on the Football League management committee and when Hardaker said, 'I don't think you should enter,' he very meekly kow-towed to him and didn't enter, but Matt Busby wouldn't have that as manager of Manchester United. He was very far-seeing and a man with an internationalist outlook.

Sir Bobby Charlton: I think that the potential of that team just before Munich – and I'm not counting myself in that – was phenomenal, and what they aspired to at that particular time was sensational. There were some fantastic players. Roger Byrne was a regular player for England, Bill Foulkes, Mark Jones and Jackie Blanchflower were really solid defenders who would be able to play now without any problem whatsoever. Little Eddie Colman was a very cultured player who was cheeky and a crowd pleaser, but very effective as well and wasn't afraid to score goals, and Duncan Edwards was maybe the greatest player I've ever seen. He died very prematurely. He was a player of such presence and such ability that it meant that Man United's potential was awesome really and of course the accident nipped it in the bud.

Bill Foulkes: Every time we entered [the European Cup], we got to the semi-final. We couldn't get past that hurdle for some reason. But when we went through to the semi-final after beating Red Star Belgrade [February 1958] I felt that we could go on winning the European Cup for the next five years with that particular team we had. We'd a lot of young players, experienced players, and we had a terrific blend.

The Munich Air Disaster

Bill Foulkes: The day of the crash was a miserable February day in Munich, sleet and snow. We'd landed in Munich from Belgrade to refuel and we were feeling very happy of course – we were through to the semi-final of the European Cup. We were taking off and the first attempt we didn't make it. Halfway down the runway he stopped, tried again, went back, tried again. Second attempt the same thing. So we went back to the terminal and we had a cup of coffee. Some of the journalists were ringing home saying, 'We're going to be delayed,' and within a few minutes – it seemed like a few minutes – they said, 'Okay, back in the aircraft.' I thought it was a little quick. There was something wrong. Anyway, I wasn't happy. I remember we'd been playing cards previously but the third time we tried to take off two boys left. David Pegg said, 'I'm going to the back, it's safer there.' He obviously felt there was something wrong, and so Albert Scanlon and myself were looking across the table at each other. I strapped myself in, very, very tight, and put my head just below the level of the seat on take-off. I just felt there was something not … it didn't get off. There was a big thud, a big bump and then another one, and I felt there's going to be another one. The next thing … nothing. I don't remember anything for a couple of minutes, and when I woke up the aircraft was sliced in half on a diagonal from right to left, virtually underneath my feet and I was looking into the fresh air. It was a terrible day. We lost eight players. Many journalists were killed. Friends of ours, too. The journalists in those days were friends of the players. Within a week, Harry Gregg and myself were playing against Sheffield Wednesday in a Cup match with 65,000 people in Old Trafford and about 30,000 outside. That was the beginning of the legend.

The Double for Spurs

Don Howe: Arthur Rowe influenced players in his side and at that time no one knew how far they would go on the management side. Nobody knew, for instance, that his right-back, Alf Ramsey, would become manager of Ipswich and manager of the England team and go on to win the World Cup. And Billy Nicholson later took over at Tottenham and built lovely footballing teams. Arthur Rowe influenced those players in the way you should play football, which was, for the sake of it, total football, 'give and go' football, 'pass it and move' football.

Bill Nicholson: When we did the double in 1960–61 we were renowned for our short game and our quick interpassing and movement off the ball, but round about that same time Wolverhampton won the Championship. Now Wolverhampton were one of the finest teams in the country and well reputed for their long-ball game, so within two years, shall we say, there's one team winning the Championship with the long ball and one team winning it with the short ball, which goes to prove that there's more than one way of playing football. We won the double in 1960–61 – the Championship and the FA Cup – and the following year, 1961–62, we won the FA Cup again, and we were very, very close indeed to doing the double again but it was our friends down at Ipswich, and Alf Ramsey, who stopped us. But the following season we were in the European Cup-winners' Cup competition and we beat Atlético Madrid 5–2. We were the first [British] team to win a European trophy.

Sir Alf Ramsey at Ipswich

Don Howe: After Alf Ramsey had finished his playing days at Tottenham, he took over at Ipswich, who in those days were in the Third Division, and he had this fantastic achievement of bringing the team from the Third Division right the way through and winning the First Division. Here again it was done with a tactical innovation. He played a deep-lying outside-left, a fella named Jimmy Leadbetter, and it really was the start of 4-3-3. He pulled him back and played him deep, virtually level with the midfield players and he had two strikers, Ray Crawford and Ted Phillips. I was playing for West Brom in those days, and we went to play there. Archie Macaulay was our manager and we knew how they played but we didn't know how to deal with it. I was the right-back in the West Brom team, and we decided that I would go down with Jimmy Leadbetter and see if I could take care of it. Obviously I was in a position that I wasn't used to playing in. If you went down with Jimmy Leadbetter, if you were the right-back, they'd get the ball and play it over the back of you, and Ray Crawford or Ted Phillips would get behind you, stretch your centre-backs and then go into the box and score goals. And it took a while for people to find a plan for coping with it. And that's why Alf Ramsey really did an Arthur Rowe. He took a side from the bottom divisions and, with a new tactical system, won the First Division with it.

Ray Crawford: Obviously Alf had looked at his players and come up with this system where Ted and myself would play up front to score the goals, but he needed someone to give us a service and he dropped his two wide men, Jimmy Leadbetter and Roy Stephenson, deeper to get the ball off the defence to serve Ted and myself. I remember the year we won the Championship we played Tottenham twice and the full-backs just didn't know what to do with Jimmy and Roy. They stood there marking the space. Jimmy came back, got the ball in space and we were able to use it without any full-backs marking them.

Ted Phillips: Oh, great bloke Alf was really. Quite often he used to come down on a Friday down on the big pitch – we used to call it the big pitch then – with the first-team players, and we used to go and sort this free-kick out, and every time we dreamt up a free-kick, if we tried it on the next day, we always scored, didn't we?

Ray Crawford: On occasions he came out with us but really he was a one-to-one man. He wasn't what you would call a tracksuit manager. He used to come round on Thursday mornings and he'd pick out players, and tell us what we'd done wrong. He had a fantastic memory. He was good at looking at the game and he would come in at half-time and he would pick out certain things that would make us better second half. He would come in and say, 'Make sure you knock the ball down,' or 'Give the ball to Jimmy, Jimmy's on his own all the time.' Everywhere we went, Jimmy Leadbetter was more or less the star player. He was getting crosses in for Ted and myself and that's where we got the goals. There was one day when our defence came out, playing them offside, while Jimmy Leadbetter, our left winger, played them onside, and that got a bit of stick from Andy [Nelson] and the boys at the back.

Jimmy Leadbetter: I was 27 at the time I joined Ipswich – I'd been to Chelsea and Brighton – and I always remember going into a shop and someone said, 'Oh, I hear they've signed another has-been' and I'm standing in the shop and they were referring to me. I didn't get in the team for four or five months and Alf came up to me and said, 'How do you fancy playing outside-left, Jim?' And I said, 'Well, the last time I played that position was at school,' because I was an inside-forward. I said, 'I'm not fast enough, as a winger.' He said, 'It's not how fast you go, it's how fast the ball goes. You go home and think about it, see what you think.' I enjoyed it because as an inside-forward you always had your back to the goals, whereas on the wing I had the whole freedom of this part of the field. I was picking up balls and passing quickly and we had two big fellas there that could finish them off. To score a goal with 10 or 12 passes you have to be accurate when you're passing a ball but if you had two accurate passes and that ball in the net you'd done your battle. Big Ted was a lovely sight with the wind blowing in the shirt, and he used to hit them from 30 yards.

Ron Greenwood's West Ham

Geoff Hurst: Cassettari's café was where we used to put into practice all our thoughts and ideas about how the game should be played, with a vinegar bottle as a centre-half and a tomato ketchup bottle as a defender and so on. We spent many happy hours at Cassettari's, talking about the game, betting on the pools. My wife could always tell when I'd been to Cassettari's at lunch-time – my clothes smelled slightly of grease.

Ron Greenwood: Malcolm [Allison] had left, of course, by the time I got to West Ham [1961], but he'd left the ideas behind. It was a question of bringing on youth. The youth policy at West Ham United had been set up by Wally St Pier, a dear old man who has unfortunately died now. He was chief scout and he had a whole bunch of people who used to scout around and get all the young, promising schoolboys at the club. There was a young player called Geoff Hurst who I'd seen play as a left-half for the youth team, and he was strong and quite good going forward, so we put him up at inside-left and he was a great success. Young Martin Peters was coming along and was quite frail, not always prominent in the side. When we won the FA Cup in '64 he didn't play because Eddie Bovington played right-half and Martin was going through a bit of a sticky period. Bobby [Moore] was there, of course. When I first went to West Ham, Bobby was in the throes of not being in the side. It was rather ironical that Geoff was taking his place as a left-half. I moved Geoff up and Bobby became a stalwart of the side and a leader and captain, and so the basis was there. Then we signed, for the record fee of English football at that time, Johnny Byrne from Crystal Palace for £63,000. Ronnie Boyce was at inside-right, Peter Brabrook and Alan Sealey were the outside-rights and young John Sissons came into the side as an outside-left. Consequently we had everything going right for us because there were players from the youth team alongside Kenny Brown, Joe Kirkup and Jackie Birkett, and either Jim Standen or Lawrie Leslie in goal. We won the FA Youth Cup in 1963. We won the FA Cup in '64, the European Cup-winners' Cup in '65. They were marvellous years and it was all to do with the players. They were so responsive, so easy to coach.

Geoff Hurst: That night when we beat Munich 1860 in the European Cup-winners' Cup [19 May 1965] was probably the culmination of everything that West Ham had worked at. I think Ron talked about it in his book. Somebody said, 'What do you feel?' and he more or less said, 'Well I just went home and went to bed and thought, "Everything I tried to do, my beliefs about football and the way it should be played, came out on the night." '

Near-post Crosses

Geoff Hurst: I think we were very innovative, not so much the near-post corner but the near-post cross from wide positions. That sort of thing, above all else, sticks in my mind. We spent hours crossing balls. Not only the forward players and midfield players but also defenders, so that whichever player got in that position, they can whip these balls into the near post. We spent hours and hours at that and the timing of the run to the near post.

Ron Greenwood: The ball had to drop roughly about between the six-yard-box line and the near goal-post. We did that to perfection time after time – Johnny Sissons, Alan Sealey, Martin Peters, full-backs, everybody – and we felt that we got it off to a fine art. We went up to Newcastle, a big Scots centre-half was playing, and Geoff had moved to the far post. Alan Sealey crossed the ball to the near post and Geoff moved in a flash on to it and flicked it into the net, and the big centre-half was stood at the back and he wondered where it had gone. It was unbelievable, and we did it time and time again.

World Football

Geoff Hurst: Ron Greenwood was really my mentor. He taught me everything about playing the game at the highest level and was a great coach, knowledgeable not only about English football or European football but world football. He saw the advent of the Hungarian successes as things we could add to our game. He took the best part of the continental game and tried to add it to the best parts of the English game. Ron wanted to play against continental opposition and we made a point of going abroad. We played in a pre-season tournament, in New York, in the summer of 1963, against eight or nine of the leading club sides throughout the world – Mexican, Brazilian, Scottish, German, Polish, Czechoslovakian – so it was a great occasion. All our ball practice at West Ham was about technique – technique in control, technique in movement, ways to move, how to move, where to run and how to run. I can sum it up by saying that Ron's teaching at West Ham was to enable the players to become top-class international players. I wouldn't say I was a world-class player but I could sit very comfortably with the great players in the world because I was taught how to play the game.

12

'He offered me x amount of money to join Sunderland'

Under the Counter

Football League rules were strict in the 1950s. There was a maximum wage, a £10 signing-on fee and clubs had the discretion to pay loyalty benefits after five years (maximum £750) and 10 years (maximum £1,000). Clubs got round this with various methods and occasionally they were found out. The biggest case of the 1950s involved Sunderland during the 1956–57 season.

Sticking to the Rules

Michael Gliksten: I can only talk about my experience of Charlton and we were very rigid in sticking to the rules. My father recognized that in his position as chairman of a public company it was very important that we should be following the rules and regulations. I know that when we went for young players, our staff would frequently come back and say, 'We can't sign them because such-and-such a club has

138

paid them so much money.' I think that that was the case in some circumstances but I think also it could have been an excuse for not having probably got in earlier and signed a player when we had the opportunity to.

Brian Mears: I think that it was an indictment, surely, on some of the players that they were asking for money to join the club. I personally didn't want to have anything to do with it, although I knew it was going on. We all knew it was going on, and, having said that, don't forget I was a member of the Football League management committee and on the FA Council, but nobody could prove anything because nobody brought forward any proof. And it was sad, really, that clubs decided the only way they could get a player was to make an illegal payment, very sad.

Jimmy O'Neill: After five years I got a benefit of £750, which was quite a lot of money in those days. The taxman took something like £250 out of it, I think, and I think out of the balance of £500 I got married, and that took care of that. I spent another five years at Everton and I got £1,000 for the second benefit after 10 years. I think the taxman again took somewhere in the region of about £350 out of that. Then I think I got an accrued share of the benefit when I left Everton to go to Stoke. I think I got about 150 quid or something. That was an accrued share of my next five years as I was starting into my third year of another five years at Everton. But they were legal payments. There was nothing under the counter.

Sir Stanley Matthews: I think I was 46 when I got a transfer from Blackpool to Stoke City. Everything was settled with Tony Waddington, the manager of Stoke City. Then I went to see the Blackpool board. The chairman was there, the manager was there and he said, 'As you know, you're being transferred to Stoke City for £3,500.' I said, 'Yes, is it possible you could waive that £3,500, and then it would go to Stoke and Stoke would put it on my wages or whatever?' And the chairman said, 'No, you're entitled to £160 and you're gonna get £160.' I said, 'But couldn't you waive it because I did give you good service,' and one of the directors turned round and said, 'We've made you a star.' I said, 'Wait a minute, when I came here 15 years ago you couldn't sell your season tickets.' Anyway, what I'm trying to say is that I got £160 from that £3,500.

Tommy Lawton: We got 'Well done' and 'Thank you' and a gold medal when we won the Championship at Everton [in 1938–39]. That's about all I got. We didn't even get a dinner or a luncheon, because they were organizing a Championship dinner for the following season and the war broke out. So that had to be cancelled and everything else, but I got a gold medal.

TG Jones: Quite unique that really, wasn't it? We won the Championship with all the blarney that goes with it, and our reward for winning the Championship was a half-day out at Morecambe. I think it was Morecambe. I didn't bother to go anyway so it didn't make any difference. That was the reward – a half-day trip to Morecambe.

George Hardwick: I believe that some clubs were a little more generous, shall we say, and prepared to take risks. I do know because little Wilf Mannion and I used to travel away with the England team, here, there and everywhere, and naturally players talk. We learned from the other players that they were getting double their salary and all sorts of different perks. They were getting their house given to them as a gift. This never occurred at Middlesbrough. Not one single penny over and above what you were entitled to did you get at Ayresome Park, sadly.

Backhanders

Len Shackleton: Stan Seymour and Wilf Taylor, the Newcastle directors, said, 'You're coming to Newcastle.' They never even asked me. I still had a choice whether I signed on or not but I said, 'Aye, okay, I'm going to Newcastle.' I had thought that if I ever got transferred I would want a share of it, so I'm thinking, 'Well, the record transfer fee is the £13,000 that Wolverhampton had got from Arsenal for Bryn Jones the last season before the war, and Newcastle have got £13,000 for transferring Albert Stubbins to Liverpool, so, £13,000 for them two, oh, I'll be worth about £5,000 or £6,000.' Stan Seymour said, 'You'll be coming to Newcastle.' I said, 'Oh, yes, and what do I get out of it?' 'Oh,' he said, 'we're prepared to give you £500,' which met what I thought was my standard, about 10 per cent of the transfer fee, so I signed. I didn't know the transfer fee until I got home and saw the evening paper. It was £13,000 and threepence. I thought, 'That was criminal.' I'd done meself out of what I thought was an extra few bob. Anyway, I was dead pleased to get £500, so we go to St James's Park, Newcastle, and there's Stan Seymour and the secretary, Frank Watt, and Stan says, '£500, Len, wasn't it, that was agreed?' I said, 'Yeah,' and he threw me down five bundles of £100, so I said, 'Thank you very much' and start to pick it up. He said, 'What are you gonna do with it, Len?' I said, 'I'm gonna put it into the building society.' 'Oh,' he said. 'You can't do that, because if you put a lump like that into a building society people are going to make two and two add up to four and they'll know where you've got it from.' Stan said, 'I'll tell you what to do, you take £100 and there's £400 that Mr Watt will put in the safe and let you come and get £20 at a time until the £400 has finished.' I thought it seemed fair enough, so I got my £100. We played Newport and I got six goals on my début. You couldn't dream a better thing, could you, really? You get transferred for a record amount of money, 56,000 Geordies there and you score six goals, so I go back to Bradford, I'm sat in the train from Newcastle to Leeds and I've counted the £100 four times before we've got to Durham because I've never seen so much money in my life. The weeks go past. I'm going to see Frank Watt, the secretary, get £20 here, another £20, until I'd got another £100. So I'd got £100 that he'd given me to start with and another £100. I go the week after and Mr Watt said, 'There's no more money in, Mr Seymour's been for it.' I think, 'Well, he's done me out of £300.' I went to see John Lee, who seemed to be a decent guy and was on the board, and I told him exactly what I've told you. He said, 'Well, that's diabolical. Can you come back tomorrow?' Obviously he'd got to substantiate what I'd said. I go see him in the morning and he gave me a cheque for £300. The moral of that is I shouldn't have got £500 but this is what these guys do to you anyway.

Jimmy O'Neill: I didn't know of any illegal payments but, when I moved from Everton to Stoke, Angela, my wife, said we could do with a new cooker and I mentioned this to Stoke. I said, 'Look, we're moving house and all the rest of it, if you could put a cooker into the house it would be very much appreciated.' And that was part of my transfer fee from Everton to Stoke. I got a new cooker out of it.

George Hardwick: We [Wilf Mannion and I] played for England against Scotland at Wembley on the Saturday afternoon, and we were on King's Cross station waiting to get the train back to Darlington, and this gentleman came up to us and began to talk to us. He was a director – I don't even know whether I should mention the name of the club, but they were a Second Division club in those days, and a club that my old mate Tommy Lawton went to in later years – and he said, 'We would very much like you both to come to join our club, we will look after you to the extent of £5,000 each, if you can get away to join us.' It was a fortune in those days, and, of course, naturally we tried all manner, but if you signed for a club at 13 you were there for life or until they wanted to get rid of you. Middlesbrough weren't ready to get rid of Wilf or I. Some players could play their way away by playing badly, but I couldn't do it. I was too damn proud, and too caring for those people that had paid their good money to come and watch us and be entertained. As I came into the tunnel, I turned round to every team I ever played in and said, 'Now look, lads, these people out here have spent a lot of money, let's give 'em a show.'

Alan Mullery: I was in the reserve team when I was 15 and then, when I got to about 16¾, Frank Osborne, the general manager, called me in and said they [Fulham] wanted to sign me as a professional on my birthday, which was in November. This would be about September, I suppose. A great old pro in those days, Roy Bentley, who was an England international centre-forward, gave me some advice. He said, 'Ask for £1,000 under-the-counter payment,' and £1,000 then was like £200,000 today, and I said, 'I can't do that.' He said, 'No, no, they'll give it to you, don't worry about it, they won't want to lose you,' so I walked into the board-room and there was Tommy Trinder, the chairman, the comedian, and Frank Osborne, who had a cigarette in the side of his mouth and drank a bottle of Scotch a day and things like this, you know, and he tossed the contract down the big board-room table, which was a big dining-room table and it was polished beautifully because I used to polish it every Friday, and the contract slid down and I looked at it and it said, 'We're gonna give you £10 signing-on fee and £12 a week to become a pro,' and in my audacity at 16¾ I slid the contract back up the table. He said, 'What's the problem?' I said, 'I want £1,000 to sign on,' and he jumped up out of his chair and he got his hat and he threw it on the table and he went, 'Get out, get out', and I got up and I walked out of the board-room and there was Roy Bentley standing down the end of the corridor and he said, 'Did you get your money?' I said, 'No, he threw me out.' He said,

'Don't worry, you'll get it.' The following day I came in and Frank said to me, 'Are you gonna sign that contract?' I said, 'No.' 'Well, I'm gonna report you,' he said, 'to the Football Association for asking for illegal payments,' and I was absolutely worried. I went home and the weekend went by. I came in on the Monday and he called me into his office and said, 'Look, I'll tell you what I'll do, you sign that contract and if you're not in the first team inside three months of your birthday, I'll give you the £1,000 out of my own pocket.' I thought, 'Well, that's not bad,' so I signed it, and two weeks before the three months were up I was in the first team, so he didn't have to give me the £1,000.

Len Shackleton: If we were playing in an important Cup tie, or an important League match, the boss would see you on £25 for a win, and £25 is a good backhander if you're only getting a tenner a week, isn't it? And the money's tax free. Well, we used to be on £25 quite a bit, especially if you're struggling against relegation and you've got to win.

Billy Elliott: I can go back to the third round of the FA Cup, Manchester United versus Bradford [29 January 1949]. This was in the days when Manchester United shared the ground at Maine Road because Old Trafford was under repairs from the war damage, and we had 82,000 there. Manchester United had mainly international players and we only had one international, Jimmy Stephen, and one other, Jackie Gibbons, who was an amateur international. We drew and the replay was at Bradford, on the following Wednesday, and we drew there and it's a known fact that the chairman at Bradford decided that it wasn't necessary to spin a coin, we would play at Maine Road as we had a bigger gate there than at Bradford, on a Monday afternoon replay. Needless to say we got done 5–0 but their income from the three games was tremendous. We got beat 5–0 but the chairman gave us £20 apiece, which was more than what we were getting in wages.

Len Shackleton: I got picked to play for the England team in Canada and America, and at the same time Sunderland was playing in Turkey. Now, the local newspaper reporter had seen a letter on the manager's desk saying that a tour of Turkey is a good tour but it's only on if Len Shackleton's a member of the Sunderland party. You see? Now he told me about that letter, so I get picked for the England tour to Canada and America, and the manager sent for me. He said, 'You don't want to go to America with England, do you?' I said, 'I've always wanted to go to America.' He didn't know I'd seen the letter about the trip, so I'm stringing him along. I said, 'Oh, I'd give my right arm to tour America and Canada with England, that's what I've waited for all the time.' He said, 'Oh, you're better off going with us to Turkey.' 'Oh, no,' I said, 'America's a lot better.' He said, 'I'll tell you what I'll do, you come to Turkey with us, and I'll give you £300 and I'll make it okay with the Football Association so you won't jeopardize your England place.'

Trevor Ford: When I wrote my book [*I Lead the Attack!*, 1957], the problem was that clubs were making fortunes out of players and not caring tuppence about them really. Clubs were selling players for a terrific amount of money and players were getting £10 signing-on fees. I mean, I cost Swansea nothing. I signed for Aston Villa for £13,500 plus a player. In those days that was a fortune, and I got £10 off Swansea. Now, they don't expect me to pay my own expenses from Swansea to Birmingham, move house and everything out of £10, so naturally I expected some help from Aston Villa, which I got. The other thing I didn't like was accepting money under the counter. Now, why should I, a professional footballer, be taking money from under the counter when I think I've earned it? The way they did it at Villa Park was tremendous, and a real joke. I used to go out with the manager after the match if I'd scored a goal and play snooker, and we'd bet £5 and he never won a game. That was his way of giving me £5 for every goal I scored.

Signing for Sunderland

Trevor Ford: I went to Sunderland because I was offered a job at £25 a week, which was more than I was getting playing football. When you think, I was on £15 a week in the winter and £12 in the summer. I started in the garage business and it was very successful. I didn't just get the £25 a week as pocket money. I had to work for it.

Ray Daniel: We [Wales] were playing Scotland at Ninian Park and Trevor [Ford] said to me, 'Sunderland are prepared to pay a record fee for you.' I said, 'Christ, I wouldn't leave Arsenal. Who wants to go from London, the best club in the bloody world, to the freezing north-east of England?' 'Well,' he said. 'There'd be a few quid in it.' So I said, 'Well, I'll have to think about it.' We went to the reception that night and my wife said to me, 'Can we go to the cocktail bar?' I said, 'What for?' 'Well,' she said. 'A gentleman from Sunderland wants to have a chat with you.' I said, 'Yeah.' Now, having already heard from Trevor, I wasn't particularly interested. I went along and this guy introduced himself, a director of Sunderland Football Club, and he said, 'We saw you play at Roker Park and we've heard a lot about you.' (Walter Winterbottom, who was then coach of England, had described me as the best centre-half in the world. I thought, 'Oh, that upped my price a bit.') He said, 'We're interested in getting you at Roker Park. We're going to build the biggest team of internationals you've ever seen.' I went back to London and we had a chat about it, and then a chap called Bill Ditchburn, the chairman of Sunderland, came on the phone, and he said, 'Ray, I'm not allowed to talk, could we meet.' I met him at the Great Northern Hotel in King's Cross and he offered me x amount of money to join Sunderland. I said, 'I've got to ask for a transfer.' He said, 'Yes, I don't think Arsenal will agree. They won't let you go but, if you insist, Arsenal don't keep unhappy players.'

Jack Ditchburn: My father [Bill Ditchburn] had quite a distinct view of the wage system. He thought players were vastly underpaid for what they were worth, and of course this is one of the reasons why they tried to rectify that. My father applied the principles of business to football in the sense that he said, 'If I had a good man in the business, he was worth paying for so if I had a good man in the football, he's worth paying for.' You couldn't pay him officially, could you, but he would apply the same principle – if he is a star then the star should really be paid a little bit more. It's a team game, of course, but being the star he would have an attraction. In those days, if you remember, you had Stanley Matthews, who was an attraction in himself. If he came to Roker Park, the gate went up. We had Shackleton. If Shackleton went to another club to play away, the gate went up. Now, if the gate went up because of the star name then surely the star should benefit from it, but he couldn't.

John Charles: I wanted to go to Sunderland! Everybody wanted to go to Sunderland because they were getting good wages. They were getting overpaid, I think, and everybody wanted to play for Sunderland at that time!

Jack Ditchburn: They became the Bank of England club because they started spending money on expensive players but the thinking was that, if you bought two or three named players before the season started, that sold your season tickets and you had the money in the bank.

The Method

Jack Ditchburn: How was the trick done which brought about the commission? There were two elements to that – the straw element and the tarmac element. (In those days the pitches were often covered with straw and they used to take the straw off for the game and pile it at the side of the pitch and put it back on.) If you had a friendly company, and the club orders from that company either too much tarmac or too much straw, they deliver and they send their invoices in, nothing wrong with that, but they overcharge for their delivery. At a later stage you raise the question of the overcharge so the company gives you a credit note. That credit note doesn't then get credited in the books of the company. How it doesn't get credited in the books of the company, I wouldn't know, but at the end of the day the club then have a surplus of money which they could deal with as they wished.

The Commission's Findings (April 1957)

Len Shackleton: The commission inquired into Sunderland about illegal payments, and they just went back a certain time. They didn't go back to when I signed, so I wasn't involved in the probe. Thank goodness they didn't go back to me. It was just about illegal payments they'd paid to players like Trevor Ford and Ken Chisholm and people like that. It was a big story at the time, obviously, because of the maximum wage. If they'd have lifted the maximum wage that would have ended all that. There wouldn't have been any need for it.

Jimmy Hill: Sunderland tried to accelerate matters and they did it outside the League regulations. In getting players to come to the club they paid them illegal signing-on fees.

Ray Daniel: We were accused of receiving x amount of money illegally from Sunderland Football Club, and then we were asked to retire to the lounge in the hotel. I think it was the Midland Hotel in Manchester. We went down and Jimmy Hill was then the Professional Footballers' Association chairman and he came down and said we were being suspended the same day. We were in a state of shock. We were advised to say nothing, because the press were all swarming around, and it takes some time to absorb what it means. We were on our way to Leicester to play in a charity match and it came on the radio that we weren't allowed to play so we all went back to Sunderland. Now this meant that we had to vacate our house in Sunderland. We weren't allowed into any football grounds. We were advised by the PFA to say nothing to the press, and obviously the press wanted to offer us money to tell the story.

Billy Elliott: It was a shock, and to my wife and to my children. Both my children were at private schools and the first thing you do is say, 'Where the hell am I going to get the money from?' because I'd had nothing. All I'd had was extra money for travelling away. I got my benefit money less tax and I got £10 signing-on fee, coming to Sunderland, less tax, so how the hell could they accuse me?

Jack Ditchburn: They were called to the first commission and the directors were called in individually and father said that he went in and immediately said they should have legal representation, which was refused. The commission, having got the information concerning the tarmac situation and the information concerning the straw, then went to the players. Finally they made their decision and fined the club £5,000 and suspended four directors and reprimanded the others. My father and the other directors were suspended for life, which of course was like taking away his arms and his legs really, because he wasn't a young man at that stage. I suppose it more or less broke his heart at the time. He wasn't a well man and it didn't have a very good effect on him. Up till that point, of course, he was successful at football. Up to the time he left, the club had played in no division other than the First Division.

Overturned Findings

Jack Ditchburn: The following day we took an opinion and our opinion was that the decision could be overturned. At that time the solicitors for the players, or the union, came into contact with us and we were then riding in harness with the players. I think they'd also sentenced the five higher-priced players and then of course the players' union, who were very indignant about the whole thing, were thinking about strikes and things of this nature. The commission had patently acted wrongly. They had abused the principles of natural justice in the way they'd conducted the wretched inquiry, and it was shameful that you had a barrister taking charge of an inquiry and denying the people who were appearing before them any legal representation. We sued the FA, we sued the League and we sued the individual members of the commission, all on the same basis. We were told that the thing would finish up in court with six of the top QCs in the country. Then they packed it up and gave us £650, I think, which was towards the costs, paid their own costs and of course set aside all the findings. I think I'm right in saying that the club only asked for the £5,000 back when we challenged them at the annual meeting and asked them why they hadn't given it back. Eventually they got their £5,000 back and everybody was reinstated.

Billy Elliott: I've never read Trevor's book to this day but I felt that if they were going to accuse us of illegal payments they had to accuse everybody, because it was happening throughout football. When we went to that commission in Manchester, Alan Hardaker stipulated that one penny or £1 or £1,000, it doesn't matter, it's illegal money, so we were dumbfounded. They tried to take our livelihood away from us but they came unstuck. We fought the case and we won it hands down and we won it with damages, so who was right? Then shortly after that they lifted the maximum wage and freedom of contract.

13

'We were going to strike'

The Two Freedoms

Action by the Professional Footballers' Association eventually led to the removal of the maximum wage in 1961, and a lifting of some of the contractual restrictions in 1963.

The Maximum Wage

Sir Philip Goodhart: [In 1960–61] the maximum wage required that no League club should pay any player more than £20 a week. There were a few fringe benefits, of course, but basically no one could be paid more than £20 a week for playing football. The system had come into being really to preserve the little clubs in the League, and it was argued by the Football League panjandrums that if the maximum wage was to be scrapped a score or more of the smaller clubs in the Football League would go bankrupt and that the game as we knew it in this country would be dramatically changed.

Bobby Robson: We were to some degree slaves. There was no freedom. We thought Stan Matthews, one of the most wonderful players in the world, earned no more than the worst right-back in the Fourth Division. We said, 'Hey, that cannot be right.'

Michael Gliksten: The maximum wage was an integral part of the Football League. It was felt that it enabled an equality of opportunity for all the clubs to hold their best players and players that they'd developed, and as a result it enabled clubs who probably weren't in highly populated industrial areas to do extremely well, clubs like Huddersfield, Blackpool, Bolton, Preston and Blackburn. If you look at the League table immediately after the war and look at it now you'll find a big difference. From my point of view I was very anxious to retain a maximum wage of some sort. I didn't mind what the maximum was providing there was a maximum, but I could foresee that if there wasn't a maximum then a club like Charlton would never be able to hold their best players. Up until probably the late 1950s, the players' wages were very much higher, proportionately, than the average working wage. I think if you research it you'll probably find that it was three or four times, and after the First World War it was considerably more than that.

Jimmy Hill: John Charles and Jimmy Greaves and people like that were going out to Italy and earning vastly different money. In the end we'd have lost all of our top-class players to other places throughout the world who had no maximum wage, so it had to end. The arguments had been made for years but the Football League had seemed unmovable on it and they had always released the vacuum by pushing up the maximum another few pounds and quite honestly at this time in 1961 if they had done that we on the committee would have accepted it, because the players would have been so pleased to have got another £10 a week to go to £30.

A Strike?

Michael Gliksten: I think the Professional Footballers' Association were very fortunate to be led by Jimmy Hill and Cliff Lloyd. Jimmy Hill was a brilliant media man, articulate, erudite, a professional footballer who presented his points extremely well, with reason, backed by the skill of Cliff Lloyd as a negotiator, and I feel that under the circumstances, and the fact that the public mood was sympathetic to the players, this was the right time for them to make their particular challenge.

Jimmy Hill: Each club has a PFA representative and I went to my first meeting of the PFA representing Brentford Football Club. When I transferred to Fulham, a chap called Norman Smith was taking his accountancy exams and had to study hard and he said, 'Would you mind taking it over.' The PFA had eight unpaid delegates, from different clubs, one of whom would be an unpaid chairman, and having suggested a change in the system I ended up as the first chairman. Well, the proposal was that we were going to strike if we didn't get the maximum wage removed. We held three major meetings to start with – one in London, one in the Midlands, one in the north – and there were players who out of fear weren't really ready to risk the money that they were getting. I think the best example of it was in the northern meeting. The story is indelible in the mind of everybody who was there. This young lad [Alan Jackson of Bury] said that his father was a miner who was very happy to earn £12 a week (or whatever it was) and, compared with that, a footballer's £20 a week was a very good wage. He didn't see any reason why he should prejudice that. And Tommy Banks [of Bolton Wanderers] said, 'I know about tha father. Tell tha Dad I can do his job down the mines but he couldn't do my job week in week out, which sometimes means marking Brother Matthews here.' He was next to Stanley Matthews, and that brought the house down, but it also brought the right result when it came to a vote. Stanley Matthews was a god and for him even to attend the meeting meant they were all whispering, 'Stanley Matthews has come.' It was rumoured that Stanley, because he was doing very well himself, not from his £20 maximum a week, but from lots of other sources because he was one of the few players then who could earn money outside his £20 a week, may not have been sympathetic. It didn't happen. He stood up and he spoke in favour of it and of course there was a big sigh of relief on the platform, because his influence would have been enormous one way or the other. He was a great aid in coming down on the side of the players.

Sir Philip Goodhart: The Professional Footballers' Association were in dispute with the Football League. I was against the entire maximum-wage system, and I was lucky enough to get a special debate in the House of Commons at the time when the whole dispute was reaching its climax. It was a very short debate but a number of MPs took part in it, and I called for a strike. A strike by the international players. I called it 'the golden strike' and I think I'm the only Conservative Member of Parliament since the war who's ever urged anybody to go on strike.

Jimmy Hill: No other profession in this country, as far as I knew, had a restriction on the top, and it was even more unfair in that a professional footballer's life is a very short one. In those days there are examples of players who played for low salaries ending up on railway-lines. They get to 30, they've been heroes for a very short space of time, they have nothing in the bank, and they can't cope with the fact that they're no longer wanted and have no earning power.

Michael Gliksten: The Football League didn't have public sympathy, so the case that the League put forward wasn't necessarily going to receive a sympathetic hearing. There was a series of meetings and at every meeting the delegates were given an unequivocal assurance that under no circumstances would the maximum wage be conceded, and at the penultimate meeting I asked Mr Joe Richards, who was then president, to confirm this assurance, which he did. Now I'm not blaming the Football League negotiating team. I think they had a very difficult position. They had to satisfy 92 chairmen and that's not easy, and then those chairmen or those delegates had to go back and discuss it with their own boards of directors. We had received this undertaking that the maximum wage would not be conceded, and then at the final meeting we were told that it *had* been conceded.

Jimmy Hill: It's a real sadness in my life that I put a proposition back across the table at that final meeting. I said, 'Look, I'm perfectly happy as long as there is no artificial limit and I'd be perfectly happy to have a maximum wage plus an unlimited performance bonus to be paid at the end of the season.' And across the table came, 'You've got what you were after, now be satisfied with it.' That was a great pity because it started off on the wrong foot. It wasn't pressure from the PFA that brought about a situation where we jumped into the deep-end straight away and indiscriminately tried to adjust to a new system.

The Immediate Effects at Fulham ...

Jimmy Hill: Without being too unkind to Tommy Trinder [the Fulham chairman], because time forgives really, he had said beforehand, when the maximum wage was there, that he wasn't free to pay Johnny Haynes, 'the greatest player in England,' a decent salary but, if he was free to, he'd be happy to pay him £100 a week, the sort of money that he might get for being at the Palladium. Of course, when the maximum wage went he was stuck. John only had to go in with the headline and say, 'There you are.' And people like Maurice Cook, our striker, said, 'Well, I may not be as good as Johnny, but I must be half as good, and would be happy with £50!'

Johnny Haynes: Poor old Tom was lumbered. He's in print as saying that he's going to pay me £100 a week, and I give him credit, he stood by it and paid me 100 quid a week, but the only thing wrong was that everybody in the country knew what I was getting. I played for Fulham for another eight years and I never got a rise, it always stayed at £100.

Alan Mullery: About 40 or 50 pros at the club were sitting in the dressing-room, going in in alphabetical order to change their contracts, but Haynesy went first because he was the England captain. He goes into the board-room, where there was TT (Tommy Trinder) and Frank Osborne and he wasn't in there a minute and he came out and walked back into the dressing-room and all these lads were looking, really excited about this situation, and he took this piece of paper out and he said, 'TT, you're true to your word, I've just got £100 a week, lads,' and he tore this piece of paper up threw it up in the air, and walked out. I'm sitting there, 17 years of age: '£100 a week? Oh, yes, please.' I was way down the list of pros, under M, so I got called in and Frank Osborne said to me, 'This is going to be the greatest day in your life.' I thought, 'Oh blimey, £100 a week, what's my Mum and Dad gonna say? The old man earning £12 a week and I'm a millionaire.' He said, 'I'm going to give you 28 quid a week.' I said, 'What are you talking about? £28 a week? You've paid Haynesy £100 a week.' He said, 'Well, you're not bloody Johnny Haynes, are you?'

... and the Effects Elsewhere

Arthur Would: I was never in support of retaining the maximum wage. But I remember when Johnny Haynes was paid £100 for the first time. I think it put that kind of player out of the scope of clubs like Grimsby and the effect of the maximum wage was to give all clubs a chance of employing the same kind of player and at a figure they could afford to pay.

Gordon Taylor: Blackpool had star players like Matthews, Preston had Finney, Blackburn had the likes of Ronnie Clayton and Bryan Douglas, Bolton had Nat Lofthouse, and I suppose they'd been able to keep those star players under the maximum wage because there was no great benefit in moving. Once it was removed, those clubs started to struggle.

Tom Finney: As soon as the maximum wage went, I said, 'You'll see that the bulk of the good players will go to the rich clubs.' In the old days you brought on players yourself or you had an equal chance of signing a player. If Manchester United went for a player and Preston North End went for a player you had an equal chance.

Michael Gliksten: When I was very young, I can remember my father talking about players who were to be transferred to clubs like Liverpool and Everton, and they said, 'Oh, we don't want to leave, we're quite happy where we are.' I think that if we had had a high maximum we could have maintained that type of situation, but the complete elimination of the maximum wage resulted in a completely different concept of the Football League.

Bert Trautmann: Manchester City had always said, 'When we are permitted officially to pay you more money, we shall pay you. At the moment it's strictly by the book.' When this new contract era started, in '61–62, I went to City and said, 'What are you offering me?' City offered me £35 a week! I was the longest-serving player. I'm not big-headed but I think I was still the best player they had and they offered me

£35, knowing they had given two other players £85 and £90 a week. And this is why I finished in 1964. I probably could have carried on another two years but I was so disappointed.

Michael Gliksten: Well, immediately, in order to meet the higher wages of the better players, we had to reduce our playing-staff, and I think the players recognized this at the time. That's why I don't think there was quite the manner of support from all the players that might have been claimed.

Retain and Transfer

Sir Philip Goodhart: When a player was signed on by a club he lost his right to transfer his services to any other club. The club owned him. When you combine this with a maximum wage, it means that the player not only binds himself to a club for his playing life but is also subjected to this absurdly small payment, and it was a medieval serf system. But you couldn't play football at the highest level in this country unless you signed on for this contract. At the end of the contract [a year] you couldn't do a damn thing, unless the club agreed to your moving and got a transfer fee for it, and you either stayed with the club until they transferred you to another club and usually made quite a lot of money out of that, or you stopped playing. At the beginning of the 1960s the big case, of course, was the George Eastham transfer, and Eastham was bought by Arsenal for £47,500.

Michael Gliksten: There were some very important aspects in the retain-and-transfer system that had to be rectified. There was the onerous condition that a player could be retained without receiving his wages, which was deplorable, but in the main the retain-and-transfer system was effectively there to protect those clubs that had developed their talent from having them poached, compensating them for the loss of that talent if those players left.

John Giles: When there were union meetings they were talking about the abolition of the maximum wage and, also, quite rightly, Cliff Lloyd was emphasizing that the retain-and-transfer system had to go. Now I don't think the players realized the significance of the retain-and-transfer system. All they saw was the maximum wage, and the abolition of the maximum wage, and the players thought they'd won a great victory. Cliff Lloyd and Jimmy Hill at the time did try to stress the retain-and-transfer system as being as important, if not more important, but the players just didn't realize and when the maximum wage was abolished they stopped going to the union meetings.

Edward Grayson: I was instructed concerning Ralph Banks, who played left-back for Bolton against Matthews in the 1953 Cup Final, and we raised the element of 'restraint of trade' in a defensive Aldershot county court action which was only half successful. George Eastham later sued Newcastle United successfully and established 'restraint of trade' as a restrictive practice under the judgement of Mr Justice Wilberforce, and it opened the floodgates.

The Eastham Case

Charlie Mitten: I knew the players would win because I was manager of Newcastle at the time and it was the George Eastham affair that brought it all to life. About 10 years before I was in exactly the same position as George Eastham and it had never changed since I'd come home [from Colombia]. I said to my board, 'Gentlemen, you're wasting your money taking them to court because he will win because I've had this all before.' They didn't believe that the players could win. My chairman, Alderman McKee, did because he was a lawyer. He knew and he said to me, 'I know what you're saying, Charles, the players will win, but the rest of the eight directors were very much against it, you see.'

Derek Dougan: Up to George Eastham it was called 'restraint of trade'. They could just retain you on the minimum amount of money. Every professional footballer living today owes a debt to a man called Cliff Lloyd. Cliff Lloyd was the greatest genius I had the pleasure of working with, the finest administrator since the inception of the game in 1863, and yet he was maligned and abused by the FA and the Football League, and by a lot of directors and chairmen. Cliff Lloyd knew the rules better than anyone else I knew, and he had been preparing since he went into the job in July 1953. Cliff knew that one day we would have to have a guinea-pig. The average life of a footballer is only eight years, and George Eastham, to his eternal credit, took almost one year out of his career. He made a stand at Newcastle.

Edward Grayson: George Eastham wanted to go to the Arsenal but because Newcastle United had this perpetually renewable contract which was the basis of their retaining his services, they would not release him to go to Arsenal even though he wanted to go to Arsenal and Arsenal wanted him. The defence was that it was reasonable in the interests of the game for the level playing field principle but Eastham was able to establish the right to hire his services for whoever's able to pay a decent wage. Mr Justice Wilberforce, a judge of great experience and learning, ruled that it was unreasonable, and there was no appeal, and thus the freedom of contract was established.

14

'Life was never going to be the same again'

England: World Cup Winners

Alf Ramsey succeeded Sir Walter Winterbottom as England manager in January 1963. Three years later the World Cup Finals were held in England. The team from the host nation won the trophy, and Alf Ramsey was knighted in 1967.

Alf Ramsey – England Manager

Johnny Haynes: Walter Winterbottom had the job a long time, from 1946 to 1962, and he was a very nice man. His job wasn't easy because he had to answer to a selection committee. He was a good manager but unfortunately he never had much luck in the big games in the World Cup Finals. In 1958 we tied with Russia in the group, and you had to replay in those days and we lost 1–0. In 1962 Brazil won the World Cup again and we got beat by Brazil in the quarter-final.

Ted Phillips: We were all out training and then he [Alf Ramsey] called us into the dressing-room and told all the players that he'd just been appointed as England manager, and everybody in the dressing-room was pleased for him. I always remember, John Cobbold, the chairman of the club, was stood outside in tears because he wanted Alf to stay at Ipswich. John Cobbold thought the world of Alf Ramsey.

Sir Walter Winterbottom: Alf decided he'd create a team and keep it as a team, keep the players, build up from them and not keep chopping and changing like happened in my day. It takes a player a bit of time to settle in a national side. He's with different players, different situations and the player has to overcome those feelings of strangeness.

Alan Ball: I can remember we were having a training session on the morning of the game in Belgrade [in May 1965], and I think we'd just done a stretching routine and Alf came over to me and said, 'I think you'll be rather pleased to know that I'm going to pick you to play for your country tonight. I think you're ready to play, and, when you do play for me, it'll be one of 10 times that you'll play for me, and then we'll find out whether you're going to be good enough to play for your country,' which I thought was fantastic because, if you know that you're going to be given a fair crack of the whip, it just takes away that initial nervousness that might stop you performing if you only have one try.

Nobby Stiles: Alf was the best in the world. He was brilliant. He was such a stickler for detail. He could remember things you'd done in a game from 12 months before. I remember us playing against Scotland just before the World Cup Finals. We beat them 4–3 there, and this was the time when you didn't have playbacks as such. There was a foul on the halfway-line and the ball had gone out of play on the track at Hampden Park, and he says, 'Can you remember what happened?' 'Well, from the free-kick

Scotland scored.' He said, 'No, I'll tell you what happened. John Connelly, our winger, went out on to the track to pick the ball up and bring it back and give it to the Scotsmen. Let them go and get it, you go and get organized.'

England as Hosts

Denis Howell: On the day I was appointed [as Minister of Sport], I said to Harold Wilson, 'Have I got any money?' To which, he gave a typical Wilsonian reply: 'No, but always remember if you've got no money it's a good time to do your thinking!' I remembered that Denis Follows [FA Secretary] had been to see Quintin Hogg [Minister with special responsibility for sport, 1962–64], and Hogg had said, 'We'll give you what help we can for your World Cup, such as supplying motor-cycle policemen to escort the teams round the country,' and Denis Follows was in despair, knowing the size of the problem and the state of our football grounds. So, as I was leaving Harold Wilson's study, having just been appointed, I suddenly remembered this. I stopped and said to Harold, 'We've got the World Cup on our hands, Prime Minister, and what's the point of having a Minister of Sport with the World Cup on his hands and no money.' To which Wilson then said, 'Well, how much do you want?' I hadn't got the faintest idea. I hadn't seen a civil servant, no work had been done on it, but I knew if I missed that moment it would be gone for ever. So, out of the back of my head, I said, 'Half a million pounds,' which seemed to me a lot of money at that time, especially as we were in the middle of an economic crisis. And I was surprised and delighted when Harold said, 'Right, you can have half a million pounds and not a penny more.' Then we started looking at the grounds.

The Team

Ray Crawford: Alf was very successful at Ipswich on a

system that he'd found and worked at, and he took it into the England set-up. And, with the better players, he was very successful. At Ipswich he had good defenders in Baxter and Andy Nelson and when he went to the England side he had Bobby Moore and Jack Charlton, and I think they played the same role. At Ipswich we had a full-back who overlapped in Larry Carberry and the England side had Ray Wilson, Jimmy Armfield and George Cohen, who he used in the same way.

Ron Greenwood: Bobby Moore, the captain, was coolness personified. I always used to say to him, 'The one thing that nobody ever finds out, you can't head a ball!' He would always position himself so he'd catch it on his chest or he'd let the ball run and turn on it, but you very rarely saw him head the ball. I didn't think he wanted to spoil his hair, you know! A marvellous man, a marvellous player.

Geoff Hurst: Bobby's strength was probably his will-power and determination. His other strength, to me, was always wanting to play under pressure. He liked the big occasion and the bigger the occasion the better he'd be. I always say he played great for West Ham, he was fantastic for England and had England being playing Mars next week in a galactic tournament he'd have raised his game to another plateau. He just relished the pressure. Martin Peters was a quieter person but deep down he had a tremendous desire to be successful and he also became a wonderful player and could have been a sensation on the continent had he played there, the way he stroked the ball and his ability to find space, and terrific in the air. Ron Greenwood said to Alf, 'You've got to come and see Martin Peters, he's a terrific player,' and Alf said, 'I'm not too sure about him, I'm not sure he can head a ball', and Martin actually was the best header of a ball at West Ham. I think Ron eventually rammed Martin down Alf's throat and of course the rest is history, 67 caps.

Jack Charlton: I was having a pint on a Saturday night after I'd played in London and we were meeting on the Sunday for the game on the Wednesday, and I stood at the bar and Alf came in and we were talking at the bar. I said to him, 'Why did you pick me, Alf?' because I was 29 when I got me first cap [in April 1965]. He said, 'Well, Jack, I've watched you play. You're very good in the air, you're quite mobile, you're a good tackler, and I know you won't trust Bobby Moore.' I said, 'What do you mean?' And Alf said, 'What I'm trying to say is if Gordon Banks gives the ball to you as a central defender, you'll give it back to Gordon and say kick it, but if you give the ball to Bobby Moore, Bobby will join in the build-up in midfield, through to the forwards, and if he makes a mistake at any stage I know, because I've watched you play, that you will always go across and play behind him and allow him to make the mistake.'

Nobby Stiles: My job in the England team was to just play in front of big Jack and Bobby Moore and any forwards who were going to attack had to come through me first. I would get back and hustle them, then win the ball quick, which was my great strength, and give it to Bobby Charlton or Martin Peters or Alan Ball and let them get on with it.

Alan Ball: Then you had one small full-back, Ray Wilson, who was as quick as lightning and was never beaten. If he was beaten, he was up and he'd have another bite, another tackle at the winger. He was totally the opposite to George Cohen, who was just sheer power and strength, so you had a mixture there. Then up front you had Geoff Hurst, who faced the play all the time – you could bounce balls off Geoff – and Roger Hunt and Jimmy Greaves. His team had that perfect balance and people complementing each other.

Jack Charlton: I said to Alf, 'What was your thinking when you balanced your team out?' 'Well, Jack,' he said, 'I have an idea and a thought in my mind of the way I want the team to play, the pattern I want to play, so I pick the players to fit the pattern, and they are not necessarily always the best players.' And I went, 'Oh, thank you very much.' He wanted to play possession football so he picked players who could play possession football. But at the same time he wanted movement forward and he picked players who could move. He wasn't too happy playing round the flanks so he didn't play many wingers.

Sir Bobby Charlton: It was made for me in a way really because I used to play on the wing and I could go from midfield and play on the wing without any problem. You had three midfield players who, depending on the situation in the match, could either be defenders or forwards. Everybody assumed that it was a defensive policy. It wasn't. It was an attacking policy just as much as a defensive policy. I think that's why England had a particularly great record away from home. It wasn't a fluke that we won the World Cup. I think for about two years we'd hardly lost away. We'd gone everywhere, the Bernabéu Stadium and places all over the world, and won.

1966 World Cup Finals – Group One

Nobby Stiles: If you read the papers on the Sunday after we drew with Uruguay, no score in the first game, you'd have thought it was the end of the world. Alf Ramsey took us down to Pinewood Studios, and Sean Connery was making a film. We had a great day. That was what great management was about. He relaxed us completely. Instead of getting us uptight and tense, Sir Alf did the opposite, so that when we came to play against Mexico it was a different ball game.

Sir Bobby Charlton: The first goal that we scored in the tournament was against Mexico and they keep showing it on television, which is very flattering. I picked the ball up in my own half and I'd nothing in front of me so I thought, 'I'll make some ground and see what unfolds.' As I got into their half I was still allowed to progress. I thought, 'Well, if they let me get another 10 or 15 yards, it might well be that I can have a crack.' Roger Hunt went on a couple of decoy runs, I think Martin Peters went somewhere, Alan Ball went somewhere else and I just kept carrying the ball and trying to change direction, or make people think I was changing direction, to give myself that little extra time, and eventually I got about 25 yards away from the goal and the defenders hadn't come to me. The Wembley pitch was beautiful and it was just running very smoothly and I thought, 'Right,' and I just concentrated on hitting it correctly and as sweetly as I could, and it flew right in the top corner, and we were on our way.

v Argentina (Quarter-final)

Nobby Stiles: Well, I could tell you about the French game first. I did a bad tackle on Simon with about 10 minutes to go. It wasn't intentional but there was talk about it. I got booked actually. I didn't get booked by the referee, I got booked by a FIFA official from Northern Ireland who was in the stand. I think it's unique. Anyway, the talk was that I wouldn't play against Argentina on the Saturday, and I was just going through the motions in training. On the Thursday coming up to the game, I always remember Sir Alf coming up to me and saying, 'Did you mean it, Nobby?' And I said, 'No, Alf, I didn't.' And I didn't, because tackling is about timing. I'd thought, 'When he turns I'm going to be there and as he turns I'm going to tackle the ball,' and as I got there he'd released it and it was a horrendous tackle. The lad never moved. (I spoke to him years later and I said, 'How did it go after?' He said, 'Oh, I was fine, I was playing in a month or so and I played for about another three years,' so that was great.) As I said, it looked as though I was going to be out against Argentina, and Sir Alf said that the biggest thing was that we kept our discipline, and I think we did. I don't think Argentina did but we kept our discipline and they were a very hard side to beat. Probably we were fortunate that Rattin did get sent off, but I still think we would have beat them because they didn't score many goals anyway.

Alan Ball: In a couple of the early games, he had played with wingers. He had John Connelly in the squad, Ian Callaghan, Terry Paine, and it was a case of whatever way he wanted to play. I think the game that changed his mind, and certainly changed my World Cup, was against Argentina, where we had to play a little bit more solid because they were a really good side. We went out with some sort of a plan. I played outside-right virtually all the game, but I had a job to do. They had a full-back called Marzolini, who was one of the best players in the tournament, and I had to stop him getting forward and causing us problems. I got my chance, because I was brought back for that game, and I thought, 'I'm going to stay in now,' which I did.

Nobby Stiles: Alf knew everything but he didn't fill your head with too much. He'd have a meeting and say, 'We'll be playing Argentina, do you think somebody should be man-marked?' Everybody thinks that all that I did in the World Cup was man-mark. I didn't, but I did it against Onega for Argentina. What Alf did was put it to the players first. He said, 'Now, what do you think?' He'd be chatting and they'd say, 'Onega,' and he'd say, 'Well, who do you think will?' and they'd say, 'Nobby,' and he'd say, 'Right, we'll do that.'

Geoff Hurst: Jimmy Greaves played the first three games, along with Roger. We hadn't played particularly well in the early rounds and in fact Roger scored the bulk of the goals, so things hadn't gone well for the team necessarily or for Jimmy, and then Jimmy injured himself against France in the last qualifying game, which we won 2–0, and I had the great opportunity to come back in. Having seen them [Argentina], in my view they were probably the best team in the tournament. They also had a very high percentage of top players and there was a little left winger called Oscar Mas who was no bigger than 5 foot, like a dwarf, but if you give him a machine-gun he'd kill everybody and he sticks in my mind. They also had a very high proportion of 'killers', ball-winners. Whereas you'll always get one or two in a great side, possibly three, they had five or six who could be a little hard, but they had some great ability and it showed in the quarter-final. With Rattin off for most of the game, we only managed to squeeze it, 1–0. The goal was a product of hours and hours of practice on the [West Ham] training field, of running up to a cone – not a live person but a cone – and, not beating 'him', actually bending the ball round 'him', so that, although the defender's there, you whip it round and he can do nothing about it. That goal was really just a simple product, Martin getting it out wide from the throw-in and whipping it in from his left foot, his bad foot, to a position on the near post, and I was there to meet it. There's a place where the ball and the man are gonna get to, where the space is the key, and the timing of the ball and the timing of the run was the key area we worked on for many, many hours at West Ham's training ground. After the game Alf ill-advisedly made his comment, calling them 'animals'. He was so incensed about the way they had played the game.

v Portugal (Semi-final)

Sir Bobby Charlton: I scored two in the semi-final. One, the goalkeeper came out when Roger Hunt was bearing down on him and instead of collecting it, the ball hit his knee and it came flying out to me. I was able to stroke it almost immediately as it came to me, and two full-backs were coming in to try and close it off because the goalkeeper was out of his goal, and Wembley was so smooth it just went straight through the middle. I was pleased about that one because I could have tried to hit it hard and probably missed. But then the next one, George Cohen, I think it was, knocked the ball down the right-hand side and we were already leading 1–0 and Geoff Hurst kept their defender away from the ball and just held it up. I'm trying to get up as quickly as I can, which I'd always been taught by Jimmy Murphy – whenever your player gets the ball always make yourself available to him in case he needs to use you. So Geoff Hurst got the ball and I got to the edge of the 18-yard box and he just laid a beautiful ball, about a four- or five-yard ball right in front of me, on my right foot and I didn't even have to break stride, I just whipped it in. It flew in as well. Yeah.

v West Germany (Final)

Geoff Hurst: The first goal was a very important goal. Germany had gone ahead and I think it's always nice in any major game to equalize pretty quickly, so it was an important time. People ask me what I felt was the best goal and people always remember the other two, the disputed one and the final one, but in terms of my professional view of it, I think the first goal was important: (a) the quick equalizer; and (b) the fact that people are very fresh in the game and you consider you should be marked very tightly, particularly as the Germans had a man-to-man system with a sweeper, so I was very proud of what we'd achieved at West Ham and the work we did on taking quick free-kicks, into space, and someone getting there. If you look at the film, the defender, Hottges, who should be marking me, is probably about five yards adrift, so that was a significant goal and one I think was the most important for me, professionally.

2–1

Geoff Hurst: Martin Peters was a good goalscorer and he got himself in that position a lot of times. He was always called 'the ghost'. He'd always work to get in there. People would never see him when the ball wasn't there. When the ball *was* there, they'd say, 'There's Martin popped up,' but he used to be there ten times out of ten. And of course he was a good finisher, as good as anybody, with either foot, side-footing, heading …

2–2

Nobby Stiles: Bally was absolutely brilliant in that Final. I always remember him running into the back of the net when the goal went in at the end of normal time. Bally runs back to the centre-circle and puts it on the centre-spot. Absolutely brilliant. And I always remember extra-time. I went to cross the ball about 10 minutes into the second period and everything drained from me. I crossed it and it just trickled over the dead-ball line, and I couldn't move. I always remember little Bally running past me and he says, 'Move, you little bastard.' He made me run, because we were room-mates. I thought there was nothing left and he made me go, because he was everywhere that day.

3–2

Geoff Hurst: My second goal was a result of Bally again knocking in a near-post cross, slightly behind me. I had to turn on it and take a few strides to get my footing. It hit the underside of the crossbar and it went miles in. I mean, it was miles over [the line]. It's never really been agreed today that the ball was in, whether they be television or magazine shots. It's interesting that people still want to talk about the goal. They say to me, 'Was it in?' That's the most-asked question. Nothing's been proved, but I always go off Roger

Hunt's reaction. He turned away, hand up, and he was a great striker and if you're not sure whether that ball is in or out, you would always attempt to put it back in the net. Roger didn't. He walked away and I always go on that and still do today.

4–2

Geoff Hurst: My third goal was just a breakaway where the Germans were bombarding us and Bobby Moore, composed under pressure, hit an inch-perfect ball to me after a couple of set-up passes. Bobby had the ability and composure in a World Cup Final to chest the ball down only a yard or two from the penalty spot. They'd lost me at that stage and gone forward. I looked across to my right because I could see Bally steaming up on my right-hand side and there was an opportunity to knock the ball square, had the goalkeeper challenged me or the defender caught me. I had a look for that, and the guy who was chasing me saw me glance and then started to go marginally away from me, because of that, and it just gave me that extra impetus to go on another two more strides. All I wanted to do was hit it as hard as I possibly could, with every ounce of my strength, thinking, 'If it goes over, then fine.' I knew it was only seconds before the end, it's 50 yards behind the goal at Wembley, and if I hit it into the car-park it'll take that few seconds and the game will be over.

What It Meant

Sir Bobby Charlton: I think all of us appreciated that when you'd won the World Cup life was never going to be the same again. I remember saying to our Jack on the final whistle, 'Well, that's it, you can't do any more than that. We're the world champions.' So, it was football's greatest moment, and probably sport's greatest moment, in our history. We were the best.

Alan Ball: We got £1,000 and it was taxed. Harold Wilson was in charge at the time, supertax was paid, so it wasn't a lot, but it didn't matter. I wasn't even interested. It was one of those things in your life that you would have done for nothing and just being given the opportunity to do it was enough for me, and to take the medal home to my father was the be-all and end-all.

Geoff Hurst: My life changed significantly. I think it changed when I was in my little house in Hornchurch and a large shadow was cast over the house when a limousine turned up to take me to a function for the top English goalscorer. I'm still fairly high profile now because of the World Cup Final. It's probably the biggest occasion we've ever taken part in as a nation and everybody from eight, nine, ten years of age at that time, and upwards, recalls quite clearly where they were and what they were doing, and everybody I meet wants to tell me.

Denis Law: I was playing golf. In Manchester. And, unlike Manchester, it was raining. There were two of us on the golf course and the guy I was playing was awful, and he beat me. As I turned the corner, all the members were at the window because they knew I was out there on the golf course, and England had won 4–2. I thought it was the end of the world. There was great rivalry between Scotland and England in those days and I was not happy that they had done it, but of course it was the greatest thing that ever happened for English football.

Imitators

Denis Law: What happens in world football is that clubs tend to imitate the team that has won the World Cup, and by

England winning without wingers all of a sudden a lot of clubs now started playing what they called a 4-3-3 system, which meant there was nobody on the wings and everything was channelled down the middle, and that for me was quite boring and it took a long time to get over that. In those days you used to ask a kid, 'Where do you play?' He would say, 'inside-forward' or 'right winger' or 'left winger'. Five or six years after that World Cup, you'd ask a young kid, 'Where do you play?' and it would be 'midfield' or 'defensive midfield' or 'right midfield'.

Tommy Smith: I think probably the worst thing that ever could have happened to us, and maybe people'll disagree, is winning the World Cup in '66 because suddenly, out of the closet, every man and his dog became a coach, and they got this badge by going to Lilleshall. I know everybody can't be a professional footballer, but everybody can be a coach. But, I'll tell you what, one hour with an ex-professional footballer of note is worth 1,000 hours of somebody who has got no experience of football, because the knowledge of the game is at the grassroots.

Beaten by Scotland

Pat Crerand: I got into the Scottish team in 1960–61 and they had great players – Alex Scott, John White, Ian St John, Denis Law, Dave Wilson, Dave Mackay, Jimmy Baxter, Billy McNeill. In '61 we had a play-off with Czechoslovakia in Belgium and they beat us in extra-time, and they got to the World Cup Final in Chile in '62. Scottish players were always lacking a bit of discipline. If Matt Busby or Jock Stein or Bill Shankly had been manager of the Scottish national side from maybe 1958 to 1970, I think you'd have probably seen the Scottish team win the World Cup Finals. That may sound daft to a lot of people but they came very close in '62 because the Czechs were beating Brazil 1–0 in the Final and we should have beaten the Czechs.

Billy Bremner: Jim Baxter was a hell of a one for taking the mickey and that's what he wanted to do [at Wembley in 1967]. I kept thinking about the 9–3 defeat, when Scotland had got a hammering, and Scotland had got thumped 7–2 at Wembley, and I'm thinking, 'God almighty, we have an opportunity here today to really take a few goals off them,' because England had a couple of injuries. I remember we were 2–1 up, and I'm saying to Baxter, 'Hey, we can take this lot for five or six today,' and all he kept saying was, 'Never mind five or six, humiliate them, take the mickey with them, that's all I'm here for.' He wanted to keep the ball up, put it through people's legs, roll it around and I thought, 'No, there's more to the game than this.' They used to call Alan Ball 'Jimmy Clitheroe' because of his high-pitched voice and Baxter was giving him the shout that day, about him being Jimmy Clitheroe. I wasn't going to give the shout because Bally would have killed me! I felt for the English players that day, too, because, like I say, they had a couple of players there that weren't really a 100 per cent and maybe we could have done better with the scoreline, but don't tell that to the Scotsman back in Scotland because that's the day they will remember all their life and that's the day that they'll tell their grandkids about, the day that they beat England after England had won the World Cup and not only beat them but beat them in their own backyard down at Wembley.

15

'Chelsea has always been a showbiz club'

Chelsea, 1962–74:
The Emergence of 'Glamour'

In the 1960s, England was at the centre of the world's fashion and pop-music industries. One football club in London became particularly associated with the rich and famous.

Birth of a Young Team

Tommy Docherty: When I arrived at Stamford Bridge as coach in February '62, we had a brilliant youth team that had just won the FA Youth Cup for the second successive time. People like Bonetti, Shellito, Venables, Hollins, Harris, Osgood, Bobby Tambling, Barry Bridges, Bert Murray. Great kids. But the older players at the club were past their sell-by date. They were just going through the motions, and that's why the club was struggling. A lot of the players weren't interested in how they were playing. They were interested in how long they were going to play, so they were coasting, so to speak. Something had to be done and we brought eight players out of the youth team into the side and we just took off. It was brilliant.

Brian Mears: Tommy Docherty was a great manager for Chelsea. He pulled the club by the scruff of the neck when we had gone down into the Second Division. He bought and sold quite regularly and gradually got a squad together. For that I admire him because it got us back into the First Division not long afterwards, and he also got us into Europe. If you remember we played in Rome, that ill-fated night when the players were attacked by the crowd.

Tommy Docherty: Osgood was a different class. He was very much a flair player. Venables was, of course. Bonetti was as good a goalkeeper as you would probably have found at that particular time, and later on we went through the transfer market and we bought probably one of the best players of the lot, Charlie Cooke, for 72,000 quid. He later became the King of the King's Road.

Tommy Baldwin: Peter [Osgood] was the best thing since sliced bread. Every important game, every major game, he scored a goal. You go back through the history books, he was there, scoring goals. He had a style all of his own, and we loved him in the team, we'd got to have him in the team. He was big, he was brave, he had tons of skill, he could head a ball, he could do almost everything.

Peter Osgood: I had some great players around me, like Alan Hudson, your Tommy Baldwins and Ian Hutchinsons, Charlie Cookes and people like this. The opposing fans used to shout, 'Osgood, No Good' but as soon as they shouted they probably made me work a little bit harder. I went to Stamford Bridge and every Saturday they used to say, 'Ossie the King of Stamford Bridge' and that was lovely. I'll never forget that as long as I live.

Nigel Clarke: There was Terry Venables, who was the leader of the pack. He was always the brightest, the smartest, the shrewdest. He knew about tactics, he knew about how to play the game, he used to enrage Tommy Docherty by changing the way they played and because he was so funny and amusing and the leader he got players like George Graham with him and Alan Harris, Ron Harris, John Hollins, their little pack that went together.

Dave Webb: There was a lot of home-grown talent and I think that was one of the unique things about Chelsea in my day. There weren't expensive buys. I think I was about 45 grand, and John Dempsey was 55 grand. Ian Hutchinson, for instance, was a £15,000 buy from Cambridge.

Tommy Docherty: The only trouble was when I sent eight of them home from Blackpool, but outside of that no problems with 'em at all because I didn't stand any nonsense. If anyone broke the rules they were on the transfer list and I got them out of the club immediately, but they were super lads, great players. Some got a little bit greedy because the maximum wage was abolished and they were all looking at a few extra quid, as everyone does in life today, and especially Terry Venables and George Graham! The players were very, very good, except for the Blackpool incident. They'd been out on half a dozen occasions on the town, wining and dining, discotheques and what not. I let them go out a couple of nights, which I thought was playing the game with them, and when they started going out five or six nights I put a clamp on. Then it was either them or me. If I hadn't sent them home on that occasion then I was as well as packing the job in because they'd have run the club instead of me, and Terry and George were very much the ring-leaders of that episode.

Ian Hutchinson: Friday night was always the fire escapes and obviously a few of the lads got caught at Blackpool when Tommy Doc sent eight of them back. There were so many things. I mean, I can remember two players at 100 feet up, hanging on to balconies, crawling along. Next thing, there's police there with guns, saying, 'Come on down.' They were the testimonial games, friendly games, so we had our fun.

A Showbiz Club

Tommy Docherty: Chelsea has always been a showbiz club. All the showbiz people used to attend the matches there, and of course on the board we had Dickie Attenborough, who was a film producer.

Ian Hutchinson: There was Michael Caine, Michael Crawford, and, obviously, the loveliest lady in the world, Jane Seymour. She was married then to Dickie Attenborough's nephew and she was gorgeous. The Chelsea set came to the games and then it just took off. To be 'in' you had to be seen to be going to Chelsea's matches because everybody was there, and Dickie [Attenborough] was filling up the directors' box with celebrities. Everyone was fighting to get into the restaurants and the bars just to see these people and then it was 'Let's go to this award,' 'Let's go to this party,' 'We've got the première of so-and-so film,' or whatever. You got free tickets just to be there and they were all 'Oh, there's a party afterwards.'

Peter Osgood: You'd see Raquel Welch, you'd see Honor Blackman, you'd see Richard O'Sullivan, you'd see Ronnie Corbett and Michael Crawford, Jane Seymour, all these sort of people, and Michael Caine used to come along. People talk about the way we used to play and the way we used to live, and I always remember scoring my 100th League goal against Everton at Stamford Bridge. I did a lap of honour and the crowd were chanting my name – 'Osgood, Osgood, Osgood'. Very, very emotional. I went into the dressing-room and who's sitting there but Steve McQueen. Now that took all my 100 League goals away from me. I just wanted to touch the great man. The Chelsea scene was incredible. I went there as a bricklayer and all of a sudden I became an international star and the rise was phenomenal. In just six months I was a top name. I was a bricklayer, and all of a sudden I was talking to people like Raquel Welch and Steve McQueen.

Jimmy Hill: Raquel Welch was at London Weekend Television; she was making a film and really promoting it, so we were to stage this meeting in front of camera, Peter Osgood and Raquel Welch, before the Saturday match, and I went along, being head of London Weekend Sport at that time. Dickie Davies was doing the interview with this young lady and she said that she wasn't very happy with something that had gone on there, with regard to the press conference and how it had been arranged, so I said, 'Well, do you want to have a spot of lunch with me and I'll willingly help,' and so she did. She prowled around this room. I was sitting down and she was sort of walking around and I was not used to that, certainly from my players at Coventry! So I said, 'Well, if you'd kindly stop walking around this place and sit down on that chair opposite me, I will try and do something to help you,' and she sat down and for a couple of days we were quite good friends in promoting that film and also getting the most glamorous figure we have seen on *The Big Match* in all its years ... including Brian Moore.

Nigel Clarke: I always remember going to Chelsea one day and sitting in the press-box and seeing Raquel Welch in the directors' box. When she went, about a quarter of an

Stan Cullis, manager of Wolverhampton Wanderers, with the League Championship trophy, 1953-54. *(Colorsport)*

Don Revie *(left)* in action for Manchester City against Birmingham City in the 1956 FA Cup Final. *(Colorsport)*

Alf Ramsey, Tottenham Hotspur and England. *(Popperfoto)*

Ipswich Town, League Champions, 1961-62. Ted Phillips and Jimmy Leadbetter are on the extreme right of the front row. *(Jimmy Leadbetter)*

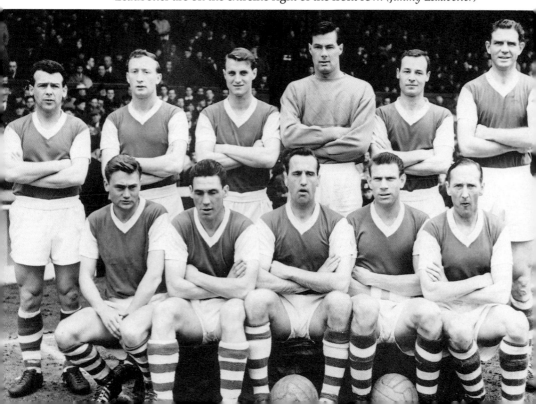

West Ham United, 1964 FA Cup Winners, Captain Bobby Moore and manager
Ron Greenwood hold the trophy. *(Popperfoto)*

Alan Sealey of West Ham scores the second goal of the 1965 European Cup
Winners Cup Final against Munich 1860. *(Popperfoto)*

Len Shackleton. *(Colorsport)*

Jimmy Hill, manager of Coventry City, poses with new signings before the 1962-63 season. *Left to right:* Hill, Jimmy Whitehouse, Willie Humphries, Hugh Barr, Terry Bly and Bobby Laverick. *(Colorsport)*

Nobby Stiles, Manchester United and England. *(Hulton Deutsch)*

Bobby Moore, captain of England, holds aloft the World Cup trophy, Wembley, 1966. *(Hulton Deutsch)*

Chelsea's John Boyle *(left)* and Tommy Baldwin with the European Cup
Winners Cup, 1971. *(Hulton Deutsch)*

Peter Osgood and Ian Hutchinson in their new pub, the Union Tavern,
Old Windsor, Berkshire, in December 1979. *(Hulton Deutsch)*

Leeds United, League Champions 1968-69 *Back row:* Madeley, O'Grady, Harvey, Sprake, Charlton, Hunter. *Middle row:* Johanneson, Belfitt, Jones, Hibbitt, Gray, Lorimer, Don Revie (manager). *Front row:* Reaney, Cooper, Giles, Bremner, Greenhoff, Bates, Les Cocker (trainer). *(Colorsport)*

David Webb scores Chelsea's winning goal in the 1970 FA Cup Final replay against Leeds United. *(Colorsport)*

George Best evades an Arsenal player in August 1970. *(Popperfoto)*

hour before the final whistle, she walked down to the touch-line and whistled to Peter Osgood and waved to him and Ossie waved back over his shoulder and that was the first indication of what a glamour profession it was. You'd get page-three girls and models and actors at Chelsea. Because it was so near the King's Road it attracted a following of pretty people, and players in those days had money in their pockets and were the new glamour symbol in sport.

Peter Osgood: Yes, Raquel came over and and she was promoting a new film and she was obviously a football fan. She came down to Stamford Bridge – I think we played Leicester – and it wasn't a very good game. We drew one each, and I always remember her screaming, 'Bye, Ossie,' and I'm still playing and I give her a wave as she went off but I didn't play very well. I think I got a bit of a going-over from Dave Sexton, because I don't think my mind was on the game. I mean, she was a very attractive lady, let's be fair, and I met her before the game. If I'd met her after it might be a bit different! But that was the exciting time, and that was the way Chelsea Football Club was.

Vidal Sassoon: The golden age as a Chelsea supporter was watching them in the sixties. There was something in the air, and I think that affected Chelsea, being in the West End. There was glamour to this whole area. We cut the players' hair, with my whole gang from Sloane Street. We had them all in and I was wearing McCreadie's uniform doing a haircut on the guy. It was just a stunt, but we were close with those guys. They were part of that social scene in a funny way. Venables, Hollins, Harris, there was certain style. Even Harris had style. What did they used to call him – 'Chopper'? Yeah, 'Chopper' Harris.

Tommy Baldwin: I used to have a drink with the likes of Richard Harris, Michael Caine, Michael Crawford and Peter O'Toole. Michael Crawford was an ardent Chelsea fan – he still is, still loves Chelsea – and he used to come to the matches and Gabrielle used to come with him. I was just getting divorced then, and we used to go to these drinks afterwards and then that's how I first met Gabrielle, and after about a year or so they went through a bad patch and they ended up getting divorced after a couple of years and I'd already been divorced and, for some reason I don't know, I just took Gabrielle out. She'd still come to the match even though she wasn't with Michael and I ended up having a drink with her and it just went on from there. They [the press] were pretty nasty about it. They said that I had stolen Michael Crawford's wife, which wasn't the case at all.

The King's Road

Vidal Sassoon: The King's Road was marvellous. It was the greatest fashion scene. People would come from everywhere with their cameras, internationally, just to see the King's Road. And just at the other end of King's Road, Fulham Road, was Stamford Bridge, and you had Osgood. Now there was a man with style.

Peter Osgood: We couldn't walk down the King's Road without being dragged into a restaurant. People loved to see Alan Hudson, myself, Charlie Cooke, Tommy Baldwin, Ian Hutchinson, 'Chopper' Harris, and they'd just say, 'Come in our restaurant and sit there, have a meal and we'll pay for it and it'll be on the house, no problem.' It's just a high profile thing. The King's Road was swinging, the Beatles were going, the Stones were going, and it was a fabulous time. I joined Chelsea in '64 and within the space of seven years [1966 to 1973] we had four Finals and four semi-finals, which was a tremendous time for Chelsea Football Club.

Terry O'Neill: We'd meet at Alvaro's, a chic Italian restaurant, and there'd be Terry Stamp, Vidal Sassoon, Nicol

Williamson, Tom Courtenay, Doug Haywood, Johnny Gold sometimes, and various others. I think all of us lived for Saturday afternoon at that time. I mean, we would all go to lunch, and then just beetle on down to the ground. And they were all our heroes. Chelsea was like a cast of a film, like *The Dirty Dozen* or something like that. Ossie was like Clint Eastwood, 'Chopper' Harris was like Lee Marvin, Charlie Cooke was James Dean-ish, Hudson was the young Robert Mitchum. They all clearly had separate identities.

Alvaro Maccioni: I became a star although I was only a restaurateur, serving food to people, but, whoever achieved something in the sixties was recognized as a star. And you became part of that crowd. I described it once as 'the beautiful people'. People would describe them as the 'in' people. I don't like to use those words, 'in' and 'out', but that was it.

Vidal Sassoon: I was in a craft where I had to be gentle and charming to people and look at their needs and cut hair accordingly and make them feel good. It was a very one-on-one emotional thing, and I needed to scream on a Saturday afternoon. I needed to get out there and be vocal, and I loved the humour that came with it. There are some wonderful incidents. One of the funniest ones was at Fulham. George Cohen, the England back, played for Fulham, and he could beat his man beautifully, and one day he had the ball and he was preparing to pass it and Jimmy Hill, who was a very funny player at times, was running through like crazy, non-stop, to pick up whatever it was that was coming, and a wag in the crowd said, 'Cohen, Cohen, give it to the Rabbi.' And the ball came over and Hill headed it into the net and it was just hysterical. It was a classic remark. 'Cohen, Cohen, give it to the Rabbi,' bump, into the net.

Terry O'Neill: The King's Road at the time was a very lovely place, all the super models walking down one street and having lunch or having dinner. It was all the girls in their mini-skirts. All of a sudden the East End became the West End and the working-class took over every creative field so it was our manor, and the King's Road was our Mayfair, and it's where we ruled the roost. It was a swinging time in that sense, but don't get thinking that it was all the drug thing. I mean, you wouldn't find drugs around sport. Drink maybe, but not drugs. But it was very easy-going. The girls loved the footballers. They loved a bit of rough, I suppose, or whatever. So it was a whole mix – lords, ladies and the working-class heroes who took it over. That's the sort of crowds you got down Stamford Bridge.

Glamour Photographs

Nigel Clarke: Terry O'Neill was to photography in those days what Osgood was to football. He was the young glamorous snapper coming through the ranks and he used to go and do the film stars and he used to get film stars and footballers together and he'd mix in that swinging world of London. I think he went on to marry Faye Dunaway. He was a glamour person and he brought photography into sport more than any other person in those days because he was a great football fan. He became a showbiz personality himself.

Ian Hutchinson: We used to go on page three with the models. The first time, I went up there with Peter Houseman, bless him, who died in a car crash. Terry O'Neill just phoned and said, 'Can you come up for a photograph?' He said it was £50 or whatever. We've got up there and there was this model. Oh, dear me. We done some silly shots, exercise shots and whatever, and he's gone, 'Right, let's do the main ones now,' and, all of a sudden, wallop and Peter Houseman, I promise you he was so naive and so quiet, his mouth just fell out. I did quite a few of those, and it just escalated and escalated until the side was broken up and then of course it all went. Instead of opening a shop or doing a photosession once a week it would go down to once a month. Chelsea were going down and down and down until they were relegated. Success breeds success and that's it. It's just a shame that they broke the side up too soon.

Terry O'Neill: In the sixties I did all the pics with the Beatles, Stones, all the pop stars, and then I went to Hollywood and did Sinatra, Clint Eastwood, Robert Redford, John Wayne. Once you get to know these people they're quite ordinary, and one always has to have idols that you want to meet or idolize through photography. So I decided to do sportsmen in the same way. I treated them like movie stars or pop stars, and I moved them from the sports pages to the centre pages. I used to try and present them in a way that they were stars in their own right. There was no football outfits. I'd do David Webb and his baby, both bare-chested, or looking like Desperate Dan, or someone else in a bath with Playboy bunnies. Or Gordon Banks. I just shot his hands with a rose; the greatest goalkeeper in the world was holding this rose and it was like a mystery picture. I either approached the players that I knew, which were mostly the Chelsea players, personally or I'd go through an agent, and at the beginning they went along with it because the agent realized it was good for them to be more starry because they might get adverts and not just be a team player. But eventually they all wanted more and more money. Then it got to a degree where it sort of took the fun and the creativity out of it. It just boiled down to money.

Dave Webb: Terry O'Neill started doing different pictures of me, and he done a marvellous one once of me daughter when she was a little baby that ended up being a double-page spread in the centre of the *Daily Mirror*. People hadn't seen footballers with their children like that before. They'd only seen them with their football kit on in the mud or whatever. I can tell you a story, but I won't tell the punch of it, I can't tell you that. Terry O'Neill done a picture and he'd got me sitting in the bath. I had me shorts on, and all these bunny girls had bikinis on, but he wanted to make it look as if we was all starkers in the bath, so he kept bubbling up all this water and bubbling and bubbling and bubbling and bubbling, but the camera kept steaming up so he had to keep going out and coming back in and then by the end of day all the bubbles had gone and he'd run out of this bubble stuff, and one of the young ladies happened to turn round and say, 'Well, if we all flatulate at the same time, Terry, perhaps we don't need any more bubble-bath stuff.' And I thought what lovely young ladies they were, working for the Bunny Club at the time.

The Occasional Drink

Tommy Baldwin: It was just fun. No one thought about the game at all. Before the game and after it everyone would be relaxed, and would talk about something completely different, about your girlfriends or where you were going at night, and after matches we would all have a good drink together. There's no worries about 'Oh, professional footballers can't drink'. We used to really enjoy ourselves.

Dave Webb: Yeah, Tommy liked a drink, like all of us did. That's why they called him 'Sponge'. He used to be in the newspapers and they used to say he was a 'Sponge' because of all the work-rate he soaked up and we all used to laugh because we all knew what he was called the 'Sponge' for. But it was quite incredible. People like him and Charlie Cooke would go out and have binges for two days and they'd come in and train, and they'd be playing on the Saturday and it was unbelievable how they performed. I'm no saint, I was just as bad in many ways. There was a famous place they used to go to – I think it was called the Candy Box – and it was open till about half-past six in the morning. All the waiters and the people that finished late in

London went in this place for a drink. I think Tommy and Charlie had season tickets.

Peter Osgood: Tom did like a drink, but he was a grafter. He worked hard, he lived hard, to be honest, but he was a hell of a player. He was Tommy Docherty's first buy. The Boss, as I call him, came from the Arsenal to Chelsea, and he swapped George Graham for Tommy Baldwin. That shows you what he thought of Tommy Baldwin and he was a great player for Chelsea and I'm glad to say he's still a great mate.

Tommy Baldwin: There tended to be two groups at Chelsea. There were the drinkers and the non-drinkers and there was about half a dozen of each. There was about four or five like me – Charlie Cooke, John Boyle, Ossie might come out and maybe Marvin Hinton and Eddie McCreadie – and we'd socialize, we'd have a drink. After games there was the two parties. Half of them probably wouldn't drink, but they'd still come out and socialize, go to the bars or the night-club and we'd all generally enjoy ourselves.

Dave Webb: It's a unique place, Chelsea. You have to be a certain type to be part of that clique. I've seen a lot of players almost in tears. They've been there for a long time, and never got accepted into the real hardcore of it. To get part of their gang, you had to perform on the football pitch and once you'd gone out there and you'd got your credibility, then it takes off. I don't know if that has always been the case since, but that was definitely the case then, with Chelsea in particular.

16

'Don Revie was a great man for detail'

Leeds United, 1961–74: The Emergence of 'Professionalism'

After Don Revie took over as manager of Leeds United, in March 1961, the club grew in strength. They won the Second Division Championship in 1963–64 and, during the next 10 years, won the First Division Championship twice and finished runners-up five times. They also won the League Cup, the FA Cup and the Fairs Cup (twice). A case study of Leeds United in the 1960s provides a contrasting picture to that of Chelsea.

Don Revie

Jack Charlton: I remember Don Revie coming. He'd been at Manchester City, then went to Sunderland and then Leeds bought him. He didn't do that much as a player for Leeds, but then he was made manager and from that moment everything changed. He'd bend over backwards to do anything to help the players: to make sure that you were informed, that you knew exactly what was going to happen, and that you prepared yourself right. Not only that, but you had to live right as well.

John Giles: Revie's big thing was his intensity. When he took over the job he wanted to be the best manager that Britain had ever known. He'd played under quite a few managers himself, and lots of them I think he didn't respect and he felt, 'When I become a manager I won't do this and I won't do that.' He was a very approachable fella, but he brought an intensity to it that I certainly hadn't been used to. He wanted to know every detail in the club, how to keep the players happy, how they were happy in their personal life. He was much more personally involved with the players. They were a fairly young group of players at Leeds – Norman Hunter, Paul Reaney, Terry Cooper, Paul Madeley, Billy Bremner – and if one of the lads was going out with a girl that he didn't like, he would say it to them: 'Get a girl that'll look after you.' He was involved that much with the players.

Norman Hunter: He was terribly superstitious. He had the same suit. He had a blue mohair suit. He must have had three or four made during a season because he used to wear it and wear it and wear it until we got beat and then he'd go and get another one. We had a run of 29 games without defeat. Well, you could nearly see your face in this blue mohair suit. Oh, very, very superstitious. When I first got in the team I picked a football up and I threw it to Billy Bremner just before we went out, and we won, and from then on the last thing I did before we went out of the dressing-room was pick a football up and throw it at whoever was captain.

Birth of a Team

John Giles: Don Revie took over an unfashionable club in a very lowly position – I think they were struggling against relegation to the Third Division – and built it up from scratch in a non-football area. Leeds was more a rugby-league stronghold than a soccer stronghold so he didn't have the traditional support that Shankly had when he went to Liverpool. Revie worked 24 hours a day, getting players in, looking after the players, getting the training and all the facilities right.

Norman Hunter: I think his first season he was battling against relegation and he bought Bobby Collins from Everton for about 30-odd thousand and he bought Tommy Younger and Cliff Mason and people like that. That turned the club round and they didn't go down. Then the next year, after about six games had gone, he put meself, Paul Reaney, Gary Sprake and a lad called Rodney Johnson in at Swansea and it went on from there. Billy [Bremner] was already there, but then you look at Paul Reaney, Gary Sprake, Paul Madeley, meself and then you go on and you have Peter Lorimer, Eddie Gray, and Terry Cooper and these were all brought through the youth system. He bought a lad called Alan Peacock upfront from Middlesbrough and then he bought Johnny Giles from Man United for about £36,000 and then all of a sudden it started to jell together and that team came out of the Second Division.

John Giles: I think he was a huge influence in the sixties. I think his attention to detail, the way that he wanted the team to plan as much as you possibly could for all events, was definitely an influence on other people in the sixties. As time went by, the likes of Paul Reaney, Terry Cooper, Billy Bremner and Norman Hunter all matured with the right values, so, as they got older and became stronger, they became better players and the team became a great team. He also had the benefit in those days of no freedom of contract. He could keep the players together, and they grew together. I joined Leeds in '63 and they didn't become a great team until about '68, which is about five years later, with basically the same players.

Syd Owen: Our ambitions for the future were to scour the country from top to bottom and get some of the best 14- and 15-year-olds to come to Elland Road from school so that we could develop them. We shall always be grateful to players like Tommy Younger and Don Weston and others who were brought into the club just to hold the situation and give us time to develop these youngsters, who we hoped would bring success to Elland Road. We even went to the degree of moving some of the families down. One example was Jim McCalliog. Mr Reynolds, the chairman, discussed it with his parents and we even moved the family down to Leeds and provided them with a house and a job so that we could get the son to come to Elland Road. Norman Hunter came from the north-east and Don moved the family down and they lived five minutes' walk from Elland Road.

Norman Hunter: I think Les Cocker and Syd Owen were already on the staff, and you also had Maurice Lindley and Bob English. When the gaffer took over he had the makings of a good backroom staff and he kept them all the time. As time wore on, you realized how good he was at organization and man-management. When Paul Madeley was coming up to signing professional, the staff said, 'Oh, he's a bit short on this,' and the gaffer said, 'I want him,' and look what a player Paul Madeley turned out to be.

Jack Charlton: We had people like Jim Storrie and Alan Peacock in the early days, and we had a period where we had John Charles back. Then the most important was Bobby Collins, I felt, and then Johnny Giles took over from Bobby when Bobby broke his thigh in Turin, and that was Bobby virtually finished with Leeds. Billy Bremner and Gilesy were certainly the two most influential players, in the centre of midfield. Norman Hunter was a power in himself in the game of football. We had people like Terry Cooper, who was voted the best left-full-back in the world during the Mexico World Cup in '70, and Paul Reaney. People like Paul Madeley. Paul never sorted out a position with Leeds United. He went through his career playing in the forwards, in the midfield, at full-back, at centre-back. He took everybody's place when they were injured, but a great athlete and a hell of a player. People like Allan Clarke and Mick Jones came in, and we were together for about six, seven, eight years as a group. Peter Lorimer and Eddie Gray. Eddie Gray had every potential to be as good as George Best, but Eddie had so many injuries during his career that he was never consistently there long enough for people to take notice.

Norman Hunter: He [Don Revie] changed the strip, from the old Leeds strip – blue and gold or something like that – and said, 'We're gonna win the European Cup like Real Madrid did.' That was his one dream, that Leeds United would one day win the European Cup, and we did play in the European Cup Final, against Bayern Munich [in 1975], but he was in the stand. He came over and watched us but unfortunately we got beat 2–0.

Jack Charlton: His idea was that we would wear a white strip, all white, because it's the easiest colour to pick out when you're doing things quickly in a game. He maybe attributed it to the fact that Real Madrid in those days were the best team in Europe and the best team in the world and they wore all white. He used to say, 'If the ball's played up here you can see somebody back there, in white, and you can turn a ball off quickly without even having to look to see that he's there because you can sense people in white around you.' And it was true.

Good Professionals

Norman Hunter: We weren't allowed long hair, we weren't allowed a beard, or a 'tache, and to this day I never wear jeans because jeans were not allowed. Down the ground, you had to be reasonably smart, and always a collar and tie on a match day. When we first started we had the old Leeds United grey suits with a huge badge on. That's what he wanted – everybody was smart and clean – and he took it from abroad, Real Madrid and people like that, and professional footballers had to look like professional footballers. If our hair got a bit too long, 'Get it cut.' Amazing.

Billy Bremner: There was never anyone who liked a bevy more than me, or more than our lads, but it was in the right place and at the right time. If you were away on a Wednesday night or something, Don Revie would say, 'Get out and enjoy yourself.' He told us, 'You're in a hotel now, remember there's other guests here.' That's all he used to say, but before games there was no way. Taboo.

Jack Charlton: If you went out after a Wednesday night and you had a game on a Saturday he was very upset. He had me in a couple of times because me and Billy got reported for being in the pub on a Thursday night. We used to go and play dominoes in the pub and he said, 'Well, as long as you don't have too much.' Don understood that you've got to let players relax a little bit as well as keep the pressure on them. Both things go hand in hand.

Norman Hunter: Very rarely did a Leeds player do endorsements and different things like that. The first person to do that was 'TC' – Terry Cooper. I don't know if you remember the old white boots. Tommy Smith wore them, and Alan Hinton, and TC was the first man to wear them, but other than that we didn't get involved in that sort of thing.

Billy Bremner: Don Revie was a great man for detail – where you stayed, what you had to eat. There was nothing too good for his players. If you walked down to the ground in the morning, he says, 'How are you, Bill?' and I says, 'Fine.' 'How's Vickie?' and I say, 'Well, she wasn't too well this morning.' Well, lo and behold, when you go home at lunch-time or early afternoon after training, there'd be a basket of fruit there for her or a bunch of flowers and 'Hope you get well soon' and all that.

Syd Owen: He was always in communication with the families. He used to send birthday cards to the players' children and the players' wives, and he would send a box of chocolates and things to players' wives when it was their birthday, and he always looked upon the family as being part of the success.

Norman Hunter: The bingo started off because we were always away on a Friday night. We used to stay at Craiglands, in Ilkley, before a home game. It's only about 15 or 20 miles down the road, if that, but he used to like to get us all together, away from the phone and the wives and the family and everything else. He used to take us over there for about five o' clock, half-past five, and then we used to have a meal and then he'd organize the bingo and carpet bowls. It's funny, you get used to things. You laugh about it now, but we loved it. There were probably more arguments over carpet bowls than when we played football.

John Giles: Later on, when we became more successful, when time dragged on in between matches, he brought in little things that would help to pass the time. The carpet bowls was one of them. We put a few quid in, drew partners and had a bit of fun. He created a family atmosphere at the club.

Billy Bremner: I never ever bloody won at the carpet

bowls. I won a few bingo things, but the carpet bowls was another thing. John Giles and the guys would take part in competitions, anything that had to do with skill. They would have oranges out in the dressing-room before games and they'd be like sitting on a chair and you had to try and kick the orange up with your left foot and kick the orange up with your right. Anything that had to do with the skill aspect, they were always endeavouring to beat the other.

Norman Hunter: I've never met a more dedicated bunch of lads in my life because we had so many disappointments, lost so many Finals, lost League titles, but the following year he picked us up again, got us fit and threw us out and those players did it week in and week out. A great set of dedicated lads, and great players, too.

'Clogging'

Jack Charlton: He brought good pros into the business, particularly Bobby Collins. Bobby would murder his grandmother to win a game. Bobby was totally 'You've got to win the game'. And that went through everybody in the team at Leeds at that time. And it got us a bit of a bad name, actually. If you kicked me, I wouldn't kick you back, everybody else would kick you back. It was that sort of attitude, protective of each other, and it certainly developed a style of team-work that probably has never been seen since.

Pat Crerand: When Leeds played Manchester United, Don used to tell his team, 'The minute the game starts, I want anybody as quickly as possible to kick Crerand and kick Law,' and we used to always fall for it because we used to forget. It used to drive Matt daft because Matt would always tell us that this was going to happen, and we knew it was going to happen, and it was unfair so you'd try to get your own back and you don't play the game properly because you're trying to get your own back on somebody that might have kicked you, and your team loses out through it. It's very difficult for Scottish players to understand that. I think Don Revie was a very cynical manager.

John Giles: When I first joined Leeds we were coming out of the Second Division and it was fairly ruthless. I think it was more violent in the sixties. I think it was a combination of a few different things: the abolition of maximum wage certainly encouraged players to look after themselves a lot more; I think winning became more important; I think there was a new professionalism and a new approach in the game; and there was a violent streak. It became more violent in the sixties right through to the mid-seventies.

Bobby Keetch: Everybody says, 'Johnny Giles, what a touch, what a ball-player. He could do this and that with the ball.' That was all true – he was a very good ball-player – but equally he could really dig in. I've got about eight stitches in my leg here, from a particularly savage encounter with Johnny Giles. Nobody would have queried it if it was Hunter, but they said, 'It couldn't have been John because John was the ball-playing little inside-forward.' I'm not saying he was dirty. He wasn't. He was just very, very hard.

Norman Hunter: Looking back, we turned games into tough, physical games where we probably didn't have to. I don't think he [Don Revie] did that intentionally, I think that was just his way in management. We spoke to him afterwards about it and he said that he wished he'd let us go out and play a lot more. That was probably a fault he had but he was still a great manager.

Billy Bremner: For about two or three years, from '65 to about '68, we were over the top a wee bit. We could play but we were a very physical side. We were so enthusiastic and so determined that none of the elite clubs were ever going to get in our way. We were like the Marlon Brandos. We weren't going to buckle to the hierarchy, and we had chips on our shoulder. At that age, 21 or 22, we probably didn't have all our act together. We won the Second Division with the greatest team you've ever seen in your life, and the first year in the First Division we bloody got pipped by goal average with Manchester United and we got to the Cup Final. We nearly did the double in our first year in the First Division and that wasn't really through our great play, that was through our great appetite to compete with the best of them. We weren't star-gazers.

Gamesmanship

George Best: In those days Leeds were one of the clubs you didn't want to play against. I mean, they were so professional, sometimes too professional. They got away with little things that they shouldn't have got away with. They time-wasted, they pulled your shirt. If it was a corner they pulled your hair, but the most exasperating thing was that they could actually play as well, which really annoyed you. I mean, they didn't have to do it.

John Giles: I definitely think that the reputation we had in the early days was exaggerated. If we won the match, afterwards people put it down to gamesmanship, and we were by far the better team, and I think it was 'give a dog a bad name' and it certainly stuck, but in the game itself, among the professionals around at that time, '67, '68, '69, '70, Leeds were the team to emulate. As a professional sportsman you always try and do what you can to win. I've seen people talking to businessmen saying, 'Well, it's disgraceful the way some professional sportsmen behave, because it's only a game.' But the same people who are talking like that are pulling strokes left, right and centre every day of their life in their own business. When it comes to sport, when it is *your* business, then to claim for a throw-in when it's not your throw-in becomes bad sportsmanship. When you're playing for your living, the sportsmanship goes out of it very quickly and you do what you can to win, and in the sixties there was a shift towards that, and I think Leeds, to be fair, were one of the leaders in that shift.

David Miller: In his playing days, Don had a reputation as a barrack-room lawyer. Don would be the person at Hull or Manchester City or Leicester who would be the leader of discussions with the management about better money and conditions. I think it would be fair to say Don was motivated by insecurity. Many footballers were. It was because of the conditions and restrictions under which they'd been obliged to play the game. When he became a manager he set out with, on the one hand, an enormous thoroughness to eliminate every possible weakness, even down to studying the characteristics and idiosyncrasies of every referee of every match that they played and working on those, and knowing the idiosyncrasies of every opposing team until it became such an obsession that it crossed the borderline between fair and unfair, sporting and unsporting, and so Leeds in the sixties led the field in manipulation of the game by having players working the referee. And it would keep on being a different player so that it wasn't the same guy every time saying, 'Ref, you've got it wrong, come on, Ref.' In the same way, when Leeds tried to delay the ball at a free-kick, it would be a different player. They'd take it in turns so that the referee wouldn't be able to fasten on to a player that was obstructing the taking of a free-kick. The goalkeeper going in with his foot up at 90 degrees towards the oncoming player was begun by Leeds with Gary Sprake. So many aspects of pushing the laws to the limit were identified with Leeds, which is a terrible shame because Leeds were such a wonderful side. Revie was a brilliant manager but he just took it to such excess that he poisoned his own pond.

Clive Thomas: The Norman Hunters, to me, were hyped up by the manager before the game – 'Got to win' – and Norman would do everything in his power to win. His tackling was fierce, but he would not kick somebody behind your back. The Bremners would be doing little things off the ball, the niggly things, and I found Allan Clarke similar, and those are the people that certainly worried me. I know Giles was a great player, brilliant passer of the ball, but one has to say that Giles was also one of the players that I watched very carefully.

Preparation

Jack Charlton: Don was an intelligent guy about football but he wasn't dogmatic. If you wanted to put an idea to Don, he'd give it thought and he'd give it a try. I remember the ploy of standing on the goal-line that we did. I came back from an England game where we'd been practising crossing balls into the middle and I'd been obstructing Jimmy Greaves and 'our kid', just forcing them off the ball, messing about before we actually went into training with the England team. I thought, 'It's got merit, this,' and I came back and I told Don. He set everything up and we tried it. I said, 'Can we swap the wingers over?' He accepted that. I had inswinging corners instead of outswingers, which were the standard practice in those days. I stood on the near post and was allowed to chase the ball, and it worked tremendously because I wasn't pushing people. I was going backwards into people to head balls. I wasn't doing anything wrong apart from chasing the ball, and I haven't got eyes in the back of me head. It worked, but it only worked because Don allowed it to work and allowed us to practise it.

Billy Bremner: In our day we never had so many players

looking at the dug-out to see 'What the hell's going on?' and 'How can we change things?' He always gave us permission to go out to change games. I was captain when I was at Leeds United but I wasn't the only captain. John Giles would change it, Jack would change things, Norman Hunter would change things. I think that's where we've lost it a wee bit. We've taken that away from the players. You ain't going to become a better player by not trying anything, by looking at a dug-out all the time, by being more of a robot while you're out on the park. Everybody used to say about Leeds United, 'Oh, they're like a machine, they go out there and they've obviously been well rehearsed and well grilled throughout the week in their training sessions.' For 13 years, all we did at training throughout the week was five-a-sides and yet people say we were machine-like. They probably thought we were machine-like because we were organized, and we organized ourselves on the park because good players can organize themselves.

Norman Hunter: If we'd lost a couple of games or lost one game, which wasn't very often, he used to threaten us all with a cheque-book: that if we weren't gonna do it he'd go out and buy somebody and put them in the team. Then he'd go through individuals, what Gary Sprake should have done and what he can do, and he'd go from Gary to Paul and all the way through the team. He never raised his voice that much but you knew. At times I used to get a little bit carried away and try and nutmeg people and beat them and he used to get hold of me and say, 'You win the ball and you give it to those who can play. That's your job.' The talks we didn't like was when we were playing a team we'd played so many times before. He'd go all the way through their team, telling us their weaknesses, their strengths, and the meetings used to go on for ages. We just used to sit there. Say I was playing against Jimmy Greaves and I'd played against Greavsie so many times it was untrue, but the gaffer would say to me, 'Norman, get him on to his right foot, don't let him go on to his left.' Well, I knew that anyway but he was very thorough on all these little points that he thought important to us. I don't think people did it as much, until he came along. We knew what their corners were and what their free-kicks were. It was very, very rare that we got caught out by somebody playing a new free-kick against us, because he had had somebody at the previous game and had got a dossier on them.

Billy Bremner: He'd talk about Alan Ball or Bobby Moore and all he would give you was his thoughts on their strengths and their weaknesses, and he would go through every individual in the team and that was his dossier. After he did that, he never said to you, 'Now listen, this is how I want you to play.' He just gave us a dossier on them and said, 'This is their strength, this is their weakness, you are good enough to go out and combat that so I'll leave it entirely to you.'

Jack Charlton: Don really got the players attuned to the fact that you weren't there to enjoy the game or enjoy yourself. You were there to get results and to win games and to work hard at your game and to produce what you had to produce. It was hard work under Don Revie, particularly the pre-season training.

Billy Bremner: His favourite saying was 'Football ain't like water, you can't turn it on and turn it off just like that.' Unless you start right, unless you prepare right, unless you play your five-a-sides as you would your games, you ain't going to do anything. So maybe that's why our five-a-sides were so competitive.

Off the Reins

Norman Hunter: After a period of time, about '69–70, he

really did let us off the reins a bit, and all of a sudden I think this country saw some of the best football that's been played. We beat Southampton seven. We beat Man United five. We beat Tottenham three or four. He said, 'Right, go out and play, don't worry so much about this and about that.'

Billy Bremner: Yes, we went out and played more fluid football and we wanted to entertain more. That was the relief in getting the Championship out of the way, because we were trying for four or five years to win the Championship, and then everybody was a bit more relaxed. I think that the reputation we got of being hard and ruthless was earned for that first four years and none of the Leeds players can ever say that it wasn't earned – we were a bit cynical and envious – but from '69 up to about the back-end of '74–75 they played some of the greatest football this country's ever seen. We never dreamed about losing games and we always went out to entertain and get forward and show our abilities. I think maybe in about four or five games in them five or six years we came as near to perfection as you can.

17

'They hated us
and we hated them'

Chelsea v Leeds United: Culture Clash

While southern teams have excellent records in the FA Cup, the League Championship has been dominated by teams from the north and Midlands. The 1970 FA Cup Final is an example of how London glamour can come out on top in knock-out competitions.

Chelsea as Opponents

John Giles: When I went to Leeds in '63, I think Chelsea had just been promoted the year before, so we met them in the First Division in the '64–65 season. They'd got involved in a youth policy obviously and they'd a lot of young players coming through. And they were very professional in their way. I think coming from London there's always going to be more glamour about a team than there is from somewhere like Leeds. My main ambition was to become a better player all the time and any distractions were distractions better kept out of the way, and I think it would be fair to say that the Chelsea players would be more open to temptation, the likes of Peter Osgood and Alan Hudson and Tommy Baldwin. I think if they relived their lives there's a few things they wouldn't have done, whereas our lads were out of the way in Leeds.

Norman Hunter: Ossie and I had a little bit of rivalry. There was two players that caused me more problems than anybody I know. One was Jimmy Greaves, the best goalscorer that I've ever seen. Greavsie scored against me every time he pulled a shirt on. The other one that caused me a lot of problems was Ossie. At 19, Peter Osgood was one of the best talents that I've ever seen. Unfortunately for Ossie he broke his leg, but he still ended up a great player.

Billy Bremner: Like I say, we were a relatively young team in '64, '65, and Chelsea were a young team and people were speculating who was going to be the better, Chelsea or Leeds, and the majority of people say Chelsea because of the flair that they had and this and that and the other. They didn't fulfil the potential that they had in '65. They looked as though they were going to be an absolutely tremendous team. It must be difficult in London for the players. In Leeds everybody knows you, you didn't do a lot and in London you can do so many bloody things. But the Chelsea thing was a nice rivalry. We could always do them in the League and they seemed always to be able to do us in Cup ties. They beat us in the fourth round of the FA Cup [1966] and they beat us in the semi-final one year [1967]. I don't think that there was any animosity between the two teams. There certainly wasn't in games.

Leeds as Opponents

Ian Hutchinson: Hate. No other word to describe it. They hated us and we hated them. They were the more successful side in those eras. Alan Hudson summed it up at one do, when there was nearly an almighty punch-up. He said, 'You're just robots.' This is Billy Bremner, Jackie Charlton, Norman Hunter, and of course it came to a punch-up and then me and Demps had to come and help out Huddy, because you blow on Huddy he'd fall over, he's not the aggressive type. Whenever we played, the two sets of supporters had pitched battles, home and away. On the pitch, oh, dearie me, I've still got the scars. There was no love whatsoever. The only person that I really got on with was Norman Hunter.

Tommy Baldwin: I thought the main instigator in the Leeds team was Johnny Giles. I'll say that straight away because Billy Bremner and Norman Hunter used to get the blame for everything. Norman Hunter was a bad tackler but he was a great footballer and a great lad. Bremner was very enthusiastic. He was small but he used to go in and he used to get kicked himself. Johnny Giles used to ghost around and you'd see someone go down in a tackle and Johnny Giles used to walk away, no one would see him. He was the one, to me, that used to go a little bit higher than everyone else, and he was very good at it, put it that way. I think Johnny Giles was the main instigator of the really bad tackles.

Dave Webb: I always remember, I got very angry one day with Eddie McCreadie. I was with him all the years I was with Chelsea. He said, 'We're not professional enough.' Him and Charlie Cooke had been on international duty with Scotland and they'd obviously been sitting down having a few drinks with Billy Bremner, and Billy's being very profound about how well Leeds are doing, and he came back full of the joys, saying, 'We've got to start doing that' and 'We should be like that,' and I said, 'Well, if it gets like that, the game's dead. If everybody gets like that, it gets too far down the wrong road.'

Ian Hutchinson: They'd stand on your foot. They'd say, 'You're only a youngster, come over here and I'll break your leg,' and 'You go past me again and you won't do it again,' just the usual things that they do, but it wasn't like one or two of them, there's like eight or nine of 'em all doing the same thing. As soon as you started giving it back to them, then they started what we called 'crying'. They used to say, 'Referee, Referee.' Oh, they were terrible.

Jack Charlton's 'Black Book'

Jack Charlton: Everybody says to me now, 'Who was in your little black book?' This was a television programme done years ago, and they said it was Peter Osgood. I said, 'No, Peter was never in it. Peter was okay.' Me and Peter had our moments on the field. He had a go at me, I had a go at him, but basically there was never any animosity between me and Peter off the field of play. None at all, or with any other Chelsea lads.

Ian Hutchinson: It came out in the press, about this black book and everybody speculated on who it was. I was 21 then, a young little slip of a lad, but we played in a testimonial, with Elton John funnily enough, down in Brighton. We were in the dressing-room and who walks in but Jack. 'Oh, no,' I said, 'I hope he's on our side.' He's muttered a few things to us, then we done the game. We went to a reception afterwards, in a lovely pub somewhere on the outskirts of Brighton. Ossie has had a couple of drinks and we've all had a few drinks and he's gone, 'Jack, what's this about this black book? What have I done to you?' He said, 'It's not you, it's that big twat next to you.' I went, 'Jack, what have I done?' He said, 'You gave me a black eye, a bruised cheek, giving it the two elbows on the corners.' (I had to go back and mark him.) I said, 'Jack, why didn't you tell me?' The other chap was Johnny Morrissey, the Everton winger. I'm not sure who the third one was. That's the two I can remember him saying. We never played against each other again. I'd have been jumping a little bit at the patter of tiny feet coming in behind me, but that's what he said at Brighton.

The 1970 FA Cup Final

Nigel Clarke: Chelsea were London's glamour team. They were watched by a crowd that came down from the King's Road and all the smart pubs and watering-holes down there, and they were playing teams like Leeds, who really represented the frozen north, the hard face of Don Revie, the hard face of Johnny Giles and Norman Hunter and Billy Bremner. It was the hard men against the southern stylists, the two extremes in football. The northern guys wanted to come down and show that Chelsea were southern softies and the Chelsea guys were guys from swinging London who would go up to Stamford Bridge and play with style and swagger and send the old northerners, with their flared trousers and sideboards, back where they belong. It was that kind of scenario. Players would tell me afterwards, 'Did you see so-and-so's gear? I wonder where he got that, from Millet's?' There was this great rivalry but it was personalized by the fact that it was 'stylish London' against 'the stodgy north'.

Ian Hutchinson: We have got a gold LP, the lads have: 'Blue is the Colour'. We were on *Top of the Pops* twice, and our record went to number four for the Cup Final.

Peter Osgood: We were flamboyant, we were happy-go-lucky. They were very, very professional in their ways. They used to do everything together. They were a machine, if you like. I think that's basically where they fell down. Over a period of 42 games they were the best. There's no doubt about that. When it came to the one-off we were so much better than them because we went out to enjoy ourselves, but they stuck to their same rigid plan.

Dave Webb: I went there to enjoy the occasion instead of going there to play football. That was the worst day's work I ever did in my whole football career, the Cup Final at Wembley, and that's why I got a roasting off Eddie Gray because I didn't go with the right frame of mind. I didn't go there as a proper professional. I was took in with the whole occasion, going down Wembley Way and seeing all the people dressed up, and I thought it was fantastic. I would have been better off to stay in the crowd with them and let someone else go and play.

Ian Hutchinson: When we played at Wembley that day, the horse show had been on the week before and they put 500 tons of sand on there. It was just like Brighton beach. It was a red hot day and we was knackered. I equalized four minutes from the end and I was absolutely knackered, everybody was knackered. I'd got socks round my ankles. We were pleased that they didn't play the replay at Wembley. They took it to Old Trafford.

Brian Mears: Wembley was incredible. I was in the Royal Box sitting next to Princess Margaret and I kept lighting her cigarette for her because she didn't have any matches. As you know, the chairmen of each club spend the first or second half next to the guest of honour, and I was a bundle of nerves, to be honest, and when we equalized that was extraordinary. I thought we'd lost it. We drew and then we went on to the replay. Now, Harold Wilson comes into this because he was at Wembley and at Old Trafford, and he had actually said to me, in the box at Wembley, and believe it or not it's absolutely true, that we would draw the first game 2–2 after extra-time. And I think it was the first drawn Cup Final at Wembley, wasn't it? And then when we went to Old

Trafford he sat two away from me, and he leaned over and said, 'Mr Mears, you're going to win this game 2–1 after extra-time.' I said, 'Can I have that in writing, Prime Minister?' It was extraordinary really, wasn't it?

Dave Webb: I knew that I'd done it all wrong and I had to put it right. On the coach coming back out, after the game, Dave Sexton came and sat next to me, and he said, obviously trying to sympathize with me having a bad time, 'What do you reckon?' I said, 'You know, I was a bit surprised, I thought you were going to change me and Ronnie Harris,' because Ronnie Harris was only declared fit the day before, he wasn't fully fit, and he came off before the end of the game anyway, and it would have suited him with his injury to have played against Eddie Gray. And so the next game, he changed it. He brought Ronnie Harris on Eddie Gray and I think Eddie Gray's still got one of Ronnie Harris's studs in his ankle. I was more suited to one of the centre-half positions, and that's where I made my mind up that it was where I wanted to play.

Ian Hutchinson: We'd always been behind – 1–0 down, 1–1, 2–1 down, 2–2 in the first game. Then 1–0 down in the second game. Then it was 1–1, and then we were ahead for the first time.

Dave Webb: We had got to that point in the game that it was achievable, and I'd go up for a throw-in. That fella [Ian Hutchinson] has now got to throw that ball 45 yards, and he does it. How he does it, I don't know. And there's Jackie Charlton, on top of his head, and I felt that I should keep going, and I just threw myself at it. There was about three white shirts, and that intimidation bit again, where I feel as if somebody's putting their foot up against me. I just threw myself at it and it hit me on the cheek. So, as I'm in the net, I look about and then I look for the ref, because anytime you played against Leeds, if you done something, and you didn't hear the whistle, you thought, 'Well, you're going to see five or six white shirts surround the referee or the linesman to try and get him to change the decision,' and I looked and they weren't doing it. They never disagreed with the decision. The linesman was heading back for the centre-circle, so was the ref, and they was all standing there with their heads down, and as if to say, 'Well, we keep getting in front, and now this team's got in front against us, what do we do?'

Ian Hutchinson: It was my mate Jack [Charlton] again that flicked it on, bless him. It was the first time we'd gone ahead in nearly four hours of football. We looked at the Leeds players and their heads dropped. I'd never seen that. Even though they pushed on and pushed on in the second half of extra-time, it wasn't the Leeds of old. I scored an offside goal, I think we hit the post or whatever and we could have won 3–1. It was a shock that Leeds had dropped their heads.

Billy Bremner: I was never disappointed if we'd lost and we'd played to our maximum. It was when we didn't play to our maximum and we lost games when I was really disappointed. Against Chelsea we dominated the play, both in the tie at Wembley and the replay. At Wembley Eddie Gray kept going past them all the time and, not only that, we felt that we were stronger on the day and we were playing better on the day. We thought we'd won the tie with seven minutes to go when Jonesy put one in the back of the net.

Norman Hunter: I've played in a few games like that. I played against Poland in '73 which was the most one-sided game that I've ever played in my life, and the one against Chelsea was very similar but we didn't beat them. We should have done and then they beat us in the replay at Old Trafford.

Dave Webb: I went up to get the medal and I couldn't get it because I'd swapped shirts with Eddie Gray. I made a beeline for him, I get there and swap me shirt with him. I put his white shirt on. I went to go up and the bloke said, 'No, Chelsea first,' so I said, 'Oh, stuff it' and I went running round the pitch. I grabbed Alan Hudson, because I felt sorry for him because he hadn't played; he'd got injured around the semi-final. I said, 'Come on, you've got to come running, you've got to go round as well.' I never picked my medal up, and, eventually, I went upstairs, and Brian Clough said, 'What you looking for, son?' I said, 'I've lost me medal, someone told me I've got to get my medal.' 'You wait there,' he said and he went off and got the people to give me my medal.

Ian Hutchinson: At the end of the game, Norman Hunter, the current England international, who'd kicked lumps out of me for four hours' football, came up and wanted to swap shirts with me, which I thought was a tremendous gesture. It's one of my prized possessions, which I've got framed in my home. We'd gone up to the directors' box then and they wouldn't give me my medal. I said, 'But I'm Chelsea.' Dr Stephen, who presented the medals, wouldn't give it to me. You can imagine, I'm dying to get my hand on this medal. He said, 'No, you'll have to wait for Leeds.' I said, 'I'm a Chelsea player', and then somebody came over and said, 'Look, that's Ian Hutchinson, he's not a Leeds player, he's got the Leeds shirt on,' and then eventually they gave it to me and of course all the lads have gone down the steps and are doing a lap of honour. I just went out in the middle of the pitch and sat down. On the BBC video – was it Ken Wolstenholme commentating? – he said, 'Who's that sitting there looking at his medal?' and there's me. It was so emotional and we were drained after extra-time.

Peter Osgood: I always remember walking down John Dalton Street. It was six o'clock in the morning and there was a lovely blonde on my arm. I'd been out and I didn't know where the lads had gone. I'd lost them and this young lady and I had had a fabulous night together, just had some champagne and different things. I don't even know her name now, but I went back to the hotel and got back to my room and all my mates were sleeping there, so I just shook hands and give her a little peck and off she went, and it was a fabulous time. This was six o'clock in the morning. And then I remember going down to Euston and it was fabulous on the train, and it was just a lovely, lovely time, you couldn't believe it. I don't think it came over to us until we got to Euston station. There was so many people there and we went through the streets of London down to Fulham, whatever, and the old age pensioners were there and I saw tears rolling down their eyes and they were Chelsea pensioners of 70 and 80 years of age. I think that brought it home to me. I thought, 'Ossie, you've arrived, this is something special.'

18

'You end up living in a goldfish bowl'

The First Superstars

Footballers' wages rose sharply after the removal of the maximum wage. With the advent of televised football and a youth culture, and the wider effects of the sixties, footballers found themselves in the forefront of national publicity, particularly George Best of Manchester United and Northern Ireland.

The Emergence of George Best

Pat Crerand: I first met George in 1963. I remember George then and he was a lovely, lovely lad. I don't think he's changed in any way whatsoever. I mean, I read stories in the papers, all the stuff that they write, and it's not the George Best I know, and I don't believe half of it anyway because George was always a smashing lad, great company, and he mixed in with everybody. He was very, very popular with all the team, very popular with all the supporters, loved by everybody. He was just a lovely, lovely lad.

Denis Law: He was probably the first superstar, wasn't he? He had the good looks. He had the long hair like the Beatles did. More than anything he had the ability to entertain on the field. He was extremely gifted. He scored magnificent goals. He had a bit of everything, and of course he was single and it was a time of the E-type Jag and all the clothes and the night-clubs.

George Best: My first professional wage was £4/1/9, in the old money, and I used to send £3 home to my Mom and Dad, so I had £1/1/9 to spend. And then when I became professional it went up to £117, which in those days was phenomenal, and, apart from the basic, we were on bonuses. We were in Europe. We were always in the top six. We had a crowd bonus. I was going out and buying cars, E-types and whatever, walking in the showrooms and paying cash. It was amazing.

Sir Bobby Charlton: Sir Matt Busby said, after the accident, that it would take about five years, and it was almost five years to the day that we won the FA Cup. That was in 1963, and I think George was a young lad then – he wasn't in the team. The year after that we won the title for the first time, in 1964, and I think it was after that that George came on. You always get a feel from the scouts and the coaches with the lower teams if there's anything special happening down there, so the first chance you get you go and have a look at him in a youth match, but everybody was mentioning George Best – 'There's this fantastic little player coming in, brilliant dribbler and brave and strong and he'll be in the first team within a few years.' One of the first matches George played in the first team was against Burnley, and an old friend of mine, John Angus, used to play right-back for England and Burnley, a Geordie from Amble, just north of where I lived. I felt I knew him quite well, and he played right-back against George Best and this little George Best tore him to ribbons really. He put the ball through his legs, and really embarrassed him in a way, and I'm thinking, 'Well, I shouldn't really feel this about somebody doing this to one of me pals,' but you'd got to admire it. Denis Law had been signed earlier than that, from Italy, and it was just magic here for a period.

Pat Crerand: In the sixties everybody all over the world enjoyed the music that was coming out of Britain, with the Beatles and all the groups that were coming out of Liverpool. The gear that they wore then was way out, the mini-skirt was in. I mean, it was great styles, great music and the football was great as well. In the sixties England won the World Cup, so England was the centre of the world at that particular period of time, and it was great to live in. Everybody had jobs, there was no lack of work. Everybody had a few bob to spend at weekends. Everybody enjoyed themselves. A great era to live in.

George Best: I think, looking back, I didn't realize how massive the sixties were. Apart from sport, in those days, you had the whole thing – music, fashion, the hippie movement – and I didn't realize how powerful it was. I do now, because I had stepped over the line from being an athlete and become – I don't know what you want to call it – a personality or pop thing. In '66, I remember a fan chasing me with a knife. He was a Benfica fan and I thought he wanted to kill me but he wanted a lock of my hair. It became a crazy situation. I was getting 10,000 letters a week from people driving me nuts. They wanted this, they wanted that, all women, and it freaked me out, and my friends in those days were the Beatles, the Rolling Stones, which was frightening. I was getting hounded. They were asking me questions about politics and such. I mean, I didn't know. What would I know? I was 17.

Temptation

George Best: In those days, as a kid, especially a kid getting the publicity I was getting, and getting away with what I was getting away with, it was very tempting to come to London and go in night-clubs, restaurants, pubs, whatever, and see all these stunning, beautiful women. Then you've got to get up at six o'clock in the morning, get back to Manchester and go training. It was very difficult. In those days it really was amazing, the women, and it was very difficult to say 'No' to it, which is why I got into a lot of trouble.

Alvaro Maccioni: I went up to Manchester quite a few times actually, on his invitation, and then in the evening we used to go out together. It was nothing like down here. Up there, it was the old England. I remember, one day, I said, 'Oh, listen, why don't you come and play for Chelsea', and he looked at me and said, 'Alvaro, if it was up to me, I'd play for nothing provided I could come to Chelsea.' That's how much he wanted to be down here.

George Best: When we used to play in London, we came down on the Friday and the format was that the boys went to the theatre or the cinema or wherever, and I used to go see a friend of mine in a restaurant called Alvaro's. I used to go in, have dinner, leave about ten o'clock, go back to the hotel and go to bed, and that was the rule. And one night I went in there and it was the middle of summer and this beautiful lady walked past, so I sent one of the waiters out and I said, 'Go and get her and bring her back. I want to talk to her.' So he brought her back and she's come in and she said, 'Who are you?' So I said, 'My name's George.' So we sat down and we had dinner. I explained to her who I was and said we were playing Arsenal the next day. So I said, 'Look, if you want to come back to the hotel, I'll book you a room,' and I'm planning all this stuff, so I got back to the hotel and Wilf McGuinness, the boss at the time, was waiting at the door. He said, 'Best, you're a bit late, aren't you?' I said, 'Sorry, Boss, I'm just going up to the room.' So I got up to the room, and I'm lying there and I'm waiting for this stunning girl to call me. She called me about three o'clock in the morning. She said, 'I'm sorry I'm late but Alvaro kept me and told me who you were and I didn't realize how famous you were.' So I said, 'I'll be up in two minutes.' So I've come out the room and I thought, 'Now I can't get in the lift, just in case anybody sees me.' So I'm climbing up the stairs and Wilf's at the end of the stairway, and I've gone through the door and he went, 'What are you doing?' I said, 'Oh, I can't sleep, I'm just going for a walk.' He said, 'You dirty little .. you've got a bird, haven't you?' So I said, 'No,' so I've dashed back to the room, I've called her back and I've said, 'I can't make it.' I said, 'I'll see you in the morning.' We got up the next morning and he's come down and said, 'You dirty little . . . how can you do that before a game?' I said, 'Wilf, it makes me sleep, some people can't relax, I like relaxing with, you know.'

Noel Cantwell: Malcolm [Allison] and I were speaking at a dinner at Altrincham one night, and at the time George had just disappeared. A lot of nice people in Manchester were so respectful of Matt that they didn't like it when this fella's gone. Malcolm had said his few words, and everybody was knocking George. So it was my turn to say a few words. Looking round, there was fellas with cigars and big fat tummies and old geriatrics, type of thing, and I happened to tell the story: if Miss World knocked at your door at 11 o'clock at night and said, 'Look, I'd like to come in,' what would you say? Excuse me, no, no, no, you can't come in, it's Thursday night, I'm playing on Saturday, away you go, you can't come in for a coffee, you can't come in for anything? If Miss World *did* put you in that position, who amongst us would say, 'No, you can't come in.' People were scowling and thinking, so Malcolm put his hand up. 'I would,' he said. So of course it got a bit of laughter. If anything, he would have been the one that couldn't have resisted.

Greg Tesser: What we started to see was footballers going to night-clubs, trendy West End night-clubs, mixing with film stars and famous artists and writers, mixing with the intelligentsia, and this was something totally new to football. I think football probably couldn't understand it; the people at the FA probably got out their coffins and almost fell over and had heart attacks. A lot of these players were befriended by these celebs but when the player didn't play so well or he got dropped you found that that celebrity tended to walk away and didn't return, which is a bit sad.

His Own Place

Noel Cantwell: I was team captain at the time. I think I was out of the team, I'm not sure, but George was a young boy, about 17 or 18, and the format was that you went through the team captain to get to the manager and I would go and speak if the person didn't want to go himself. So George came to see me one day. He said, 'I think I would like to have my own apartment, my own flat.' Now this was an unheard-of thing at most football clubs at that time, because people were put in digs, and you had a supervisor who reported to the manager if anything went wrong. So George said, 'I think in the interest of Man United it would be a good thing if I had my own place.' So I thought, 'Well, tell me the argument.' He said, 'Well, look Noel, if I go out at night and I've got my own place, I can bring a girlfriend back to my place, whereas now if I go to her place it's about an hour later before I get back to my place.' So I said to him, 'George, I think you'd better go and argue that one yourself with the Boss.'

George Best: I got hold of a friend of mine who was an architect and I said, 'You've got to build this place. All I need is a snooker table and a sunken bath and whatever else you build around it.' But all of a sudden it became like a goldfish bowl. I mean, Sundays, they had coach trips turning up, parking on my lawn, trying to get over, nicking my goldfish, smashing down the trees. It became a nightmare. It cost me £40,000 in those days and I sold it for about the same price about nine months later because I couldn't live there.

Pat Crerand: I think the club had done as much as they could with George. So I don't think George would disagree with the fact that when things went wrong he was more to blame than anybody else. George was in a strange situation, as well, which was very unfortunate. It was the swinging sixties and the media were getting into sport in a big way and George was the hero. They must have driven George potty. He couldn't go anywhere or do anything. It must have been a very difficult life for George at that time. Probably his only release was playing football on a Saturday.

'El Beatle'

Pat Crerand: We went over to Portugal and we beat Benfica 5–1. We weren't expected to win the match. We'd only beaten them 3–2 here in the quarter-final and Benfica had won practically every game they had played in the European Cup in Lisbon [18 out of 19]. I think that was the best performance I've ever seen from any team. George had one of those nights when everything went right for him, and the team were magnificent that night. The football was of a standard that you had to play or be there to see. When George come back from Benfica in 1966, everybody called him 'El Beatle'.

George Best: In those days I started believing what they were writing about me. When we played in Portugal, I bought this big sombrero and leather coat, because I knew they were going to take my photograph when I came back. I did it on purpose because I knew it was going to be in the papers. At the time I thought I was taking advantage of them, but it backfires. You end up living in a goldfish bowl. I was on the back page *and* the front page of one national newspaper, and there's not many people do that, but it's a big mistake.

Greg Tesser: Yeah, the George Best phenomenon was extraordinary. I mean, there were certain players who were superstars in their way – the late Bobby Moore, for example, Peter Osgood, Charlie Cooke, Rodney Marsh – but they were mild behind George Best because even people who didn't care too much about football would follow the fortunes of George Best. You were guaranteed to sell any product with George Best's name on it. The poster we did of George Best, with long hair in a King's Road shirt, sold 50,000 copies. I can't see it happening again, and the reason it happened was because he was the first of this new breed of footballer, when he was christened El Beatle in Portugal. Nobody had ever seen a player look like that. A player who admitted certain things that he shouldn't have done. A player who wasn't the typical sportsman. If you've got something unique you're bound to succeed, but as far as the other players were concerned there was a lot of jealousy, there's no doubt about that, because he was earning a fortune. Other players said, 'We're nearly as good as George Best,' but it wasn't only his ability. He had something that was unique.

George Best: When you're flavour of the month they come to you, and Denis Compton is a pal of mine and the same thing happened to him – he did the Brylcreem thing. When I started I was doing everything. I did sausages. I did oranges. I did aftershave. They came and asked me to do it, and when it comes you say, 'Yes, I'll do it.' You're a kid, what do you know? Someone phones you up and says, 'We'll give you twenty grand to stand up and say you eat sausages.' What are you going to say – no? And I did it, but it was hard, it really was, because I ended up getting in fights in the street with people who didn't eat sausages, and, being an Irishman, I don't mind fighting. I'll fight any wanker. I got into so much trouble and ended up getting arrested and going to prison because people wanted to come up and fight.

Bobby Keetch: I had a taste, just a taste, of what George Best had, and really I had enough of it in a very short time. I gave up football for a couple of years because if you're captured in a bar or restaurant by a nuisance, they're never brain surgeons or great writers; they're normally absolute idiots who just drive you mad. George Best's life has been made a nightmare. I've been around plenty of times when people have just walked up to him, punched him in the eye and said, 'That's because my girlfriend fancies you.' It looked as though he was a troublemaker, but there are two sides to those stories and George suffered because of the constant glare on him. As I say, I had it in a small way and I just said, 'Well, I don't really want that in my life any more,' so I gave it up.

George Best: I couldn't hide, and I tried. That's why I disappeared so many times. I kept packing in just to get away from it all, trying to find havens to disappear to, and I couldn't. I mean, I used to go to Spain, and that's the worst place in the world to go to to get away from anything, and then I went to America and I tried all sorts of places to hide. I've gone to Malaysia, I've gone to Mauritius, I've gone to South Africa, Australia, Hong Kong, and, I don't know why, they know you're there. It's a big compliment but it's hard.

Frank Butler: There's a great story about Georgie Best

which is absolutely true. When we went to the World Cup in Mexico, we offered Georgie Best £10,000 to fly down with us and I would ghost his story, his comments on the World Cup, and it took me at least a fortnight to contact George. I kept leaving messages and the like. Then I said to the northern correspondent, 'Get hold of him, get him on the phone.' So he got him on the phone and I said, 'George, there's £10,000, first-class fare, come down and just talk to me down there and I'll write the column for you when I'm there.' And George's remark was marvellous. He said, 'Oh, Frank, I'd love to, but I've got a little colleen I'm going to Majorca with.' I rather admired him for that. Money didn't mean that much to him, so he went to Majorca instead. I liked Georgie Best. He never did anyone any harm except himself.

Derek Dougan: I shared many a room with George between 1965 and 1972 and I'll never forget when we played down in Wales. We were playing the match at Swansea and it was the time that he was doing this advert for the egg – 'E for B and Georgie Best' – and it became a catchword. We were down there in the rain and about 80 kids came out of the school, and all these wee Welsh kids were chanting, 'E for B and Georgie Best.' I couldn't believe it. Then I'm going into the hotel on the Saturday morning and there was a wedding in there, and the bride left the groom's arm and came over and all she wanted was a photograph taken with Georgie Best. We went down into the town after training, because all Irish guys like a cup of tea, and went into a little café. I couldn't believe it. Where did they come from? There must have been hundreds there. Pat Jennings and I were with him. No one asked us for *our* autographs – all they wanted was George Best's autograph. And that guy signed all of those kids' stuff to a point that he had two little blisters on his fingers. He's very much maligned. I've seen him do things for mentally handicapped kids, for kids with disabilities, but unfortunately it never makes the news.

George Best: It really did become massive. I mean, when I was a kid I was getting letters from Harold Wilson. He was writing to me as a fan! I was being invited to 10 Downing Street. I was going to say hello to the Queen. I had the biggest superstars in the world inviting me to go along and say hello to them! It was frightening what was happening to football. It wasn't just sport, it was showbiz. When we used to play at Old Trafford, we had Albert Finney coming there, Tom Courtenay, Lulu, the Beatles, the Rolling Stones. It was like a Who's Who of Showbiz. It was more than sport.

London's 'George Best' – Peter Marinello

Peter Marinello: I was 19 at the time when Arsenal came in to buy me. I went down there and had a look. I was told there was two or three other clubs prepared to pay that fee. I didn't really want to sign but I suppose I thought, 'Well, Hibs want rid of me, I'll sign and see how it goes.' I'd never been to London before and I was quite amazed with all the hullabaloo and all the commotion that my signing caused, and for the first year at Arsenal I was run off my feet, and the training was a lot harder at the time. Well, it was the end of the swinging sixties and it was the seventies and life was good, money in my pocket and I was doing the modelling and I was writing an article for a daily newspaper, and I suppose it was too much, too quick, too soon, for a young lad, but I enjoyed it. It was good at the time.

Terry O'Neill: Peter Marinello was typical of the sort of guy produced out of all this new-found stardom. I remember seeing this very nice face, very nice guy, dressed in all this 1970s gear and I really felt sorry for him. He looked like a boy in a man's world. I couldn't even understand what all the fuss was about, really. I just felt sorry that I thought, 'This guy's not going to make it.'

Peter Marinello: The first game I played in for Arsenal was against Manchester United at Old Trafford and obviously there were comparisons again with George Best, although George didn't play that day [10 January 1970]. He was suspended, and I think he was in Ireland or somewhere, and I actually scored the first goal, which was probably the worst thing with all the pressure and all the palaver. I got the ball on the halfway-line, beat two or three players and stuck the ball in the net, and the spectators, or the press, expected that every week, and it was just unbelievable that the first game had to be at Old Trafford. We actually lost 2–1 but I scored the first goal and I enjoyed the game. If George Best had been playing that day, it might have took the pressure off me a little bit.

Malcolm Allison: This young fella come down from Scotland and he went to Highbury and he had a reputation before he started, so the professionals, the full-backs playing against him, said, 'I'll see to him early on,' and they marked him tight and they hit him and they were very strong with him, and they just marked him out the game. I mean, there's no way they were going to have another George Best taking them apart.

Peter Marinello: I was probably thrown in far too quick and expected to be a world-beater, which the media built up. I felt I had it in me to do it but everything just got on top of me. Maybe I spent too much time on other things and maybe if they had protected me I might have been better. But it's hard to protect somebody 24 hours a day, I suppose, and so I was maybe a bit big-headed.

Nigel Clarke: We wanted a London George Best, I suppose, and Peter was glamorous and trendy, long hair, good-looking boy, smart, a very pleasant lad, good footballer, but so much was expected of him. He joined Arsenal, and every move was photographed, everything he said was blown up and made a headline of. Tremendous pressure. A good footballer, he never quite made it at Arsenal and he was submerged by it all, the tremendous demand to be a star. They wanted him to be the next George Best and he couldn't be.

Peter Marinello: The offers were coming in. At one time I was making more money outside the game than what I was playing. The Milk Marketing Board came in and they wanted to do a campaign, put me on the posters and do a television campaign, and then there was the mail-order catalogues. They wanted me to wear all these clothes, and I used to get letters from girls and then they were from men as well, because I used to wear all this gear and it made me look a bit feminine, aye. One company wanted to turn me into an international make-up artist. Crazy offers. Actually one publishing company approached me to write a book. I'd only played about 40 or 50 games for Hibs, played about half a dozen games for Arsenal, and they wanted to write a book about me. I thought it was pretty funny.

Nigel Clarke: Yes, he did adverts and was quite a promising face of television but it never happened for him on the pitch and that's where he had to make his mark. He could make as many adverts as he liked but unless he was doing it on the pitch that was no good. Arsenal dropped him, he disappeared from the scene, made a couple of comebacks but the pressure was far too much for him. A great shame because he was a nice lad.

Peter Marinello: I was transferred six or seven times and I probably made in excess of £70,000 just in transfer fees. One transfer fee I got was £33,000, just to sign on for the club, although at that time the tax was high. I came out of the game with quite a bit of money. Enjoyed myself. We had nice homes. Probably the worst thing I've ever done was getting involved in business because everything came too easy. I trusted people. I got involved with people who were less than honest. They preyed on my name and I used to get them money and I signed personal guarantees and it was a complete disaster. Most football clubs look after you well. I was probably shielded. Everything was done for you when I was playing football. When you bought a house, the secretary or the directors organized it for you and you just signed a piece of paper, and you were protected, and I suppose when I finished I'd a lot of money to invest and it was a disaster, but life goes on. I'm enjoying myself now and I've got myself involved in youth football and amateur football, and I coach kids.

19

'I'd be opening garages and presenting things'

Hot Commercial Property

This chapter charts the emergence of agents, who initially represented players in their dealings outside football and then increasingly became involved in all aspects of a player's finances and career. The coming of 'freedom of contract' in 1978 increased the number of transfer deals and contractual negotiations.

Agents

Ken Stanley: It started with Denis Compton. Bagenal Harvey was a friend of Denis's, I think, and he simply said to him one day, 'Bagenal, for goodness' sake do something with this mail of mine,' because he had about two lockers full of mail. I think Bagenal then realized the potential. The first thing I remember that Bagenal did for Denis was the Brylcreem advert which was on every hoarding, every poster, and I think that was really the beginning of it. When I heard about Bagenal, I thought, 'Well, that's a jolly good idea.' At that time I had a table-tennis hall in Burnley and I signed Jimmy McIlroy, who was a terrific player, and Colin McDonald, who played in goal for England, a fantastic goalkeeper who had an unfortunate accident. I didn't really do anything for those two players.

Bobby Keetch: Johnny Haynes was the first player I'd ever heard of with an agent, a chap called Bagenal Harvey, but I don't think he fitted the picture of a modern agent. He was a very well-spoken, gentlemanly type of guy who lived in a cottage in the country. I think the big difference was that Bagenal Harvey got a commercial contract for Johnny Haynes and earned his money from that. No way did he negotiate a salary for Johnny Haynes, or his personal terms, and live off his wages, which seems to be part of the set-up today.

Johnny Haynes: I knew Denis Compton because he was reporting football for the *Sunday Express* at that time, and I got a phone call one day and it was this Irish voice saying he was Bagenal Harvey. Denis was the Brylcreem Boy at the time and when he finished that contract I got it, thank God, because I was with the same agent. I did photographic work for three days and got a cheque for £1,500, and I was only getting £1,000 for 12 months' wages at soccer.

Ken Stanley: I'd worked very hard at the table-tennis hall. I bought a cinema, converted it to a five-a-side stadium at Brierfield and I worked very, very hard but finished up as a glorified youth officer, not making any money. I moved from Burnley to work for Mitre in Huddersfield and it was there that I signed Denis Law. Denis joined me as a 17-year-old and then things really began to happen with Denis. In the world of soccer Denis is the one that helped me and through Denis all the boys started to join. I started working in the bedroom, creating ideas, creating books and different things. I didn't even have a telephone. I used to go round the corner and use the public telephone and I've even phoned Denis from that public telephone when he was in Italy.

Nigel Clarke: I think the only agent around was a fella called Jack Turner who handled Bobby Moore, but he was on his own and there wasn't a soul anywhere near Jack, and players were just grateful to talk to the press, grateful to get their names in the papers. I sniffed out something at Chelsea one day and put it to Ossie, and Ossie, being sharp, said, 'Well, yeah, it's true, but it will cost you.' Well, it was no good me going to the newspaper and saying, 'Look, I've got this good story, can you help us out?' They'd have said, 'No way.' So I paid it out of my own salary. I said, 'Look, here's £25, that's all I can manage.' I think I claimed it back on my expenses over about 10 weeks. It was quite an innocuous story, something about another player being dropped by Tommy Docherty because he was about to buy Tony Hateley, I think. In those days stories that made the back pages were things as innocuous as transfer requests and injuries and I wanted so badly to be in there, to be first, and to show I was a good reporter.

Greg Tesser: As I'm concerned with Peter Osgood, the promotion started when I first met him. I think it was in '68 and he was going through a very rough time at that stage. He was in and out of the first team and his confidence was at a very low ebb. The company I was involved with had just printed and published a rock-star poster of George Best, and it sold 50,000 copies, so I thought, 'Let's do a little library of these things', and Peter Osgood, to me, although he wasn't playing very well, was the next one on the list. I said, 'We'd like to do a poster of you, Peter', and we did it and it was very successful. Then he said to me, 'Look, I haven't got an agent or anybody to help me to promote my name, can you do it?' Of course, as a Chelsea fanatic, I immediately agreed. He was

a very good talker, he looked good and he played football to
perfection and he was also, back in the sixties, a rebel. Apart
from George Best, he was the ideal vehicle to promote. The
only other experience I'd had in promoting stars was a few
years before when I was a publicist for the Yardbirds, Eric
Clapton, so I transferred my knowledge of rock publicity to
the football scene and Peter Osgood, to me, was absolutely
perfect.

Ken Stanley: I didn't really achieve as much for Denis
Law as possibly I could have done because at that time
Denis was quite happy to do the job as a plumber might do –
he played his football and went home. He married a super
girl, Di, and he had a happy home life and he wasn't
particularly keen at that stage to do all the extras. It was
through Denis that George Best joined with me and then of
course, when George signed up, things started to change
because the telephone never stopped ringing with George.
He was in such demand. My favourite saying used to be,
and it was quite true, 'You could put George's name on
stair-rods and sell them to bungalows.' The fan mail came
from all over the world, from every walk of life, and even
that long ago we had a fan club in Japan. We had the most
fantastic clothing contract in Japan for George. I would
never do anything without discussing it with the manager. I
would always phone Sir Matt and say, 'I'm thinking of doing
this, is it okay?' and if he approved then I would go ahead.
There was the George Best instructional strip which the
Daily Express published and then we syndicated it
worldwide and made it into a book, and then the BBC did a
television series, all from that strip, and it was peak viewing.
It didn't take a great deal of George's time, once we'd taken
the necessary pictures.

George Best: Ken's a lovely man but he was in at the start
when we didn't have agents. I mean, there's a lovely scene in
a film called *Charlie Bubbles* where they sit round and talk

about you like you're not there, and Ken was a little bit like that. He used to sit there and say, 'Right, this is the cake and I've got a quarter, you've got a quarter, you've got a quarter.' And I used to sit there and think, 'What are they talking about? They're talking about me like I'm a piece of cake.'

Greg Tesser: We [Peter Osgood and I] got a column in a *Shoot*-style magazine called *Striker*, a kid's comic thing. We then got a column in the *Daily Mail* which I think paid us £80 a week in 1969 (quite a lot of money in those days), a big sponsorship endorsement deal with Bukta, the sportswear company, opening of shops, supermarkets, appearances on television and a lot of radio interviews, which was the obvious thing. But the biggest coup I think I ever had, I became very friendly with a photographer called Terry O'Neill, who later got married to Faye Dunaway. He was also a Chelsea fan and he was the official photographer for Raquel Welch, and *The Times* newspaper did a big interview with her and she was talking about England and saying how much she loved football, particularly Chelsea and Peter Osgood, which of course was total rubbish because she didn't know one end of a football from the other. The fact that he was now idolized by this film star was extraordinary, so that led to lots of very, very interesting promotional work for him.

Ian Hutchinson: I had an agent called Ken Johnson, who got me the John Collier thing and the *People* newspaper. It was just starting then, but there was nothing like agents taking percentages off your wages. I think Ken took 10 per cent of all he earned for me outside the game. That was fine.

Francis Lee: Our average gate [at Manchester City] in those days was 37,000 and you'd get a lot of fan mail, a lot of people writing and asking for photographs and things like that. You'd get a lot of letters from nutters. Every time you had a derby match you used to get 20 or 30 death threats.

After I started to play for England I wrote an article for the *Daily Mirror* for about five years, and I did a lot of sponsorship and advertising and things like that. At one time I was probably earning more outside the game than I was inside the game.

Jeff Astle: I had a bloke named George Bartram. I think he were Morecambe and Wise's agent in them days. He got things for me that I would never have got meself. I mean, I opened things like big plays. I went to Shrewsbury Flower Show, which is one of the biggest in England, and things like that. It was extra money but I enjoyed it. I'd be opening garages and presenting things and it was extra money for me and I thought it was a very good idea. In the late sixties and seventies, there were more footballers doing things out of football, joining in with quiz shows and things on television. I enjoyed *The Golden Shot*. I'd been on *A Question of Sport* and a lot of programmes like that, and I'd met a lot of people in show business.

Greg Tesser: The obvious television programmes were *Match of the Day* and *The Big Match*, but what was starting to happen was that big football stars of the era were being asked, either through phoning up themselves or through an approach to their agents or whatever, to be on all kinds of TV programmes. I think Martin Peters or Geoff Hurst were in *Till Death Us Do Part*. It was a totally new thing, a footballer being used to sell comedy shows. Vince Powell contacted me, and said he'd like Peter Osgood to be in an episode of a top comedy programme called *Never Mind the Quality, Feel the Width* and the only way I could get him into the programme was to have a match going on. Somewhere in this programme, with this little tailor's shop, you panned out to this football field near the Thames Television studio and Osgood was playing football. He must have been in it for no more than about five minutes and I think he said one line, but he got huge billing for it, in the *TV Times* and all that.

Ken Stanley: When George Best joined me, things really started to move and, from Denis and George, I got a whole host of footballers. They're too numerous to name and they were all terrific players: Gordon Banks, Jack Charlton, Billy Bremner and Emlyn Hughes, etc. Then, of course, that led to being the first agent for the World Cup with Sir Alf. I had an association with the team in '66 in so much as at that time I was working for Mitre Sports and I arranged tracksuits for the team and hold-alls on behalf of the company. Through that I made an association with Sir Alf and Harold Shepherdson and after they'd won the World Cup it was really a time when the players should have made an awful lot of money and they didn't. After that they created a players' pool and I was fortunate enough and honoured enough to be asked to act as agent for the players' pool. One of the biggest promotions was the Esso coin that came in the '70 World Cup. The World Cup record, 'Back Home', was fantastic. We did the record in about two or three hours and I think it was 'Top of the Pops' for about three weeks.

Frank Butler: When I went to the World Cup in Rio [in 1950] I sat with the players, played pontoon with them and we chatted. They were glad to give you interviews. We never paid a penny for an interview. I remember going back to the World Cup in Argentina [in 1978] and it was 'them and us'. In our day I used to travel first-class and the players travelled economy. In the end we all travelled first-class but the players got the best seats. You'd ask them a question and they'd say, 'Well could you see my agent?' or 'Could you see my business manager?' I have paid Don Revie £25,000 for two stories, and Georgie Best another £20,000 and never saw them because the agent came and you sent a ghostwriter and you spoke to them on the phone and things like that. You can't blame the players but, to my mind, it got absolutely stupid.

Terry Venables: I was about 19 when I met a chap called Kenneth Wheeler, who was one of the first agents. He introduced me to a ghostwriter called Gordon Williams, and we became very friendly and eventually wrote books together. We would write stories in the *Topical Times Annual*, or whatever annual it was, and he would get £25 and I would get £25. So he said, 'You write it yourself and you get the £50.' I thought, 'Well, I'll cut him out straight away', and invested in a typewriter and wrote a few short stories. Then we got together and wrote a football novel called *They Used to Play on Grass*. Gordon, of course, was the maestro, and he helped me a lot, but I think I contributed quite a lot. Then we wrote the Hazel books, which later became a television series.

Jeff Astle: I was a big star in them days in the First Division and there was a lad named Carl Wayne who was the lead singer in the Move and he had just made this song called 'Blackberry Way' which was in the hit parade, and he decided it might be a good idea to cut a record [in 1969]. I weren't a bad singer really. I was a church lad all me life, in the church choir, and I was all for it really. So to cut a long story short, we went to the studios and he helped me out and he sang in the background. It was a very catchy tune. In fact it come on the wireless a few times. Once we were playing in London and Ed Stewart was the DJ on the kids' programme in the morning and somebody asked for a request and we all sang it on the bus when we were travelling down. It were called 'Sweet Water'. It had a very catchy chorus and we used to sing it in the showers, all the lads at West Brom, Len Cantello and Asa Hartford:

Sweet water flows through my fingers and through my toes.
See my sweet water run, see it sparkle in the sun.

Tommy Docherty: I first noticed agents in 1974–75, as manager of Manchester United. One or two players said to me, 'Can I bring me agent to see ya?' I said, 'No way. Your agent can't score any goals or win any matches for me. He can do nothing for me. I will deal with you. If you want to go out and discuss what I've discussed with you with your agent, you go ahead and do so, but there's no way your agent is coming in here.' There's one or two good agents, I must admit, but eight out of 10 are gangsters.

Jon Holmes: When I was at university I read a book by Mark McCormack called *Arnie: Evolution of a Legend*. It wasn't a particularly good book, as it happens, but it described the way that McCormack used golf to enhance Arnold Palmer's public profile in the same way that Palmer's increased public profile improved the position of golf. I think sports representation was at a very early stage then. McCormack was the man who started it. I didn't have much ability myself [as a player] and my knees fell to bits at a very early age so the only way I was going to stay involved in sport was in some form of business connection. After spending a short time in journalism, after I left university, I started to work in sports management as a sideline, a part-time activity, when I went into the financial service industry, and it grew gently, as it were, from there. I started in 1972. I was probably the first who came from a financial background. I was fortunate in that working in Leicester we had clients at Leicester City and one of the most prominent players at Leicester at that point was Peter Shilton. We started looking after his personal financial affairs, and from that I then started looking after his commercial affairs, in a broader sense. The first commercial deal was probably a boot contract with somebody like Gola in the early seventies. The first transfer deal we did was when he moved to Stoke in late 1974 and at that point we negotiated with Tony Waddington [Stoke City manager]. I don't think that had been done too much at that time. Stoke were certainly a bit surprised and I think they thought our approach was a wee bit more commercial than anything they'd encountered before. There wasn't freedom of contract, as it's called now, so, if you wanted to move, whether you were under contract or your contract had ceased, you had to ask for a transfer or the club had to place you on the list and then a deal had to be agreed, and thus the player was very much in the dark about what was going on. That situation doesn't exist now. So that's the major difference. A player at the end of his contract can talk to whomever he chooses.

Freedom of Contract

Gordon Taylor: When I joined the PFA full-time in 1980 I saw literally drawers full of correspondence where the previous secretary had tried in vain to arrange meetings with the Football League, where Alan Hardaker was the secretary. They had been conveniently diverted and prevaricated and as a result there was a need to get together. I think this was a reaction from the League after the maximum wage was removed, saying, 'You know, that's one battle we lost, we don't intend losing any more.'

Derek Dougan: We set up the Professional Footballers' Negotiation Committee and that had its first meeting in February 1975. There was only one item on the agenda and that was freedom of contract. We were told quite clearly by the League and the FA, more by the League, that we would not get freedom of contract without a fight, and we decided that we'd take up the fight, and we spent the next three and a half years getting through to the players what the consequences of giving 100 per cent support to the PFA would mean to the future. It soon became apparent that we wouldn't get total implementation. Freedom of contract to me is that at the end of a contract on 30 June, as of 1 July I could move to any other club in the world, without any restriction, but it wasn't possible. We wanted to get the player to be able to move from club A to club B as cleanly and as quickly as possible, and it took three and a half years to go from freedom of contract to a watered-down version of freedom of contract, which meant really that I didn't remove the shackles altogether. I literally compromised and I had to live with my conscience. I do believe that if we had implemented freedom of contract any time between 1975 and '78, it would have been a financial saviour for the game. With total hindsight, it [the compromise] wasn't in the best interests of the game, because suddenly, after '78, the transfer system spread out of control altogether. They were paying fortunes. And I'll give you one club in particular that lost a fortune on the transfer market, and, years later, is still paying the price for it, and that was Manchester City, who literally threw good money after bad.

Transfer Take-off

Malcolm Allison: First of all, let's get it straight. When I'd been there four days Peter Swales and Tony Book went and signed a fella called Bobby Shinton, who, to me, was a player without a position. Paid £400,000 for him. After that Peter Swales went and signed a fella called Steve Daley. We went to play Southampton and the chairman never came but he went and saw the chairman of Wolverhampton Wanderers. They agreed a deal for £1 million plus VAT and then I came in on Monday morning and Tony Book said, 'We've signed Steve Daley.' I said, 'How much, what've we signed him for?' He said, 'A million pounds'. I said, 'What? A million pounds?' I'd already agreed with John Barnwell [manager of Wolves] to buy him for £650,000. Then ten minutes later Tony Book came back to me and said, 'They want £1,100,000.' I said, 'Whoa, we don't want him.' Anyway, the chairman, Mr Swales, agreed to take him. Then there was another boy they wanted, a boy called Michael Robinson who Ken Barnes and Tony Book had watched, and they'd all watched, and they kept on to me about this boy Michael

Robinson, and I'd seen him play once. I gave in to them, I let 'em sign him. Then I signed a boy called Steve McKenzie. He was a 17-year-old boy from Crystal Palace and I liked him and I thought he was going to be a very good player, but they wanted £250,000 for him – Terry Venables was the manager. So I went to the chairman and I said, 'Look, we can buy this kid for £250,000.' So he rang up the financial adviser for Manchester City and he said, 'Malcolm wants to sign this boy for 250, what do you think?' So this fella – I forget his name – said to the chairman, 'Yes, okay, sure.' He thought he meant £250, but it was £250,000. Yeah, the chairman was Peter Swales and the manager was Tony Book and I was the coach.

Peter Swales: I had it in my brain in those days that I wanted to be bigger than Manchester United, which really was a bit silly because I should have let them get on with their own business and got on with my business, but we came very, very close to their average attendance in the late seventies. It didn't quite come off for us but it was worth the try. We were the first club to sign three £1 million players. Trevor Francis was one, Stephen Daley from Wolverhampton and Kevin Reeves from Norwich, who was unlucky with injuries. Malcolm will say that I picked Steve Daley. I would argue with that, but I wouldn't want to fall out with him after all these years. It was the manager's job to pick the player and the board's job to negotiate the fee. In those days, of course, you could pay over any number of years and that encouraged you to take ludicrous gambles. You mortgaged your future, but they were exciting days.

20

'Things began to deteriorate'

The International Team in the 1970s

England's attempt to retain the World Cup, in Mexico in 1970, progressed smoothly until the quarter-finals, but then West Germany overcame a 2–0 deficit to win 3–2 in extra-time. It was England's last appearance in the World Cup Finals for 12 years. They failed to qualify in 1974 and again in 1978.

The 1970 World Cup Finals

Alan Mullery: I think Alf and every England player believed that we were probably the strongest squad that England had ever had in the whole of their history. It was a much stronger squad than in '66, and that's no disrespect to the squad playing in '66. We all believed we could win it, no problems at all. We had so much confidence in him as a manager and in the players. The rivalry for places in the team was amazing and we really fancied our chances.

Geoff Hurst: We felt very confident because we'd

achieved it before and the squad were four years more experienced. We'd got the Bobby Charltons still around, the Gordon Bankses, the Bobby Moores, myself, Martin Peters, Alan Ball, so we had a nucleus of the team, and some very significant introductions to the team as well, notably Alan Mullery, who played that Nobby Stiles role as well as Nobby if not better, if that were possible, and Franny Lee, who I think gave us more variation up front and more flair than, say, Jimmy Greaves, Roger Hunt or I had. He was a significant addition to the team, a tremendous professional who could play wide and was very difficult to pick up.

Sir Bobby Charlton: Tommy Wright and Terry Cooper had come in at full-back, Keith Newton and Francis Lee had come in, and we had good build-up. We had successful matches, we'd done well in South America, and everybody expected us to do well. I think we played Romania first and we beat Romania. Brazil had beaten Czechoslovakia in the first round of games, and in the second game we were due to play Brazil. So we had both won our first matches and it looked like we still could progress in the tournament. The Brazilian match was going to be a crunch match, psychologically. It didn't matter that we lost because everybody expected that we would beat Czechoslovakia, which we did, but there was so much emphasis put on this game. This was potentially the rehearsal for the Final and it was a brilliant game. We played well, they played well, we defended well, they defended well, but everybody was probing all the time. We had the type of players to probe. We could have scored, they could have scored. Not a lot of chances, but the one goal was scored by Jairzinho. Pelé got this ball and waited for somebody to come and challenge him – I think it was Terry Cooper – and he laid a little ball off to the right to Jairzinho who thumped it in. After that we still had many chances to equalize and get back in the game. That was a sensational match, maybe Bobby Moore's greatest game. Any little bit of danger he nipped it in the bud, and he didn't tackle one man, he was tackling them all, and all crucial tackles. And if you're playing against a great side like Brazil, you know you can't make mistakes. And we didn't really make one. Gordon Banks was absolutely out of this world. Without question the best goalkeeper in the world at the time. He made that save from Pelé's header. From about six inches from the floor, he flicked it over the bar with his little finger. Pelé now says he couldn't believe that it actually wasn't a goal, but Gordon had been doing it all the time.

Geoff Hurst: I think if you put it into perspective I'd say that the Brazilian team that won it in 1970 were in many people's estimation the best team ever to have won the World Cup and one of the best teams ever – Jairzinho, Pelé, Tostao, Rivelino, Gerson, Carlos Alberto and so on. We lost 1–0 but we could easily have won 2–1 or 3–1, so we matched probably the best team in the world, ever, so that gives you an indication of how good we were at that time.

Jack Charlton: Everybody expected the Final would be between England and Brazil, and it would have been apart from the fact that Germany got back into a game which was dead. I sat and watched the game. In fact I walked out of the stadium, I couldn't watch any more when they made it 2–1 towards the end of the game, and then I came back and I was just in time to see the German winner in extra-time. But at 2–0, I mean, the game was dead and buried. Everybody blames Alf for bringing our kid off in that game, because he brought him off in a vital stage of the game, but Alf felt that Bobby had played in every game up till then and he maybe needed a rest. A lesson I've learnt. I very rarely use substitutes unless I have to, because that game taught me that if you use a substitute when it's not necessary, when the result is good and everything is going fine, you might upset the balance and structure of the team and lose the game.

Alan Ball: The worst memory of my lifetime was sitting in the dressing-room after being beaten by the Germans 3–2 after leading 2–0. But we were part of a magnificent tournament and part of an England team that played some cracking football, and they were marvellous games.

Alan Mullery: I became good friends with Pelé over the years and he said the only team they feared in Mexico was England, especially after the way we played against them. In a way he was delighted that England went out to West Germany but in another way he was disappointed because he thought that the Final would have been a much more even contest if England had got to the Final instead of Italy, because they absolutely murdered Italy.

After 1970

Sir Bobby Charlton: After the World Cup of 1970, there was no reason to think that English football wouldn't continue to be good. We'd just failed but we'd done really well. New players were coming in and they were still good players. So I think that we had every reason to be optimistic over the next few years. Qualification became more difficult because teams you took for granted at one stage were suddenly emerging with proper coaching. A lot of them were going full-time professional. It's not so long since a country like Holland were an amateur part-time professional team, but they all started to play full-time professional football and they had proper coaching, so eventually they were going to improve and make it more difficult for the teams that had had easy rides before that. So I think that was why we declined slightly. It wasn't so much that we declined as the others improved.

Brian Glanville: Things began to deteriorate when he [Alf Ramsey] began to deteriorate as a manager. Nobody seems to be able to crack it for all that long. He was immensely the best we've ever had in England for the national team and he had a sublime period from 1966, when he won the World Cup against all the odds, right through to after the 1970 tournament, when England were terribly unlucky not to qualify for the semi-finals, which they would have done if Gordon Banks hadn't drunk the fatal glass of beer and got ill. That was the main reason we lost to West Germany. But then things began to go wrong and by 1972 it was quite clear that this wasn't Alf as we knew him. There was a very embarrassing semi-final first leg at home to West Germany at Wembley in the European Nations Cup. Gunter Netzer just ran riot and Germany won very easily. I believe it was 3–1. Then we went over to Berlin and we needed to get the two goals back and Alf just panicked and put out a totally defensive team and we got a rather humiliating, grubby 0–0 draw and Gunter Netzer came off and made the rather classic remark, that 'the whole England team has autographed my leg'.

v Poland – World Cup Qualifier, October 1973

Norman Hunter: From my point of view it was my chance to establish myself because it was the first time he'd left Bobby Moore out. It was a good side because it was Shilton, Madeley, McFarland, Hunter, Hughes, Bell, Currie, Peters, Channon, Chivers and Clarke. Well, that's not a bad side, and we went into the game and Alf had built us up to say that we were better than Poland, I can remember that, and we *were* a better side. I have never played in a more one-sided game in my life. I think there's a few funny stories. Brian Clough called the 'keeper Tomashevski 'a clown' and he was absolutely brilliant on the night. For 45 minutes we camped in their half. Tomashevski was brilliant and we just couldn't score. Then 20 minutes into the second half the ball was played out and I came across and it was going to be a 50–50 ball and I'm thinking to myself, 'Right, tackle him and get the ball into touch', but then he slowed up, and I did the silliest thing I've ever done in my life. I usually go with my left foot, and I went with my right foot, and I thought to myself, 'I'll just try and keep this in', and I missed it, and the rest is history. He went through and they scored. Even then, we hit the woodwork, Allan Clarke scored, and it was just one of those things. That was probably one of the worst moments and the worst feelings I've ever had in football.

Peter Shilton: It was my first important game for England. I think the Poles broke down our right-hand side. I remember Norman Hunter ran across and I think most people thought it was his ball. I think Norman did. The fella managed to get past Norman and cut inside and squared the ball to a fella on the edge of the box. He shot. I thought at the time that it had gone through Emlyn Hughes's legs but I don't think it did. He hit the shot pretty well, I tried to scoop the ball up with my arms and the pace beat me. I look back now and think, 'Maybe if I'd just blocked it with something, maybe a foot, or just tried to get a hand to it and block it, maybe I would have made the save,' but I was still pretty young in those days, and possibly I tried to make a perfect save.

Sir Alf Ramsey Sacked (May 1974)

Peter Swales: My first meeting with the FA Council I sat next to an old gentleman who was asleep most of the meeting. (It couldn't happen today, I must promise you, this was 20-odd years ago.) We had some forms to fill in, so I woke him up to fill this particular form in and one of the questions was something about injuries, and the answer he put down was something to do with his leg, injured in the Boer War. That was my first experience on the Football

Association Council. He must have been in his late eighties, but that doesn't apply today. They've got younger, thriving people.

Brian Mears: Being on the Football League management committee, you had to be on the FA Council and there were certain committees, including the international, the disciplinary, the referees' committee and so on. I was asked to stand for the international committee, which I did, and I was appointed to it. Dick Wragg was the chairman. The first meeting I went to Alf Ramsey was sacked, and, if you look back on it, it was not a proud day for the England international committee, because here was a man who is greatly respected now, as he was then, by his players and by the whole country for winning the World Cup. Fantastic achievement. And there I was, a very minor player, sitting in judgement on somebody who I admire. But what can I say? I was part of the committee. But it was a sad day really, a very sad day. I was thinking about it this morning and I thought how extraordinary it was that Ipswich Town produced two managers for England – Alf Ramsey and Bobby Robson. The Cobbolds must have known a thing or two about managers.

Ted Phillips: We'd just left work in London. I'd got a mate with me and I saw Alf waiting for the Ipswich train, the one I was going to get, and I took my mate over and introduced him. He was highly honoured to shake the England manager's hand. We get on the train and I said, 'Gonna have a beer, Alf?' And he said, 'I'll get 'em.' So he went up to the counter and he's got himself two miniature Scotches and got me a couple of cans and I said, 'What, you turned to Scotch now, Alf?' He said, 'Oh, I have an occasional drink.' So I got off at Colchester and he continued to Ipswich and the next morning I got on the train, opened the paper and there it was: Alf Ramsey sacked as England's manager! He never said a dickie bird to me at all. That's the type of bloke Alf was, wasn't he?

The Don Revie Era, July 1974–July 1977

Billy Bremner: When he told me he was going with England I was down at the ground. I says, 'Well, there's no other job that you would leave here for, obviously,' and he says, 'No, no other job.' I says, 'Well, we can't blame you because that's the pinnacle of anyone's career, to be national manager. I know how much you would like to be the England manager, I'd like to wish you all the best and I hope you are successful with them.' Throughout the place everyone was demoralized, and we felt that the Leeds United directors probably didn't endeavour enough to keep him at the football club because he may have decided to stay with Leeds United. What people tend to forget about Leeds United, the great team, he only ever bought three players – Gilesy, Clarkey and Jonesy – and he hadn't bought any of the next lot that was coming up. They had all come from Scotland Schoolboys, Wales Schoolboys, England School-boys. He had developed this youth policy and when he left that seemed to fizzle out.

Alan Ball: He had a special thing at Leeds, didn't he? He brought these lads through, and let's be fair, they were a terrific side. I had the honour to play against them quite a lot of times. He had a family there that were special. To become England manager, you've got to take people from all over the country, from different clubs who play different ways, and you've got to mould them into a team. I think Don Revie found that difficult.

Don Howe: If the England team were playing in an important World Cup qualifying game on a Wednesday, in those days the players had to play in a hard First Division match the Saturday before, and Don Revie and a lot of the England managers thought it wasn't right and I completely agree with them. You didn't have enough preparation time. You would get together perhaps on the Sunday night, or the

Monday morning, and half a dozen of your best players would be injured and they couldn't take part in any of the training and the practice sessions, so you were virtually going into an important game on the Wednesday evening without any get-together and work as a team.

Norman Hunter: I think he tried to take a League situation into the international scene and it doesn't work, because you've got players from different clubs and you've gotta treat 'em slightly different. He tried the bingo and the carpet bowls with England. Well, it was not done. And I think he made far too many changes. He chopped and changed the side, whereas at Leeds the team picked itself. He hardly had a settled side when he was in the England job.

Phil Thompson: I remember one of my first games. It was an under-23 game with Don and we went away and we played indoor bowls, and I went back and tried to keep a straight face and tell the stories to Ronnie Moran and Joe Fagan and Bob Paisley, that we've been playing carpet bowls and bingo. It was 'big grins on the faces', but this is what Don had had great success with at Leeds, so he's saying, 'Well, why change things?'

John Giles: I think he was amazed at the lack of professionalism and knowledge of the players coming in, compared to the Leeds players that he had, because he'd had some of the Leeds players for 14 years, week in and week out. If things went wrong he could put it right, and they would understand and get used to the approach, whereas players coming into the England team were coming from different clubs who wouldn't have the same professional approach and he wouldn't have the time to do things with them that he had at Leeds. I also think he underestimated when he was at Leeds the actual playing strength of the players, because Don always gave great credit to the opposition.

Phil Thompson: It was Leeds and Liverpool who were always at the top of the League at that time, always going for Cups and so on, and I thought it [Don Revie's appointment] was the best thing that could have happened. Okay, I'd heard about his dossiers and all this and I thought, 'Well, basically, you can take them or leave them.' But I thought it was a great future for the game with Revie, but it wasn't to be. I think Don Revie got together something like 88 players in Manchester for his first meeting of players, everybody who he considered had a possibility of playing for England. So you can see that 77 people were going to be disappointed from when the first team was picked. We went with England and he put too much emphasis on the opponents, whereas we'd always been brought up at Liverpool to say, 'Let the opponents bother about you,' which I think is a great way to do it, but Don had us with these statistics about players. You know, he's great with his left foot, bring him on his right foot, and he's great in the air, and he can swivel in the air, and he's like a ballerina, and he pirouettes and everything. And eventually you went into games thinking, 'This player I'm playing against is one of the best players in the world,' and that's not really what you wanted to know. You wanted to know that the opposition are a load of garbage, as Shanks would tell us, and you were the best in the world, you were going to beat them. I think this was his letdown. I think it left a sour feeling with everybody when he actually ducked out of a sinking ship.

John Giles: They didn't have a successful time, and I think there was a lot of talk that he was going to be sacked, and whilst he was still manager of England he arranged a job in the United Arab Emirates and he did that on the quiet and then he left the Football Association to go to that job. But I think where he upset some people was that he gave the story to a national newspaper before he informed the Football Association about it. I spoke to him after and he certainly felt that they were setting somebody else up to take his job, so he was going to pre-empt that.

Billy Bremner: I think he regretted how he left England, obviously, because what people don't realize was that Don Revie was flagrantly proud of being English. Nobody could say anything about England as far as he was concerned. I think people think, 'Well he got his money and went away with the Arabs and blah, blah, blah.' I've never spoken with him about it but that must have been a hard decision for him, and the manner in which he did it, because it stunk of greed, which was certainly not like him. I don't think he was ever a greedy man. I've never found out he'd been a greedy man. He must have had some inside information about what was about to happen to him as the England manager and he jumped the gun. It's a shame really because he got terrible publicity over it, and the guys that really knew him, ie the players, knew he was certainly not like that as an individual. I know he's done things that helped people. Managers have been sacked at football clubs and he's put them on the payroll at Elland Road as scouts and you didn't even have to scout but he'd make sure that their families were all right, and when he needed friends a lot at the finish there weren't many there.

Sir Bert Millichip: I was actually with the England team in South America and I was informed, as a member of the international committee, that Mr Revie had gone to watch a football match somewhere in Europe and would be joining us later, and we met up with him in Brazil, I think, and were immediately informed that he was saying that he was prepared to give up his job but he wanted compensation. We were astonished that he was suggesting that he should leave, even more astonished that he should be asking for compensation, and we came to a general agreement at that time that we should offer no compensation, and that was maintained throughout, and it eventually ended up in court proceedings.

Frank Butler: I was a very great friend of Don's but I was a bit upset when he quit the England team as manager. You see, he didn't do it openly. The team went down to South America, Don didn't travel with them, and then he decided he was going to join the Arabs for a fortune and I think he let England down. We spoke to his agent, and I think we paid £25,000 for two articles, saying why he left and that. I'd called him 'Goldfinger' and I hadn't spoken to him for years and he said, 'Oh, Frank, you were very, very tough with me, weren't you?' I said, 'Well, weren't you wrong?' He said, 'Yeah, I shouldn't have done it that way,' and poor Don is now dead. It's very sad. He ended up in very bad health and died very early.

Brian Clough: The People's Choice

Peter Swales: It was the greatest interview I've ever taken part in. I still smile about it now. I've interviewed managers for Manchester City and I've been involved in interviewing managers for England over the years but the Cloughie one was something different. We had a chairman in those days called Sir Harold Thompson who was quite a strong personality, and he didn't like Cloughie too much really, if I was honest, but public opinion forced us to give Cloughie an interview. I think Sir Matt Busby was on the committee then, and Sir Bert Millichip, who's the current chairman of the Football Association, but Sir Harold Thompson was in the chair and he was going to tell Cloughie exactly what he thought about him; he was going to tell him what was required to become an England manager and he was going to read the riot act to him. We interviewed him at nine o'clock on a Monday morning at Lancaster Gate, and the streets were crammed with press and media because Cloughie was the biggest name in football. We were all sat down at five to nine, round the table, and Sir Harold was raring to get at Cloughie, and Cloughie came in on the stroke of nine o'clock. Sir Harold pointed to his seat, which was at the opposite end of the table, and before Sir Harold had a chance to say a word, Cloughie looked at his watch and said, 'I hope if I get this job I don't have to come at nine o'clock on a Monday morning' (with a few expletives in the middle) and that really floored Sir Harold. From then on Cloughie was most charming, and he dominated the meeting and got on top of Sir Harold. The interview was really good enough to have got him the job but he was never going to be England manager, unfortunately.

Brian Clough: I just told them exactly the truth, that I was the best man for the job. They were worried that I was possibly going to take over the Football Association, which I would have done. I couldn't have stood for committees, and meetings with people who didn't have the remotest idea about football, 19 people round a table.

Sir Bert Millichip: Mr Clough was always the public's choice, and certainly they didn't cease to remind us of that over a considerable number of years following that decision, but it's not for me to say why Mr Clough was not considered as the right and proper man for the job.

Peter Swales: I think we felt – I didn't have a very strong voice in it but I probably felt the same – that he was too controversial to be England manager. It was a different type of FA than it is today. It was much more the old-school-tie Association and he was a bit too controversial for us. We settled in the end for Ron Greenwood, who was a smashing manager.

Ron Greenwood: When Don packed up it created a bit of a fracas in the Football Association, and there were many leading people who looked for the job. I think Jack Charlton always said that he put in an application but didn't get an interview. Bobby Robson was interviewed. Lawrie

McMenemy was interviewed. But prior to that they'd appointed me as the coach, or the team manager, to fill the gap until the final decision was made, when all these other people were interviewed. We played a friendly game at Wembley [v Switzerland] but we drew 0–0, so the first game wasn't a great success. Then we had to go to Luxembourg and we won 2–0 when we were supposed to win by about six or seven. Then of course the next game was against Italy at Wembley and it was a question of winning, which we did. We won 2–0, but we didn't go through [to the 1978 World Cup Finals] on goal average because of what had happened before under Don. So I served those three matches as a caretaker manager. By that time I'd promoted myself to general manager at West Ham United and let young John Lyall take over. So when the Football Association were looking for somebody to take over mid-season, as it were, I suppose I had the background as regards being in charge of England Youth and the under-23s and the 'B' team, and I had the necessary qualification. I think what went in my favour was the fact that they didn't have to disturb a club situation by taking their manager away mid-season, because we're talking about just after the season started [1977–78]. I think that's why I got chosen as a caretaker manager and then it was up to me to prove that I could do the job, and so after the Italian game, because that was quite successful, they made the appointment and I was selected to be the full-time manager.

21

'You've got a street riot on your hands'

The 'Hooliganism' Era

Football attendances declined during the 1970s, partly because of increased hooliganism at matches. Although hooliganism was far from a new problem – it had been rife in the 1890s for instance – it received copious publicity in the 1970s, especially via television, and undoubtedly became more of a problem. Eventually, outbreaks of hooliganism inside grounds were controlled, although the problem continued to be present in the streets, and abroad when English clubs travelled in European competitions.

An Emerging Problem

Harry Jacobs: I was in Crewe Alexandra's ground in 1937. It was December and Crewe were playing New Brighton. Both teams were in the Northern section of the Third Division, and it was a needle game, a Cup tie. Crewe were winning [1–0] and they only had to get the next 10 minutes over and they were in the draw for the next round (when the big teams came in). The south side of Crewe railway station was the boundary of the ground, and the engines started throwing off steam with their whistles – no doubt the crowd had let them know what the result was – and they were stoking up their engines. It was rather a dark, overcast day, and a gust of wind seemed to blow the cloud over the top end of the ground, where I was standing, and the referee abandoned the match. Well, this incensed the players, and the crowd suddenly realized what was happening, and started to encroach on the ground from two sides. A policeman pushed through the players and put his arm round the referee, and I heard him shout, 'Run for it.' Together they ran down the field, and as they got to the halfway-line, the policemen who were on duty at that end of the ground came forward and smoothed a path for them and they ran right through the crowd, on to the terrace and into the referee's hut where he got changed. I know this is true because I was the policeman who put me arm around him, and I took punches on my left arm, and when we arrived at the dressing-room the pair of us fell into the dressing-room exhausted on the floor.

Jim King: I started travelling away in the mid-fifties [with Everton] and it was pretty depressing travelling by train. I think it was the aftermath of the war, and the train service hadn't been renewed or revitalized or anything and we were travelling away in old coaches, no corridors on the train, no toilets, and we were all herded 12 to 14 in a compartment. I can remember going to Old Trafford with my brother and we'd been standing with United fans. They'd beaten us, we got back to the station and we were herded together. Then the police lined us up and kept us there until there was enough to fill a train. We waited for a long time. We finally got on the train, and of course there was no toilets. I was bursting to go so I stepped on to the platform, and a sergeant come at me with his baton: 'Get back on.' I said, 'But I'm going to the toilet.' He says, 'Get back on.' I said, 'What am I going to do?' He says, 'Do what you always do, all over the compartment,' and this is the way we were being treated at this time.

John Fitt: We went to Workington and the Workington fans threw stones at us, because Reg Davies, the [Millwall] goalkeeper, got involved in a fight with the Workington centre-forward. It was round about the 88th minute and the referee got fed up with it. He just blew the whistle and rushed off and we all thought he'd abandoned it, and it was only the next day we found out that in fact he hadn't abandoned it, and it was 2–2, because Workington equalized in the last minute. That was 1961 and I was 18 and I was a bit scared that day, I must admit. But it was very unusual to see any violence from anyone.

Jack Curtis: The worst-behaved crowd I've ever been in was at Leicester City when Leicester City played a friendly match against Glasgow Rangers [February 1967], and I sat in the stand talking to a man with a Rangers scarf on. A very sensible, nice man, very pleasant indeed, until they ran on the pitch, and he's jumping up, and it's the jeers, the jeers, the jeers, and halfway through the second half there were empty whisky bottles flying all over the place.

Ken Sheehan: I think I first noticed it when Millwall had that very good run in the late-sixties, when people like Keith Weller, Gilchrist, Cripps, Len Julians were playing for them, and at that stage there was a lot of hooliganism starting and I remember going to Crystal Palace on one occasion and after the match walking down the main road and suddenly a sea of youths came down the road and all we could do, all anybody could do, was jump out of the way. They virtually took the whole street over and that was the first time I really saw the power of all these youngsters getting together and frightening people.

Maud Gascoyne: We had season tickets [at Nottingham Forest] and we were in the stand on the halfway-line and the Leicester supporters picked up stones and threw them at us. It really was frightening. So I said, 'That's it, if that's football I'm not going any more.'

Barrie Fay: It gradually got worse, 1969, '70, '71, '72, that period of time. It was a hard time to be a proper football fan. West Ham wasn't the nicest crowd in the world, and we [Liverpool] played them twice in a month [January 1976]. We won luckily in the FA Cup and paid the price for it – no windows on the coach, no jacket on me back. You was followed and you was in two minds what to do – run, fight, or just play it calm and hope the police were round the next corner.

Mark Sambrook: Throughout the seventies you didn't need to plan things. I mean, you could go to Halifax and get your face kicked in in a Fourth Division game between Halifax and Rochdale because the crowds were such that it attracted loads of kids. I know very few guys who are my age now, who were teenagers then, who didn't get involved in fights at football matches. You didn't have much choice. Either you went with your Dad in your parka and you still got a decent chance of getting your face beat in, or you went with the lads (which had much more kudos attached to it for teenagers). We didn't particularly plan meeting fans from other clubs because you knew you couldn't avoid 'em. There wasn't that sort of sinister element of plotting to have riots somewhere. It just happened.

Edward Grayson: By 1974, it was very much a recognized problem which exploded in a very sensational manner with the Nottingham Forest–Newcastle Cup tie at St James's Park. Newcastle were losing at home to Nottingham Forest and the Newcastle fans decided to try and prevent that defeat by going on to the field and stopping the match. The ultimate decision of the Football Association was to order a replay, and Newcastle went on to lose the Final 3–0 to Liverpool. If the Football Association had had the moral and intellectual courage, and the guts to kick Newcastle United out of the FA Cup on that occasion, it might have stopped the increase of hooliganism which ultimately led to the Heysel Disaster [1985].

Chief Inspector Bryan Drew: I joined the Metropolitan Police in 1974 and almost from the very beginning I was involved in policing football, predominantly at the grounds in West London. My initial experiences were large crowds, very, very noisy, where disorder was, in a lot of cases, the norm rather than the exception: such events as trying to take the opposing supporters' end, where you would have fights between one group of supporters trying deliberately to infiltrate the home end of a ground, and events like that, where you were continually busy trying to keep people apart during the football matches.

Brendon Batson: When I started [in 1971], there were hardly any black players. I was a London lad and I knew of Clyde Best, Ade Coker, and the Charles brothers, Clive and John, and there were players in the lower divisions like Ces Podd and Joe Cooke. When I went to West Brom [in February 1978], Cyrille Regis and Laurie Cunningham were already there. I think we were the first team to field *three* black players, and Ron Atkinson [the West Brom manager] nicknamed us 'The Three Degrees'. As more and more black players came into professional football it seemed to antagonize those people with racist views and attitudes. Instead of making it better it made it worse in a way. You went through a whole thing – chants, bananas being thrown, and them spitting at you. You used to get really personal letters. I remember when Cyrille was called up for England a letter came through with a bullet, saying, 'This has got your name on' or something to that effect. We used to joke about it. Laurie used to get some really nasty letters, and he'd just pin them up on the noticeboard for all of us to have a good laugh. But we didn't used to talk about it and say, 'How are we going to deal with the problem?'.

Taking an End

John Fitt: The first sign of any sort of aggravation which I saw was when Millwall were playing Walsall in December 1965. They were near the top of the Third Division. Walsall had a young Allan Clarke and George Kirby, an old stalwart who used to play for Southampton, and it was 1–1 in the second half. The fans got frustrated and some Walsall fans started singing and chanting. In those days you could walk round three sides of a ground, and I was behind one goal and I said to my mate, who was standing next to me, 'Ken, where are they going?' There was a drift of people just walking all the way round the ground to where these Walsall fans were singing, and you could see what was happening, but the police did nothing until there was an actual scuffle. In 1966, just after England won the World Cup, there was a record in the charts, 'Distant Drums' by Jim Reeves, where he's saying, 'I hear the sound of distant drums, over there,' and very quickly football supporters changed that into 'I hear the sound of distant bums, over there.' You could see that there was a cynical change in supporters' attitudes. They started attacking verbally the other supporters, and, what with the development of the motorways and maybe young people earning more money, they could travel to more football.

Mark Sambrook: I remember times [with Stoke City] when the pitch was invaded before the game, thousands of people running across the pitch to get at the other team's end. Bolton springs to mind round about '73–74, a Sunday Cup game where it lashed down with rain so the pitch was really muddy. I remember running across the pitch with several mates before the match, people losing their shoes, the police running after you, fights on the pitch because the police were trying to stop you.

Ken Chaplin: It was a great day in January 1975. We hired a train fom Euston and went up to Burnley with four British Transport police. We [Wimbledon] had a great game and beat Burnley – the first non-League club to beat a First Division side for years. The unfortunate part was coming back. As the train pulled out of Burnley station we were told by the police to pull the blinds down: 'You're gonna get stoned as you get down to the bridges.' We drew the blinds and stones were hitting the outside of the carriage. We were on the floor listening to the Cup draw. We were about 10 minutes out of Burnley when they came up with 'Leeds v Wimbledon' in round four. But it was a great day out.

John Fitt: And I remember one game, a local derby – Charlton versus Millwall in 1977. In those days fans used to wave scarves above their heads, singing, and there was a mass of red singing, 'Charlton, Charlton,' and suddenly, about 20 minutes before the game started, a hole appeared in this mass of red and it spread. It was like a stone being dropped into a pool and the ripples spreading out, and the ripples disappeared and it was all as it was before, but what came back was a mass of blue and then it was singing, 'Millwall, Millwall,' and that was the first time that I had seen an end being taken. I think the terms they used were that Millwall 'steamed in' and Charlton ran.

Dale Campbell: We used to get in there in dribs and drabs, go to the back and then there's, say, probably 40 or 50 of you, and you used to shout your team's name and you was behind them and you pushed forwards in the terrace and that was it. When you look back at it, you could have killed somebody, stamping on them and that lot, but luckily enough it never happened. And then the police come rushing in and you was like jumping on the pitch then to get into your own end, so you didn't get nicked. You'd gone in somebody's end and you've had a bit of a scuffle, you've jumped on to the pitch and your adrenalin was high. You used to walk back round the ground while the game was on and you thought you was an hero coming back into your own end. It was a nice feeling.

In the Streets

Brian Belton: Someone would see a hat in the back of a car and say, 'I like that hat,' and they'd smash the back window and take the hat and pull the hat down over their head. It wasn't particularly an act of violence, it was a ludicrous, hysterical act. Throwing a toilet out of a train window was funny. It's a set of surreal actions, to take a toilet out of an old train and through a window. When you're in a group and when you see this person walking around with a toilet, it's funny, and the toilet goes whooshing out of the window. We knew we could go into some of these little railway towns like Carlisle, Stockport or whatever and we could walk up and down the High Street and everyone would look at us and everyone would be frightened of us and we wouldn't have to do very much, just shout and swear a bit: 'You're gonna get your fucking heads kicked in.' I mean, anyone can say that. Of course, if you're from a particular cultural background, when you hear someone say, 'You're gonna get your fuckin' heads kicked in,' you think you'll get your fucking head kicked in but hardly anyone got their fucking head kicked in. Of course, the local bobbies responded, whereas in London the white shirts wouldn't take any notice of you, basically because they grew up with it.

Dale Campbell: One did go out of hand one year at Middlesbrough, where a football supporter died on the street. We didn't mean it. We just happened to appear on the street at the same time as a few Middlesbrough supporters and it did get out of hand. It was just a normal Saturday, going to Middlesbrough. Got up there, had a few beers, had a bit of a scuffle before the game and all that lot. We got in and there was bits and bobs going off in the ground. When we came out we thought the streets would be empty but they was full so we was all in the escort but some of us wanted to get out, and a few of us did get away from the police and we ended up chasing about 50 down the street, but we didn't realize when we got to the bottom of the street that there was loads more Middlesbrough supporters there. Some of us had milk crates in our hands fighting 'em off cos there was too many of 'em, but he just got hit on the head, that was it, a punch, and you know he went down that hard he hit his head on the kerb, didn't even turn up blood. Just one of them things. Nobody meant to do it, it could have been the other bloke. I mean, the other bloke who hit him had a gash in his head of about eight inches from a belt buckle. The police weren't there at the time, but some of us got caught, some of us paid for it. At the end of the day we all went to jail for it, but I don't regret it, I won't regret it, no.

Brian Belton: I remember being on the station at Crystal Palace and it was incredibly crowded, and a copper come on with a dog and this dog was going wild. I mean, it really was, and it was pushing young fans back and they were balancing on the edge of the platform there, on the verge of falling off the platform. Now, what do you do? So one of 'em has kicked the dog, the dog's moved backwards and of course you've got a disgusting display now, if you come at it cold, of a dog getting a good kicking. No one wanted to see that happen but is it the fan's fault or is it the cop's fault? I mean, it would seem to me that time and time again it had been about clumsy policing. I remember coming out of Tottenham. We'd done nothing. Yes, we had boots and braces on, so we were stuck in a prison cell down on Silver Street for hours and hours and hours. You take a load of adolescent young men that have got certain types of role models in this world, what they do is they go along and they shout and holler and then the crowd starts to move and it gets more and more beefed up, someone breaks a window, in comes coppers, local people, and you've got a street riot on your hands.

Barrie Fay: I've seen a sports shop in Geneva destroyed in about 30 seconds. Phew! Gone! There were security cameras to this place, three floors to it, and it was just decimated within 30 seconds. They just waltzed in and waltzed out with what they wanted. Nobody said a word and nobody did anything. I couldn't believe it. I was just having a pint and phew! Big bags of swag and away they went, and no doubt it'd be on sale in Merseyside the following day or the day after.

Brian Belton: Little traditions grew up. I had this mate and part of his role was to kick a window in. He got very good at kicking big windows in without getting hurt, so you knew that at some point in the afternoon, either when you were going in or when you went out, that this guy was going to kick a window in, so all the time you're waiting for this and checking him out. It's like one of these constantly recurring jokes and of course when it did happen you were so pent up. He got very good at timing this joke so it was hilarious, and of course everyone would run away. One day he actually got his foot stuck in the window and he had to go to hospital and even that was funny. I mean, there's nothing quite nicer than the sound of breaking glass when you're about 15, it's an exciting sound.

Barrie Fay: St Etienne was well underprepared for the visit of Liverpool fans. They were not going round beating locals up or anything like that. It was shops with stuff outside, and they couldn't believe it. Drugs played a major part, I suppose. A little bit of blow, a little bit of dope, a few too near with the beers. The lad that thought he could fly off the bridge with his Union Jack and didn't make it, and when he hit the floor he realized he couldn't fly.

Mark Sambrook: I think the first sinister element I remember was some of the London clubs leaving calling cards. That type of behaviour. People being severely injured. Weapons were being used, in terms of actually taking weapons with intent to hurt somebody rather than finding somebody throwing pieces of concrete at you and doing the same back to protect yourself. I remember a kid in London on the Tube getting killed, either Millwall or West Ham, I can't remember. He was thrown out of a train and there was a train coming the other way and he was killed, and I always remember that was significant for me because it's like, 'Oh, I don't fancy this game any more, it's not a laugh any more.' Plus, Stoke were crap in the late seventies and early eighties so I just lost faith in watching them.

Prevention

Denis Howell: I had to segregate fans because we'd got these terrible fights going on. I thought the only way I could deal with it at that moment was to make sure that the two sets of rival supporters were kept apart. And we also did other things. For example, again without much authority, we said, 'No drinks on trains, no drinks on coaches,' and I also said, 'The away supporters should not arrive too early.'

Mark Sambrook: I mean, Coventry, for instance, in the seventies, they used to take your boots off you. If you had docs [Dr Martens] on they used to take them off you before you went in the ground. You used to have to watch the match in your stocking feet and they'd line the boots up by the turnstiles and you got your boots when you left at the end of the match. Of course you knew half the time you'd get back and somebody's nicked your boots because you've got a better pair than they have, so you went in something really old if you were going to Coventry because you knew you were probably going to lose them anyway. You also knew at Coventry that you wouldn't get arrested, they'd just eject you from the ground and let you back in about half an hour later when you'd cooled down.

Sir Bert Millichip: I sat on the commission that first ordered Manchester United to put up fences. I think they were the first club in this country who were ordered to put up fences. That would be in the late 1970s.

Irving Scholar: In the early 1980s hooliganism was probably the biggest single problem that football faced. Each week there was an outbreak, each week it was headlines, each week there were further and further problems, and it was getting worse, not better, and of course eventually the government started to take an interest, bearing in mind the government of the time were on the platform of law and order. I think the biggest single change took place in the mid-1980s when you had the introduction of closed-circuit television.

Chief Inspector Bryan Drew: I think some clubs were looking at rudimentary closed-circuit televison cameras during the seventies. This was later supported as an initiative by the Football Trust, who from then up to this date have funded closed-circuit television cameras, and I think there's now a system at every Football League club. Prior to Hillsborough [1989], the main reason that we used them was for public order, to identify. The emphasis has changed now inasmuch as they're there primarily for public safety, but of course the two are so closely interlinked anyway.

Irving Scholar: We invested a lot of money on making sure that it was as safe as it possibly could be, and we brought in security staff as a matter of course, way before other people, and the whole idea was that we wanted to make it a safe place. Spurs certainly had a hooligan problem in the 1970s, but by the 1980s I do believe that that had changed considerably.

Chief Inspector Bryan Drew: I think it was long suspected, and people have long known, that alcohol had some part of play in the disorder associated with football and the first piece of specific legislation was the Sporting Events (Control of Alcohol etc) Act, in 1985. We had the Public Order Act in 1986. Following on from Hillsborough, we had the Football Spectators Act which introduced, amongst other things, 'football restriction orders', which was an attempt to ensure that people convicted of the same type of offences would be stopped from travelling abroad in the future, either to support a club team or the national team. And, lastly, in 1991, we had the Football (Offences) Act, which made three specific offences: running on the playing area; racist or indecent chanting; and throwing of missiles. We have a number of specific pieces of legislation relevant only to football.

The 'ID Card Scheme'

John Fitt: There was one boy I used to teach and he called himself a Chelsea supporter, and that particular season [1984–85] he went to three matches: Chelsea versus Millwall in the FA Cup fourth round, West Ham versus Chelsea and Luton versus Millwall. Three matches, and they were all potential troublemaking matches. I think you multiply that by a few thousand and you might get the problem. Millwall at that time were getting 6,000 average home gate. They were near the top of the Third Division and that particular day they took away 8,000 to Luton. I think most of the yobs in London went up expecting a fight, and I think they were probably the ones who started throwing the seats, and unfortunately that probably did more to damage Millwall than any other incident I can remember, and I think it prompted our dear lady to come on television again to criticize the state of the British game and what she would do about it. Luton brought out identity cards and Mrs Thatcher tried to pass a law using the Minister of Sport at the time, Colin Moynihan, who was completely behind it but, fortunately, in the end, Lord Justice Taylor threw out the idea as unworkable.

Chief Inspector Bryan Drew: Mrs Thatcher got fed up with the way that certain supporters, when they went abroad, were dragging the name of this country through the mud, perhaps the final straw being the European Championships in Germany in 1988. Large numbers were arrested, and that called for a further look at what we were doing, which prompted the formation of the unit that I now work in and prompted calls for a national membership scheme. The ID scheme had a lot of supporters and a lot of opponents. It has been enshrined in legislation in the Football Spectators Act and it would only require a statutory instrument to bring it into being. I think it would probably have led to more problems from a policing point of view rather than less problems.

John Fitt: Mrs Thatcher seemed totally reluctant to actually address the real problem, which was a social one. I don't think closing grounds or introducing identity cards would have changed anything. It would have just switched the trouble at the time to outside the grounds. I mean if you're a hooligan you're looking for ways to spoil other people's lives and you do it in other ways. Football was just a handy medium at the time.

22

'Money was very, very tight'

Football's Shifting Balance Sheet

With the removal of the maximum wage, and a continuing decline in attendances, clubs began to feel the pinch during the 1960s. Over the years, many clubs had received significant amounts from funding-raising efforts by supporters' clubs. But, increasingly, more income was needed from outside the game if clubs were to survive, particularly during the 1970s when the threat of hooliganism affected attendances still further.

Bankrupt – Accrington Stanley (March 1962)

Ruth Chadwick: I think it came as a bombshell when we went out of the League. There's a lot of people who've never been to a football match since. They were very upset about it. What were we going to do without a football team?

Joe Devlin: When I joined them, in '53, Walter Galbraith had just taken over as manager. I was the first Scottish signing. He signed Les Cocker, Wardle from Stockport,

Harry Eastham from Liverpool and one or two others, then maybe about five or six Scottish Jocks. We finished halfway up the League, which was great because the season before they'd sought re-election. The following year we had a tip-top year and finished second to Barnsley, then the next year we finished third. Crowds were buzzing – 10,000, 12,000, 14,000 – and they were great for about four or five seasons. Then you could see this demise coming in.

Mike Ferguson: Accrington were the first team then to start playing these floodlit friendlies. I came here from Burnley on the bus, when Joe was playing, and I watched them play Tottenham, St Mirren, Third Lanark, East Fife, Blackburn Rovers, Burnley, and this place were full.

Joe Devlin: And they were one of the first to start with a lottery. There was a little guy called Albert Lucas who ran it, and Stanley were getting the wages every week out of this, and then they made it illegal to run these pools for the survival of the club.

Mike Ferguson: We then had the situation where Blackburn had been in the FA Cup Final in '60, and Burnley had won the Championship [in 1959–60] and were in the European Cup the year after, and we're stuck in between them. They signed me in the summer [1960] and we'd only eight players. We started training and they started to bring more players in. Even at that stage I realized how financially badly off the club must have been. We played Colchester once, the first game of the season, and we left at 4.30. (There were no motorways.) About 10 o'clock Harry Hubbick stopped the bus and we got off at this transport café for pie and peas, and we were playing at three o'clock! It were a red hot day, we drew 2–2, got back at two, and everybody thought, 'What a good day that's been.' We went weeks without getting paid. It never seemed to bother me as a young player but it obviously must have bothered the older players because they had families. It came to the stage where we hadn't had any wages for quite a few weeks and Jimmy Harrower took me into his office one morning with Jack Wigglesworth, the secretary, and said, 'Mike, Workington have offered £3,500 for you, and we'd like you to go because it will help us over a sticky period, we'll be able to pay the wages.' I was 17. It were a dreadful situation for me to be put in. I had a little think about it and I decided, 'No.' I walked into the dressing-room – it was after training and all the players were having a shower – and, I'll never forget, big George Forrester said, 'Well, son, what are you doing?' He frightened me to death, he did. I said, 'I'm not going.' He said, 'Smashing, son, you've a career in this game, not the Workingtons. Don't worry about us, we'll survive.' George had family like a lot of them had. It were a terrible burden for a long time; if I had gone, Accrington might have been saved, who knows? When it came to the time of finishing it were a dreadful time. We still kept playing. We never dreamt that it would happen. We just turned up for training and they said, 'Don't get changed.' Cliff Lloyd was there from the PFA, the manager was there, the secretary. They said, 'We're finished,' and that was it, everybody just went home. I walked round the back of the school and waited for the bus back to Burnley. I know now how people feel in industry when somebody just comes up to them and says, 'You're finished today,' because I've had it done to me. I had a fantastic time at Accrington. I had a lot of help from the players and I went on to play with some of the greatest players in English football with Blackburn Rovers in the First Division.

Voted Out – Bradford Park Avenue (June 1970)

George Hudson: Jimmy Scoular came in with high hopes and did a good job. He got us into the Third Division [1960–61] and we were doing quite well in the Third Division and then we had a bit of a bad spell. The directors, as usual, had no money to help the club and we went down in the Fourth Division. We started putting out appeals to the public to support us because the gates were getting down to four and five thousand, which was too low. I think the biggest problem was when Kevin Hector left us [1966]. We finished 23rd and the next three years we were 24th. The money was so short that we did all the terracing of the Low Stand, which was down at the bottom, and we painted all the walls of the ground. I was there five nights a week because I only lived two minutes' walk away. There was about 20 on the supporters' club committee and they were all really good workers. They used to steward the stands for nothing. We never thought we'd get thrown out of the League. It never entered our heads at all. We thought we'd automatically get re-elected but we got thrown out. There was no way back in those days. I cried my heart out. We went into this Northern Premier League. The first game at home was Netherfield and naturally you think, 'Oh, well, we'll go straight back,' and Netherfield beat us 2–0 at home. We went to Valley Parade in '73–74 season and then it was the '74 season when we finished completely. We went into bankruptcy for £60,000. That's all, £60,000.

A Club with Ideas – Coventry City

Jim Hamill: King's Lynn was the start of it. We got hammered into the ground in a Cup match against King's Lynn [November 1961], and Mr Robins, the senior man, sacked the lot and brought in Jimmy Hill.

John Haddon: It was completely different to anything that had gone before, in the whole of football really. Never had you seen anyone like Jimmy Hill before, and he did a tremendous amount of good, as a manager, for Coventry City. He put us on the map. He may be fortunate that he had a very active supporters' club behind him at that time.

Jimmy Hill: Derek Henderson, a journalist on the local paper, wrote about 'the Sky Blues' one Saturday night and I said, 'Hey, that's a great name for us, let's latch on to it and promote it,' so everything became Sky Blue. We had Radio Sky Blue and, in the days when people used to come long before the kick-off, we had a radio programme which would run from three-quarters of an hour before the game up until the kick-off, with events before the match. We did all sorts of things. We had women's netball, dogs jumping over fences and things that wouldn't damage the ground, but we entertained them and Charles Harrold, who was a professional broadcaster, was superb in that role.

Charles Harrold: I joined them sometime around August 1963. Sky Blue Radio was what other people would call a PA system, an announcement system, a Tannoy system, but it was a lot more than that because I remember Jimmy Hill used to believe that it was our one really great form of communication with the people. Before the game we had a record request programme, which was part of the entertainment, but all the time we were passing information to them, about the team and the players and so on. To give you a little example, if a chap got injured during the game and he could take no further part, as soon as we were able to establish the extent of the injury, we would tell them. We used to feel that if a person came to the game, we didn't want him to go home and discover things that he didn't know about because he'd been at the game. We monitored radio programmes. Towards the end of the season, when other results were vital to us, we set up arrangements and had direct phones through to press men on these grounds, and every 20 minutes or half an hour, they'd give us a score. We had a little chime. Whenever I was going to use the Sky Blue Radio, we had a chime, the first few bars of the Sky Blues song. When the ball went out of play – we never made an announcement while the game was going on – this chime would go and the whole ground would go absolutely silent, because they knew there was something good coming. Then we would tell 'em the score and the whole place would go mad and that would set the team going more, and so on. Sometimes something would cross Jimmy Hill's mind while the game was going on, and he'd lean over to me and say, 'Look, tell 'em so-and-so.'

Jimmy Hill: Then there was the Sky Blue Express. We had problems on the railway at that time; it wasn't hooliganism, it was called vandalism. Those who were travelling to watch matches were breaking up railway carriages, so it was suggested to us by the head of the local railway system that it might be a good idea if the club booked the train and paid for it. We called it the Sky Blue Express and we garlanded it up with bits of sky blue and flags and things like that and we wired each carriage for sound so we could keep them interested in the club news, and then they began to play bingo on the train. Then one day we had a group in the guard's van so that they could dance on the way to the match, all ideas to stop vandalism, so it wasn't just a gimmick.

Charles Harrold: I can remember the greatest trip of all. We went to Preston and the coach at the beginning of the train was an old freight van that BR had let us have, and we cleaned it up and decorated it and that was the bar and the canteen and whatever. In the centre of the train was my control wagon with all the other carriages, and our last carriage was another freight van which we dressed up and it was a disco. We had a rock band here from Coventry and people danced all the blinking way to Preston. What a train!

Jimmy Hill: The Sky Blue Song was another thing – 'Let's all sing together, play up Sky Blues' – which was written by John Camkin and me one night over a glass of gin and tonic.

We used the Eton boating song which is not a shouty chorusy song. When it was sung, when we were losing at Highfield Road, it would almost make you cry. One of the most enjoyable moments of my life was the Cup Final [1987] when they beat Tottenham and I heard the song sung at Wembley. The most disappointing moment of my life was when we decided to let the whole city know when we'd scored a goal. We tried to get a firework, or something that would go up and make a noise over the city, so that everybody on Saturday afternoon would know when the home side scored. We went to Brock's, we went everywhere, and in the end they couldn't supply us with anything. Do you know how many goals we scored in the first game? Five, against Crystal Palace, and I cried, because we would have got headlines. I still never forgive those who make fireworks.

Charles Harrold: In those days programmes were little bits of paper kept together with a staple, weren't they? They were a penny or tuppence. They weren't worth any more. We set about creating a magazine. It was a magazine programme. We developed the shop, which was a kind of a hole in a corner when I first came here. We rebuilt an area and made a really big shop, and that was highly popular. We had a Sky Blue Club which was open to supporters. I think everybody in the club was trying a new way of running a football club.

Jimmy Hill: We needed to find a way to get one more mention in the *Coventry Evening Telegraph* of George Curtis and Mick Kearns's testimonial against Liverpool. George came into the office – a very persuasive man, George Curtis – and said, 'Are we getting anything in the *Telegraph* tonight because it's a once-a-lifetime chance for a player to get money.' I said, 'Well, George, they've done very well for us.' He said, 'If you rode your horse round, we could get a mention.' Well, there's no argument to that, so I said,

'All right,' got on to my friend Ted Edgar, who provided a horse for me and his England showjumping jacket and hat. There were 25,000 people there and they saw the manager on a horse, going round before the match started.

Charles Harrold: He was a spectacular sight, going round the running-track, and behind him, in a giant Rolls-Royce, was the chairman, as proud as he was. So it was an extraordinary night, and I remember Bill Shankly was standing next to me by the tunnel, and he looked at this and he watched Jimmy Hill going round on this horse and he turned to me and he said, 'Well, I've seen it all now, haven't I?'

Insolvent – Chelsea

Brian Mears: We'd been ambitious enough to want to build a new stadium, and the first part of it was the East Stand, and that was completed in August 1974 in time for the first game against Carlisle. We started off by losing 3–0 at home to Carlisle and eventually we were relegated in '75. That was a disaster, financially, because that stand had cost us £2½ million, and we still owed the bank at least £1½ million. Eventually we sold Ray Wilkins to Manchester United for £900,000, but we had to face up to the fact that we were insolvent. So we called a creditors' meeting in the main restaurant in the new stand, and there were probably 140 to 150 creditors, including the bank, the Inland Revenue and Customs & Excise and so on. There was only one way to deal with this and that was to stand up, as I did, and say to them, 'Ladies and gentlemen, I'm very sorry that you're here on this occasion, when we have to tell you that we are unable to pay our debts. If any of the creditors in this room wishes to put us into bankruptcy then so be it.' I sat down to dead silence. Eventually somebody stood up and said, 'No, I think I speak for all of us when I say we're prepared to give you time to repay.' I admire them for not pulling the plug, but you can understand what would have happened if a company had done. They wouldn't have been the most popular in the country, particularly in London. So we were able to repay our debts, and look at the new stand now. Look how much money it's generating now. It's incredible. Huge amounts of money with the restaurant, the prices of the seats, the bars, the sponsors' days and so on. So I'm very proud of that stand, and hopefully I left Chelsea a better place than when I found it.

Bringing Money into the Game

John Haddon: If you go back to 1960 and 1961, the [Coventry City] balance sheets for those years say, 'Without the financial help of the supporters' club we would be in grave financial debt,' and that's actually on their balance sheet. In those days we were putting about £4,000 a year in.

Arthur Would: Eventually we came to the involvement derived from the pools. We agreed to license [copyright] the use of the fixtures, as had to be done. The case was fought with the pools promoters and won by the League. From then we derived the income from the pools promoters. The effect of that, of course, was that Grimsby Town's fixtures were as good as Arsenal's fixtures in terms of pools income.

Barrie Gill: I went on from television to become the marketing manager of Ford of Britain, and one of the first things I did was persuade Ford to become a sponsor of the England team for the 1970 World Cup in Mexico. We decided that football suited our profile. Every one of that squad got a Cortina, and it was done in the England colours with the England badge. I'm a Leeds United fan and Paul Reaney, who was in the squad, broke his leg playing at West Ham the month before he should have set off, but we actually made another car and gave him a car, which he never forgot. The day after we announced the sponsorship we had trouble at home at the Halewood Plant because the unions wondered why we were spending this money on football, and we had to explain what the coverage meant in terms of pounds, shillings and pence and how it would help them. We created the Ford Fair Play League [1970–71], where every team would get points for the goals scored (because there had to be a plus side) but would lose points for a booking, for a penalty against them, etc. To our horror, every month Oldham won it. They got more and more money and built a stand with it.

Denis Howell: We set up the Football Trust [in 1974], again in quite a surprising manner. Alan Hardaker brought Cecil Moores of Littlewoods to see me and to say that the Spot the Ball football competition wasn't paying any tax, and football pools were paying too much tax (30-odd per cent). We had just put through the Safety of Sports Grounds Act [to become law in 1975], which followed from the terrible tragedy at Glasgow Rangers [1971] and the Wheatley Report [1972]. The government took the view – and the football people didn't like this – that if you attract the public on to your premises, you have an overriding responsibility for their safety. The Safety of Sports Grounds Act was based on that principle, but I had got no money to help them do this job. So when Hardaker brought Cecil Moores to see me it triggered off a thought-process. Moores had said to me, 'I'll give you seven and a half per cent of the take,' which seemed a good chunk. I went and saw Dennis Healey [Chancellor of the Exchequer]. Dennis Healey confirmed to me that he had no knowledge of Spot the Ball coupons, and no intention of putting a tax on it. I said, 'Can you give me any money for Safety of Sports Grounds?' He said, 'No.' So I said, 'Well, I can get my own money if you agree not to tax Spot the Ball,' so we did that little deal, and I went back and sent for Moores and Hardaker. Cecil Moores was overjoyed

Sir Alf Ramsey training with the England players, November 1970. *(Popperfoto)*

England vs Poland, 1973. England trainer Harold Shepherdson consoles Emlyn Hughes at the end of the game, while Kevin Keegan and Norman Hunter leave the pitch. *(Colorsport)*

A confrontation between a football fan and a policeman at the Chelsea vs
Tottenham Hotspur game, April 1975. *(Hulton Deutsch)*

England fans in Switzerland, June 1981. (*Hulton Deutsch*)

Phil Neal and Alan Hansen hold the European Cup trophy at Wembley in 1978 after Liverpool's second successive triumph in the competition *(Colorsport)*

Brian Clough and Peter Taylor, who steered Nottingham Forest to successive European Cup Final wins in 1979 and 1980. *(Colorsport)*

Ron Greenwood, manager of England 1977-82. *(Colorsport)*

Bryan Robson in action against France during the 1982 World Cup Finals.
(Colorsport)

England's Terry Fenwick heads for goal during the 1986 World Cup quarter-final against Argentina. *(Colorsport)*

Bobby Robson, England 1982-90.
(Popperfoto)

The 1990 England World Cup squad, before the third-place match with Italy.
(Colorsport)

Paul Gascoigne. *(Colorsport)*

Workmen remove fencing at Spurs' ground White Hart Lane in April 1989, shortly after the Hillsborough Disaster. *(Popperfoto)*

The new Kop, Anfield, Liverpool 1994. *(Colorsport)*

and promptly upped it to 10 per cent. I think it got to 14 or 15 per cent before VAT came in. That was the first big move after the World Cup to get substantial money in for all Football League clubs. The Football Trust was set up by the football authorities. The money's been extremely well used, I think. The Trust has done a first-class job.

Derek Dougan: When I went to Kettering I was appointed head cook and bottle-washer, the first chief executive ever to be appointed in football. I realized that money was very, very tight and I was looking at all sorts of ways to bring in money. The local tyre company was called Kettering Tyres – 'KT', like Kettering Town – and I had meetings with them and talked them into sponsoring the club for the remainder of the season. It was January 1976. By that time I was into sports retailing and I got a manufacturer to make me a special shirt with 'Kettering Tyres' on it, and also I had them make me another shirt with 'KT' on it. The result was that I got an awful lot of publicity because I had looked up the FA Handbook and in there it said that they had actually thought about the introduction of sponsorship and names on shirts, but they had never ratified it. The next thing was that the FA came on to the club secretary and said, 'Do you know that you can't do this?' The result was that they brought me up before the FA disciplinary hearing. They slapped our wrists, let us off without any fine, and simply said, 'If you do that again, we've got the power to actually close your ground', and I couldn't believe it. The next day they actually did a deal and allowed the competing Finalists to wear Admiral on the shirts because they'd gone into a commercial sponsorship deal with Admiral, the sports manufacturers. And I thought, 'Well, there's one rule for the little plebs and there's one rule for the FA, and it's par for the course.'

Alex Fynn: Once upon a time I was important in the advertising business. I worked on the Health Education Council account, and the main part of that account was anti-smoking. I had the idea that if we sponsored a football team we could break the ban on shirt advertising. At that time there was no shirt advertising for televised football, and I thought that Spurs, who needed a sponsor, would be perfect for the anti-smoking message. So we went to talk to Tottenham and it never happened because I think the officials at the Health Education Council caught Ossie [Ardiles] and Ricky [Villa] having a quick surreptitious drag, but I think we sufficiently impressed Spurs that they thought there might be something in this marketing lark after all. They came to see us at Saatchi and Saatchi and we persuaded them that it was worthwhile trying to promote attendances. The thing about football is that it's inconsistent. One week you can be good, one week you can be bad, but at the beginning of a season expectations are high and advertising can fuel those expectations. We persuaded Spurs to run a television-and-radio campaign to promote season-ticket sales and attendance at the opening games, and it was very successful. The selling-idea was: 'This Saturday Spurs are fielding 30,000 against Coventry, make sure you're one of the team.' The advertising had the players coming out of the tunnel and behind the team were the fans. In fact, one of the fans was a grandmother called Mrs Ridlington, and she became so popular that when the team didn't do well, later on in the season, you would have the cry from the stands: 'Bring on Mrs Ridlington'.

Barrie Gill: In 1982 we were one of the agencies asked to present how we would handle central sponsorship for the Football League. We made our presentation and we won the right to create and market central sponsorships for the Football League, and about three weeks after we were appointed we persuaded the National Dairy Council to come in with the Milk Cup [1982–83]. The press picked it up so well that when Liverpool beat Tottenham Hotspur [in the 1982 League Cup Final], the *Sunday Times* had a cartoon of the then Tottenham manager putting out a note saying, 'No milk today, thanks.' The nice thing about the Milk Cup and why we wanted it more than anything else was that every little club got a home game in the home-and-away first round. So we were able then to market with the dairies. At the same time we were persuading Canon to become the first-ever sponsor of the League. Halfway through our negotiations football agreed to shirt sponsor, if you remember, which was a major problem. The first season that Canon sponsored the League, JVC and Sharp, i.e. Arsenal and Manchester United, were battling for the Championship! Liverpool had led the way with shirt sponsorship with Crown Paints, so it was getting more commercial. A major meeting was held in Birmingham, a sort of football blueprint for the future where we presented our sponsorship plans, some of which were knocked back because all the clubs wouldn't agree. It sounds familiar, doesn't it? Two chairmen stood up and said, 'Do we want these people? Do we need them? Why deal with them?' And Jimmy Hill stood up and said, 'I think we should thank CSS for finding us the first-ever sponsor,' and I'll never forget him doing that. The first night I heard 'Here's James Alexander-Gordon, Canon League, Division One' was one of the most exciting moments of my whole life. The Canon League was an unmitigated success. They carried on for three years, by which time they'd got from 18 per cent to 80 per cent awareness, and they are an object lesson in how to end the sponsorship. They made a presentation on what Canon had achieved, what they'd done, how well it had worked, to pave the way for another sponsor. Unfortunately, football really was in a mess at that time and the sponsor we found was *Today*. The idea was that *Today* would become the paper of record for football, but, if you remember, they changed ownership.

The Whole Club

Graham Taylor: My apprenticeship, so to speak, at Lincoln, which had been for five years, had taught me to be more interested in the club as a whole as opposed to just the team, because at any one time a team can win or lose with things outside of your control. When Watford came back and showed a further interest I agreed to meet Elton John and I chose to go to Watford because I had a gut feeling that things might happen there, but it also enabled me to have a look at the whole club, every aspect of the club, and be part of it. I'd done a lot of similar things at Lincoln, where I took the players to the people and would organize visits to where our supporters worked. I remember at Lincoln I used to go on to the Tannoy system before a home game, half an hour or so before the kick-off, and tell the supporters my feelings about the previous game we'd played and what we were looking for and what we were expecting today, so you'd got a great togetherness. I carried those things on at Watford and I found that people generally responded to that. We appointed a girl called Caroline Gillies as our marketing manager, and we appointed promotions and public relations officers in our very early days. We were very, very family orientated. I think I'm right in saying that as a Third Division club Watford were the first club to have a family enclosure. It became special for a period of time and it set a tone and I think a lot of the very big clubs now automatically work at these things.

23

'Liverpool were a multi-national side'

A Run of Club Successes in Europe, 1977–85

The first British team to win the European Cup were Celtic in 1967. A year later Manchester United became the first English team to take that trophy. English clubs followed this with success in the Inter-Cities Fairs Cup (later the UEFA Cup) – six successive wins between 1968 and 1973. Between 1963 and 1971, English teams also won the European Cup Winners' Cup on four occasions. But the European Cup itself proved elusive for a period after the Manchester United win. Then, in 1977, came a watershed which saw English clubs consistently winning the European Cup: Liverpool (1977, 1978, 1981 and 1984), Nottingham Forest (1979 and 1980) and Aston Villa (1982). Here we look at Liverpool and Nottingham Forest.

The Shankly Foundations, 1959–74

Denis Law: He [Bill Shankly] asked for extra money to buy a player at Huddersfield and the board refused, or they didn't have it, or whatever, and then he went to Liverpool. We all wondered – had he stayed at Huddersfield could Huddersfield have been the great team that Liverpool became through the sixties, seventies and into the eighties?

Tommy Smith: Shankly was football. Say you went in during the morning and said, 'Good morning, Boss.' 'Aye, son, good day for football.' And, if it was raining, 'Aye, son, good day for skidding the ball.' Everything was associated with football. Our favourite used to be maybe on a Thursday morning. We'd be doing something and hear, 'Put it down, boys.' We'd all say, 'Well, that's it, five-a-side in the car-park.' We'd go in the car-park, there'd be 10 groundstaff lads, Bob Paisley, Joe Fagan, Reuben Bennett, the Boss, and about three bin-wagons used to pull up outside and all these bin-men used to get out and play footie on the side in the car-park.

Pat Crerand: When you look at Bill Shankly and Jock Stein and Matt Busby, coming from the mining areas just outside Glasgow, they had a great belief in people. They were brought up real working-class people and they had to look after one another, and I think that was probably part of it because they had a great belief in football teams, that those 10 people you went out on the pitch with were your friends and nobody else.

Larry Lloyd: I think we were playing Ipswich, Liverpool versus Ipswich at Anfield, and we were top of the table, Ipswich were near the bottom. We were already in the dressing-room getting ready and Shankly just stood there watching all the Ipswich players file past, into their dressing-room. The next thing he burst into our dressing-room and said, 'Right, that's it, you'll have no problem today. I've just seen a centre-half whose glasses are like milkbottles. They're that thick, he's blind. I've just seen a little boy that plays midfield, his legs are like that, he won't be able to run.' So it got to ten to three – three o'clock kick-off, of course – and we were all ready to go out, fired up, adrenalin flowing and everything. He said, 'Take your shirts off.' 'What?' 'Take your shirts off.' So we pulled the shirts off. He said, 'Throw 'em on the floor.' So we threw them on the floor. 'This is a new one,' I thought. 'We've not heard this one before.' He said, 'Now, you lot go and have a bath, I'll throw these shirts out on the field and the shirts will beat Ipswich by themselves.' In the cold light of day you think, 'What a stupid story.' You tell that to anyone not involved in football, they think, 'Dear me, that's silly,' but, no, it seemed to work.

Tom Saunders: Well, you see, he was the simple man who would have made a great teacher because he had a wonderful way with words. His enthusiasm was enormous, but he didn't understand the jargon as it came into the game. I well remember him one morning pinning me up against the wall down there underneath where the dressing-rooms are and saying to me, 'Tom, what the bloody hell are they talking about, this overlapping full-back?' And I would explain in simple terms to him what that meant, and he said, 'Well, what's new about that? We've been doing that for donkey's years.' So perhaps it's a simple game and perhaps we're complicating it too much.

Larry Lloyd: Shankly wasn't really one for team talks but we had one this particular Friday morning and he had a little football field with magnetic men. He had a set of 11 red magnets and a set of white magnets. Obviously we were red, Liverpool. He was going through all the movements – nobody knew what he was on about, to be quite honest – and Bob Paisley, then his assistant, said, 'Boss, wait a minute, I can count 11 red magnets but I can only count 10 white ones.' He'd kept one in his hand and he threw it across the dressing-room and said, 'Well, he can't play anyway.'

Tommy Smith: I spoke to a chap about 12 months ago on business, and he said, 'You don't remember me, I worked as a student in the Holiday Inn.' I said, 'Oh, aye.' Even for home games we used to go away Friday night and a lot of the young lads were just married and had kids and they wanted a decent night's sleep. He said, 'Can you remember, you always used to have a bit of an argument on match-day?' I said, 'No, not really.' He said, 'Well, we used to get told by Joe Fagan and Bob Paisley to give you the wrong meal. If you wanted steak, we'd give you fish, and by the time you left the hotel, you'd tear the head off anybody.'

Ian St John: The training at Liverpool was devised by Bill Shankly and I think he went back to his roots of schoolboy and youth football, kicking a ball around the streets. We had shooting boards and we had what they called the 'sweat-box', four goals in a square, and if he was going to punish us in any way we went in the 'sweat-box'. But it was terrific practice. You'd go in as a pair and one guy would hit it and it would come off the boards and the second guy would hit it, so you had the four boards you could hit. You could volley it sideways, you could let it go past you and volley it to the one behind, and you worked like in a squash game. We worked in short spells, maybe a couple of minutes, and it was great, developing great kicking, great volleying and great timing. We used to play little heading games as well, and little two-a-sides. It was just your own boyhood games again. Shankly was ahead of the game, and I think that's why Liverpool have been so successful over the years. It was Shankly who set it all up and the whole thing just carried through.

Tommy Smith: Shanks loved the kids of 15 and 16 because he used to play five-a-side with them. He taught you good habits in the five-a-sides at Melwood. If you went to fetch the ball behind the goal, he would insist that somebody else followed you, and on the way back you did one-twos to get to know your players, which way you kick a ball and that. To my mind those little things, which don't sound a great deal, meant an awful lot.

The Key to Liverpool's Success

Ian St John: The mix has got to be right, of the Scots and the English, and throw in a Welshman, Irishman, whatever. I always think the English have very good, upright, strong professionals, dedicated professionals. The good English players, the ones who win Championships, are good lads and reliable, and I think you need the Celts, I think you need the Scots, maybe the Irish, the Welsh, to add the little bit of something else in the mixture. It's like baking a cake, and the extra ingredient to make the really good cake has got to be that we [the Scots] are probably more flamboyant, more fiery than the English.

Alan Hansen: Liverpool were a multi-national side, and they were all very, very competent players, they all had good techniques. The whole system was based on 'pass the ball and move' and 'keep a hold of it', and we had the players that could do that. I think if you play week in, week out, with certain players, then you get to know the system you're playing, you get to know the players you're playing alongside, and we were a very, very capable outfit.

Ian St John: I always remember Bob [Paisley] saying, after we'd been in Europe a couple of years, 'What we've got to pick up from these fellas is that we can't go and win the ball individually, we're to win the ball collectively.' You couldn't go chasing in there expecting to get the ball, because these fellas would just knock it around, kill you off and move on. We never ever went for the ball individually, we would always go on instruction from the back-up lads, say, 'Okay get 'em, push 'em this way, that way,' and we would crowd around a ball to try and stop them doing that. And so we learned that from them. We also learned to keep the ball more. In our early days at Liverpool we were very direct with our football – 'Let's get at them and surge' – but we became patient through European football, knocking the ball around ('Don't give it away, let's keep it'). Going away from home, it was 'Kill the crowd [noise], take your time.'

Alan Hansen: Right from pre-season training, everything was done with a ball. Obviously you did some hard stuff, but the whole system was geared to passing and moving. You used to have a stupid thing – well, I thought it was stupid (at first) – where if you passed it and didn't move two or three yards you were penalized, and that soon taught you that you had to move. Ronnie Moran would be standing there, shouting, 'Right, you didn't move, you lost the ball.' When you played it, it was 'move two yards to the right' or 'two yards to the left'.

Tom Saunders: Training is one thing and tactics are one thing, but really it is about quality players, which they had in those days. You would never see here, for example, a player coming anywhere near the bench looking for instructions of any sort. They were the top men and once the game started they got on with it, and they were not restricted. Many people came here to watch training sessions in those years thinking there was some particular kind of magic, and they'd come down to Melwood and we'd allow them to watch and, after the training session, they would feel as though they'd been cheated. They would say, 'Well, you mustn't be showing us it all. You must be hiding something from us.' The whole method was simple. It was based on a rapport with management, good management, good players and the freedom to express themselves.

Alan Hansen: Bob Paisley used to say the first two yards of professional football was in the head. When he first said that, I thought, 'What a load of rubbish', but the more I played the game, the more I realized he was spot on. If you're quick up there [in the head], you've got a chance. Dalglish wasn't the fastest in the world, but when he was at his peak you could play it in four or five yards either side of him and he would collect it. Now just imagine how much confidence that gave the player in possession when he was passing.

Nottingham Forest

Alan Hill: When Brian Clough came [in January 1975], the club were possibly on their way down to the Third Division. They finished 16th in the League, and I thought, 'Something's got to happen for this club to survive.' Brian had a presence about him, and he paid a lot of attention to little details. He looked after the washing-ladies and tea-ladies and treated everybody the same. You could see the confidence building up in the club and then he started bringing in better players, quality players, and it started to snowball. After the second season, Peter Taylor came along, and they were a great partnership. Brian would fire the bullets and Peter would go in and sort it all out.

Brian Glanville: Clough was an astonishing manager but very much in his own way. He was accused of being a bully, he was accused of ruling by fear, but it doesn't alter the fact that he had incredible success, and most of the really famous players who've played for him will still absolutely swear by him. He behaved very much like a pre-war manager – you didn't see him much – and therefore when you did see him it was an occasion.

Larry Lloyd: I think all good managers – and I emphasize Clough was a good manager in his day – tend to concentrate on your strengths as opposed to your weaknesses. In my case, I could head the ball and I could tackle, but I couldn't run, so when I got the ball I gave it to someone who could run. I gave it to somebody like John Robertson and Archie Gemmill and Martin O'Neill, who could pass the ball. I knew my limitations. He had someone else playing next to you who would cover your weakness, and perhaps my strength would cover his weakness, and that's all about good management.

John Robertson: When Brian Clough first came into my football club, everyone, at that time, picked on all the things that I *couldn't* do, as far as football was concerned – I couldn't tackle, I couldn't head, I wasn't the quickest person – but it didn't seem to worry Cloughie at all and he concentrated on the things that I was good at. He was the one that moved me from midfield to left wing, and from then on I went from strength to strength, because he knew that I could go past people, he knew the final product was good, and he was more positive, rather than worrying about the things I couldn't do.

Peter Shilton: Funny enough, tactics never really came into it. We played a certain way at Forest. Everybody knew their jobs and we basically let the opposition worry about us. Oh, certain games, we maybe took the wingers back a little bit, from 4-2-4 to 4-4-2, and let them come on to us and then hit them on the break. But we never went into anything elaborate. If we played well, and everybody did their jobs well, we knew we were good enough to get results.

Larry Lloyd: We were stood in the tunnel waiting to come out of the Bernabéu stadium there in Madrid [1980 European Cup Final], and, as it happens, I was lined up next to Kevin Keegan [Hamburg]. Having known Kevin for five years when I was at Liverpool, playing in the same team as him, I said, 'Hello, how are you doing, Kev,' you know, the usual small talk you make, because we got on fairly well at Liverpool. I said, 'Kevin, I've gotta tell you, see him at the back, Kenny Burns?' Now, you've got to picture Ken, bless him. He's no teeth and he's chewing a bit of raw meat. I said, 'Kev, his job is to murder you,' so I tried to throw that in at Kevin. Whether he took it or not, as the game went on, Burnsy was giving Kevin Keegan so much stick, he [Keegan] was going farther and farther back and he ended up playing next to his own centre-back. As a tactic, the little conversation Kenny and I had had – 'I'll look after the big boy, you look after Keegan' – had worked. We didn't really have to be told that. We knew.

Viv Anderson: I think European football suited us because of the players we had. They were all comfortable on the ball, they all could pass and move. We thought, 'Just another game in Europe and we'll go out and beat these with no danger.'

Peter Shilton: Every game was treated the same. We used to have a team meeting on maybe the Friday morning, but that sometimes involved the players just sitting in a room, having a drink or whatever they wanted to have after training, and maybe Brian Clough and Pete Taylor would come down after an hour and say, 'That's the team and we'll see you tomorrow.' Other times they'd come in and they'd laugh and joke or they'd bring certain points up, maybe about the way you live and the way you prepare yourself and the sort of things you eat. They had a unique style. They didn't get too elaborate in terms of tactics. But if they felt that the opposition had one or two weaknesses that we needed to exploit, they brought them out.

Larry Lloyd: I think I was on my first or second day's training when I came from Coventry. At Coventry they had a wonderful training ground and all the facilities, and we were down at Holme Road, the Forest training ground, and it was just a ploughed field on the banks of the Trent. It was all stinging nettles and everything along the path. 'Take your tracksuit bottoms off,' said Clough. 'Pair up, jump on his back, pair up, piggy-back.' So I had another lad on my back. 'Right, run through those nettles.' The stinging nettles are bringing up white lumps, horrible, and we had to run through them. Nobody refused to do it. I looked around and I thought, 'I better do it as well, but why?'

Alan Hill: He'd have them going through cow-pats, in and out of trees, anything to make training different. One particular day we were walking along the embankment of the River Trent and he says, 'Right, first one to the bottom step and back,' and it was a bit icy and I think Birtles went head first in the River Trent.

John Robertson: When I played for Brian Clough, I just wanted to get a 'well done' from him. When I was playing, if I ever did anything right he always used to get his little hand up and he'd do that to me and call me and when that happened I used to feel 10 foot tall.

Larry Lloyd: John needed that 'well done', he needed that pat on the back. I couldn't give two monkeys whether he said 'well done' to me, and he knew that and he used to go the other way, and give me a rollocking. Clough knew I used to fall for it and, running through that tunnel, my attitude was 'I'll show that big so-and-so.' I didn't need a pat on the back, I needed that wind-up to go out and show him what I could do, but that was once again the value of the man.

Peter Shilton: Brian Clough and Peter Taylor were a little bit unusual in preparations. I think one story was that we played Liverpool in the second leg of the first round of the European Cup [in September 1978]. We'd beaten them 2–0 at home, and we travelled up to Liverpool on the morning of the game, ready to have lunch, a sleep in the afternoon and go to the game. And just as we were getting outside Liverpool, Brian Clough turned round and said, 'Does anybody want a beer?' which any other football club in the country just wouldn't contemplate. But one or two players said, 'Oh, I wouldn't mind a beer, Boss.' When we were having lunch, he said, 'If anybody wants a glass of wine, you can have a glass of wine or two,' and they did. Not every player, obviously, some didn't want to drink. It was his way of making the players have a good sleep in the afternoon and taking the pressure off and saying, 'Well, look, nothing's too serious.' And we went out and we got a 0–0 draw and ended up in the Final of the European Cup.

Larry Lloyd: We were playing Queen's Park Rangers in the FA Cup [1978]. We were drawn away. We drew at Loftus Road, and on the Tuesday, the replay here at the City Ground, we drew again, so that meant there was a toss of a coin to decide where we were going to play the second replay. We won the toss and it had to be played on that Thursday. Clough was on one of his several holidays in Majorca – I think he used to have three or four a year – so Peter Taylor was in charge. It was a Thursday night, it was twenty past seven, 7.30 kick-off, no sign of Clough because he's away, isn't he? Suddenly the dressing-room door literally came off the hinges, and he stood there and he pointed his finger at every one of us. He said, 'I have just broken up my holiday to come back to gee you up, thank you very much,' and he walked out. No team talk. We won the game 3–1.

Peter Shilton: He used to like a game of squash on a Saturday morning and sometimes you'd come in for a match at two o'clock and you'd find him sitting in the dressing-room with his shorts on, and his rugby shirt on and he'd just come out of the shower, and he would look so relaxed about it, and then he'd shoot off up to his office, and then come back to the dressing-room just before the kick-off.

A lot of it was psychological. A lot of it was just the way Brian Clough was, I suppose. These days you get sport psychologists and this type of thing, but basically it's all the same philosophy in terms of being able to work out players' mental attitude and being able to relax them at the right times.

Viv Anderson: I'd just dislocated my knee and I got a phone call at four o'clock in the afternoon: 'Come to the ground.' So I go to the ground and he sits me down and a lad called Mark Proctor, and he said, 'I want you two to go to Derby on loan.' Being born and bred in Nottingham, I said, 'Well, Nottingham lads don't go to Derby, that's the last place they go. They'd rather go to Timbuktu than Derby.' He said, 'Well, you're going anyway.' I said, 'Well, I don't want to go.' He said, 'Well, we're going to Pete Taylor's house and you can tell him to his face.' So he drove us to Pete Taylor's house and we had a cup of tea with his wife and he said, 'I'd love you to come and play for a month, blah, blah, blah.' I said, 'I'd rather stay at Forest Reserves and get fit there, Pete, but thanks for the offer.' So he went back in to tell Mr Clough and Mr Clough said, 'Well, that's it then. You're not coming back with me, you'll have to get your own way home.' This is at seven o'clock at night, it's pitch black. I'm saying, 'You're joking?' He says, 'No, you get your own way home.' So me and Mark Proctor ended up going over back fields, climbing over fences. We ended up in a pub about nine o'clock at night, sitting there. We ring a cab, I get home and my wife goes, 'Where the hell have you been?' I says, 'It's a long story.'

John Robertson: In the late seventies and early eighties a British team was winning the European Cup nearly every year and I don't know why. England as a nation hadn't done really that well, but the teams that were winning European Cups were of mixed nationality – Scotland, England, Irish and Welsh. I don't know, maybe it's a case for a Great Britain team.

24

'A forward-thinking, forward-passing, forward-moving game'

Coaching Ideas of the 1980s

The 1980s debate about tactics centred on what became known, rather simplistically, as 'the long-ball game'. The best-known instigators of 'direct football' were Graham Taylor at Watford, Dave Bassett at Wimbledon and Sheffield United, Steve Coppell at Crystal Palace and Jack Charlton with the Ireland national team. All these managers have achieved success with limited resources.

The Winning Way?

Charles Hughes: I qualified as a teacher at Loughborough College, and then taught at schools in Lancashire. I became a qualified FA Coach whilst I was at Loughborough College, then I started doing courses for the FA during vacation time when I was teaching. I was invited to apply for the post of assistant director of coaching, manager of the England amateur team and manager of the Great Britain Olympic

293

team, and I got that appointment, and started on 1 January 1964. We had considerable success with the England amateur team until 1974, when everyone was declared 'players' and the amateur team ceased to exist. We played 77 games and we lost only 12 of those games and I think won 49. I started analysing football when I came to the FA in 1964, and I looked at all the teams who'd been successful in the World Cup between 1966 and 1986 – Brazil and Argentina, Italy, West Germany (as they then were), ourselves and Holland. We also had a look at Liverpool. We analysed those games to find out what strategies seemed to be most effective. Not systems of play. Not whether they played with wingers or whether they played with sweepers or whether they had man-to-man marking or whether they didn't, but the general strategic concept both in attack and defence. The conclusion is that the whole object of the game is based in this simple concept: that it's a forward-thinking, forward-passing, forward-moving game, but it has to be done under control and therefore you have to develop the techniques that make that possible.

Charles Reep: In 1990 there appeared in the FA Cup Final programme a whole page advertising the FA book with the winning formula. The public were informed that Charles Hughes was a pioneer of performance analysis, that he'd done all this great work and that he was the man that had done the whole thing. I'd been at it for 50 years before that and I'd got indisputable evidence that I was the pioneer. I wrote to the FA and demanded an apology. I had a letter back from Kelly to say that he was sorry but he couldn't see his way to publishing it. Now I had the choice of taking the FA to the law. I made inquiries and discovered I should have to employ a barrister and the costs would be enormous. With my income as a pensioner I couldn't possibly face the dangers. I had to let it go.

Jack Charlton: Ninety per cent of goals are when

something's done quickly. You get more oohs and aahs from a fella who pulls out of his situation and hits a ball from the right-hand side of the field to the left-hand side to a guy in a good position, who pulls it down well and takes the ball and exploits the situation, than you ever get from all your passing movements of 10 or 20 passes across the back. Be clever across the front, but don't be clever across the back, because that's where it'll cost you games.

John Cartwright: Charles Hughes's theory is that the quicker you get the ball forward, the more pressure you can put on opposing defences, and, by not having so many passes in your attacking play, the amount of chances of making a mistake during that passing sequence is reduced, and in some respects he's absolutely right. But the problem is that we're dealing with human beings, and human beings are not machines that can go on for ever and ever running at the same pace and doing the same things all the time. His football is dehumanizing in many aspects. We require, in this country, more art, skill and grace in our game, and imagination. The imagination part of Charles Hughes's theory is non-existent.

Charles Hughes: By and large, about 85 or 90 per cent of goals are scored from five consecutive passes or less. Now five consecutive passes is quite a lot of passes. I'm not saying, and nor is the analysis indicating, that teams will not score from more than five passes, but it won't occur very often. The evidence is that when you get into high passing movements, consecutive passing movements, you're actually decreasing your chances of scoring.

John Cartwright: He's right that most goals are scored from a shorter series of passes, but if you take that theory onwards, I mean, are we then going to say that most goals are scored with, say, one pass which means they should just kick the ball forward? That you cut out any qualities of skill and understanding in play that people want to see in midfield and from back positions, and just have a game where you have six foot sixes or six foot sevens playing up against six foot eights or six foot nines, and the ball is constantly kicked backwards and forwards up and down the pitch? If this is the sort of game style that we want to see, fine, but I don't think the majority of people want to see that.

Charles Hughes: I think so many denigrate what I'm saying. They would say it's all about 'the long-ball game' or 'kick and rush' or words to that effect, and that is absolute nonsense, unless they're saying the Brazilians and the West Germans and Italy and Holland and Argentina have all done what they're saying and not what I'm saying, but I've actually analysed what they've done to win their World Championships. Now they may not agree with me but the facts are there for all to see. You'll find that a very high incidence of goals are scored from regained possessions in the attacking third of the field. Some have exaggerated and reduced it all to the long-ball game, and I do urge people not be fooled by that but to look deeper and say, 'What's behind this? How have all these teams won the World Cup?'

Bobby Robson: I got along with Charles Hughes very well indeed. He's a good colleague, very intelligent, a very able person. He had good ideas, a way of thinking, and saw football in a slightly different way. He was a man of statistics and he could say, 'Well, if you do this and this, you will achieve that.' He would tell you to concentrate on your set-plays. He would tell you also that getting crosses in was very important to the game. I didn't agree with everything he said, but I agree with some of what he said.

John Cartwright: Direct play forces people to knock the ball forward at every opportunity, right or wrong, and because of this we do tend to give the ball away when there are many opportunities to keep possession of the ball. We are probably one of the worst nations in the world, at all levels, in sustaining a lead. Charles Hughes, in his book, says that football's a forward-thinking, forward-running, forward-passing game. Well it's not. Football is a 360-degree game. It's a game that you can play backwards, sideways and forward, and the most important thing is to be able to distinguish what it is required at any particular time.

David Miller: What hasn't been properly explained about Hughes's system is that it's not a bypass for being able to play the game. The statistics may be true and will actually work better for skilful players than for unskilful players. Saying Brazil or Hungary at their greatest scored 80 per cent of their goals from fewer than five passes may be true but you've got to look at what those teams were doing in the rest of the match. They win a match, say, 3–1, but do you talk about those three goals, which in total occupy maybe 75 seconds of a 90-minute match, or what were they doing in the other 88 minutes 45 seconds? You've got to look at that because maybe that had a huge bearing on how they came to score those goals by five passes or less.

Tom Saunders: The great man Shanks here used to say, 'Tom, the game's about long balls and short balls,' and I don't see that as being any different. The much-maligned Charles Hughes at the FA once went to town a little bit on this business of playing the numbers game. That is, if you dispatched the ball early enough, the number of goals might be more favourable than they would be if you knocked it about for five minutes in the middle of the field. Now the fella's been crucified ever since and I think possibly a little bit unfairly. But the great man was right: the game's about the long ball and the short ball and it's a matter of having good enough players to work out when the time is to dispatch it.

Jimmy Hill: Football is a game of 'slow, slow, quick, quick, slow.' If it's 'quick, quick, quick, quick, quick,' there's no breaking up of the rhythm, there's no deception, there's no slowing a man down. I know a lot of players who are not particularly fast, but they beat people because they slow their opponent down to trick their way past him. It is the change in pace, the change in a tactic, that is the deception, not the flat-out aggression and pace, steam-rolling the enemy into submission, and that's what we tend to do within our League.

Watford, 1977–87

Graham Taylor: I remember playing for a man called Jimmy McGuigan [at Grimsby Town], and the ball was played up front, it came back to our midfield players and we used to 'play it through'; so you 'play it up', 'get it back' and 'play it through'. Nobody ever talked about 'long ball' then. People talked about 'the third man running', so the ball was played from the back up to your front man, he played it back to your midfield man and your midfield man played it into space behind your defenders for a third man running through. Never mind about Watford, we were playing that at Lincoln. We were scoring goals. We played with wide men and we got the ball in early. It began to hit the media when suddenly Watford were coming out of the Second Division and into the First Division, and we upset people because suddenly we beat the big clubs. We were doing it because we'd got good players. We'd got John Barnes, an outside-left who loved the ball at his feet and loved to take people on and could bend crosses in. We'd got Nigel Callaghan, outside-right, who off half a yard could hit in quality crosses. He didn't need to beat people, he could drive balls and ping them in. We had a centre-forward called Ross Jenkins who was 6ft 4in and had lovely chest control, and we had a fella called Luther Blissett who wanted the ball in front of him, so why give it to him with his back to the goal? What we then added was to say, 'Why don't we assume we're 1–0 down and play like that, why don't we speed everything up?' Watch any team and, if they're 1–0 down with five minutes to go, they speed the game up without anything from the coach or the manager.

Charles Reep: I wrote to Graham Taylor, and it was a long letter, five or six sheets of foolscap, about what I'd done for Wolverhampton Wanderers. He rang me up and said he was very interested indeed. It was August 1980. We met at a hotel in Exeter. I had breakfast with him, and stayed there for two or three hours talking. I kept some records for him, and he saw that it was quite good and I asked him if he would care to put us on a contract. My friend Simon Hartley lived in Watford. He could see every match and report to me. We were to have £6,000 as a bonus for promotion, and we got it. As easy as that. I got a £2,500 retainer fee so I was in the big money.

Graham Taylor: Well, Charles Reep wrote to me as he's written to many many people and unfortunately you need to put a morning to one side to read the letters he sends you. I put it to one side, and I read it eventually, and I thought, 'This fella has got something.' Reep had a system that recorded the movement of the ball and exactly what happened. He is a very intriguing man, a very clever man, and he bombards you with a lot of figures and a lot of facts but he had a tremendous wealth of information going back many years. You'd be a fool not to at least think about it and many people have. I disagree with some of his things and eventually we did part company. He would say that you've got to put in more 'long passes and you've got to regain the ball back'. You can't do the two. If you're winning the ball back in the opposition's third or half of the field, it's staying in there so you can't put the long passes. But it opened up my mind to looking at professional football not only from an art point of view but also from a science point of view. What

I would like to say is that in 1975–76 I hadn't met Charles Reep, but Lincoln scored 111 goals and won the Fourth Division Championship. I was already keeping a record of how many goals we scored and conceded from restarts, and therefore I do take umbrage a little bit when people assume that Graham Taylor got involved with this fella and it all stemmed from that.

Wimbledon, 1981–87

Dave Bassett: I was at Wimbledon as a player for three years and we won the Southern League title three years on the trot and had some great Cup runs. We got into the League after those three years [1977]. Allen Batsford was the manager, and I was helping him, but he left at Christmas and Dario Gradi became the manager. I was assistant manager and coach with him for three years before he went to Crystal Palace and then I became manager. Wimbledon wasn't expected to last because of it being around Chelsea, QPR, Crystal Palace, etc, but Ron Noades, who was the chairman at that time, had a dream that Wimbledon could get in the First Division in 10 years, and his dream came true eventually but he wasn't there as chairman. Well, there's a lot of claptrap talked about the direct style. Some people say that you just welly the ball down the field and you get goals. Well, it's not quite like that. A lot of thought went into what we did, believe it or not. At Wimbledon we felt that we wanted to get the ball into their half of the field where we could get good crossing positions or good shooting positions or situations where we could pass a ball which resulted in a shot at goal. If we could pass the ball forwards we were prepared to do that. It amazed me how people reacted, but I think a lot of it was jealousy because Wimbledon came through the divisions. They got in the First Division and we finished sixth in our first season there. I think a lot of teams tried to pick up things that

Wimbledon have done. We see that most goalkeepers dribble out of the box now and deliver the ball on. That was something that Wimbledon did before anybody else. At the end of the day it's about scoring goals. It's no good playing a wonderful passing game and ending up 0–0 each week. Directors are interested in their business and their club. They're not interested in the beautiful game or the passing game.

Crystal Palace, 1984–93

Steve Coppell: It always amazes me that the long-ball theory is looked upon as being simple – 'you just welly it and you win games' – whereas the passing style of football is harder because 'there's more coaching involved'. My experience is that long-ball teams are coached, they are told what to do, they are allowed to express themselves but only in certain areas of the field, whereas passing sides are just told to go out and play. The Liverpool sides are famous for their training in five-a-sides whereas the more direct teams spend a long time getting formulae right and getting positions right and the shape of the side correct and they spend a long time in dead-ball situations. Reality states that the passing game is expression without the coaching whereas long-ball football is more about coaching. A lot of people say that bad players can play that style of football. They can, but they can't play it successfully. You need good players to play that style successfully. I was fortunate. Over five or six years we got together a side which was excellent: Ian Wright, Mark Bright, McGoldrick, Salako, Andy Gray, Geoff Thomas, Young, the goalkeeper Nigel Martin. We had some good players and with time we gave a little bit more expression to the very rigid framework we started with.

Ian Wright: If you look at the goals that me and Mark [Bright] scored at the time, the style we was playing was beneficial to everybody in the team because he [Steve Coppell] had to make use of the players he had. He didn't really want me to take many chances just over the halfway-line, that kind of area. If I was gonna do any of my flair stuff, or anybody in the team was gonna do any flair stuff, he'd rather them do it around the penalty box. He did always stress to me that I wasn't picking the right places to try and do the flair stuff but he never inhibited me. He always wanted me to express myself in the last third, and George Graham's the same.

Steve Coppell: I wanted to win football games, and I felt, given the kind of players I had and the financial resources I had available, the style of play that I was adopting was the best way for me. If I'd been at another club where there had been greater financial resources then I certainly would have adopted a different style of play. I used to go and watch other teams and I obviously used to watch Wimbledon, who are just down the road, and I looked at what I used to term 'the Rag, Tag and Bobtail outfit'. They had great spirit for each other, and played a style of football which perhaps wasn't pleasing on the eye but which was exciting. I used to go to Wimbledon and see fabulous goalmouth action every game. Wimbledon won more games than they lost and they were up at the top of the table and having seen that I felt that, looking at my problems, the solution, being pragmatic, was to adopt a more direct style and please my chairman, who was employing me to win games.

25

'How do we replace the back streets?'

England: The Greenwood Years, 1977–82

Ron Greenwood took over as England manager after the sudden departure of Don Revie. His England team reached the 1980 European Championship Finals and the 1982 World Cup Finals. On the surface, England had some fine players – Keegan, Brooking, Robson, Coppell – but some people were concerned about whether the supply of naturally talented youngsters would continue indefinitely.

Club and Country

Bryan Robson: I didn't have any problems at first because most of my early games were in the Home International Championships, playing against British players, so that made it easier to step into the team. Once you start playing against the top continental teams, it's a different ball game. I mean, their pattern of play is totally different to the way that the British teams play. You get more time on the ball to start with, and, as a midfield player, or a defender, they drop off you and drop back to the edge of their box but play with the sweeper system. You've got to have a lot of patience on the ball and you can slow the game down to a walking pace, if you want to, but then once you try to break them down you've got to do it really quickly and very precisely, and I think that's what players find very difficult to change to because in our League it's 90 miles an hour all the time. They go into international games and they try to play that way and you keep giving the ball away because you're rushing everything, when you've got more time on the ball than you think.

Steve Coppell: The problem with playing for England, I think, is familiarity and feeling comfortable. It took me about 10 games to feel comfortable in the environment. When you first go away with England you meet up on a Sunday, or whatever, and you're conscious of everything you do. Even when you sit down at a meal you want to use the right knife and fork and you want to eat properly and you don't want to do anything which draws attention to you. Football humour is cruel. Other players will make fun of you, pick you out, so you're very much shrinking into the pack all the time, and it was only after I'd played a few games and I knew the people, the physio, the doctors, the manager and the coaches, that I felt comfortable and felt as if I could express myself properly.

Don Howe: I remember one time we were playing Brazil. It was virtually in May and there were about two League games left, and the Brazilian game was important to us. You know you're going to get a full house so you want to play well. On the Monday morning, when we get to training, we had six players who could train. A lot of the players had pulled out through injuries with their clubs, some of the players who arrived had got injuries that had to be treated, so we're starting to get ready for an important game against Brazil and on the Monday morning before the Wednesday night game, we've got six players to work with, and that's how bad it can get at times and it's not the right way to do things.

Sir Bert Millichip: I take my mind back initially to the chairmen at the Football Association during my time there. When I was first appointed it was Sir Andrew Stephen, the chairman of Sheffield Wednesday, who did not give his entire time and attention to it. He was a doctor. Sir Harold Thompson, who followed him in 1976, was an academic from Oxford University, a man who had been involved with the amateur side of the game with Oxford University and Pegasus but with no professional experience, and a man who did not give his full time and attention to the job because he was an active academic. I do recollect the day of my appointment, when I was interviewed by a television crew, and Mr Croker [FA secretary] was standing at my back, and I was asked the question, 'Do you intend to put your full time and attention to the job?' Mr Croker and I answered at the same time. I said, 'Yes, I will,' and he said, 'No, he won't.' That was perhaps the first disagreement between myself and the secretary at the time, although we patched it up very quickly.

System of Play

Ron Greenwood: If you've got one side that plays 'a long-ball game', for the want of a terminology, and you've got another side that wants to build up from the back, you've got to be careful how you pick players from those two different systems so they could fit into a system which we wanted to play. The system I wanted to play was basically the continental type of system, which could combat, both defensively and in attack, the type of play that the other countries played. We felt first and foremost, when I first took over, that two wingers would be the ideal situation for us. That's what was the old traditional type of English play, and we felt that that was the best pattern on which to build. It's no good having a system whereby you bring somebody in and it takes them about a dozen games before they know what the system's all about. In the main, on the continent, they've played with a sweeper system for years now. So consequently when, say, for argument's sake, Beckenbauer used to play the sweeper, if he got injured somebody would come in and play the same way as he did, because they did it at club level, and so that was the uniformity and the continuity which would enable them to play. I used to laugh and say we played 22 different ways in the First Division.

Steve Coppell: Ron Greenwood's background was the academy of West Ham which was an adaptation, I suppose, of the Tottenham 'push and run'. It was a passing game but he selected players who were successful in other environments. The dominant personalities of my era were the Emlyn Hugheses, the Kevin Keegans, the Trevor Brookings, Ray Wilkins, Bryan Robson coming into the frame, and these were hardened professionals, all of them, and I think they perhaps dictated the style just as much as the manager did. The manager selected the players, so he knew exactly what was going on, and I think he gave the players that freedom to impose themselves. Ron Greenwood always used to say, 'There isn't one captain in this team, there are 11 captains.'

Phil Thompson: We played with a flat back-four at Liverpool, but Ron Greenwood came to me one day and he said, 'We realize as a flat back-four we may be going to get caught out for pace or whatever. You've got big Dave Watson with you, let Dave come across, more central, let him deal with any long balls, you drop off and play more of a sweeper and it'll be a doddle to you. You then have a look. If there's anybody coming, running through, beyond the two full-backs and the centre-half, you can then just step up if you want to play them offside. You sort everything out and you organize the way you always do.'

Ron Greenwood: When I first took over the England job I felt that it was a question of understanding, and I went round to every club that had an international player. I'd go to the hotel where they were staying, and I remember going to the Liverpool one. (Liverpool were very successful at the time and I selected seven of them for one game.) They were playing at Middlesbrough at the time and Kenny Dalglish had just signed for them. It was comical, actually, because he said, 'I'm about the only one that can't come in there,' because he wasn't an Englishman, and he laughed. I felt that this was important to get to know the players and to get their views of what the international set-up was all about. How did they look upon it? How did they feel about the international set-up? What I was doing was probing *them* to find out what *they* felt, and it was invaluable in many cases.

The 1980 European Championships

Ron Greenwood: It was comical, really, because to qualify in that league we lost one point only. When we got to Italy for the Championships our first game was against Belgium and we were unfortunate, really, that we had one or two injuries. We'd beaten Spain 2–0 in Spain about two months before and everything was perfect with Keegan, Francis and everyone. The first game was against Belgium. Francis was injured and he couldn't play, and the pattern lost a little of its impetus. We drew with Belgium. We then had to play Italy on their own midden, as it were, and we didn't disgrace ourselves and we were a bit unfortunate not to have got a draw. Italy beat us 1–0. We had to go to Naples to play Spain and we won that one. So we ended up winning one, losing one and drawing one, but it wasn't sufficient to get us through.

Qualifying for the 1982 World Cup Finals

Ron Greenwood: The game in Norway was a disaster. We didn't have the side that we really wanted out and we made mistakes and one or two players were a little bit late covering and it was a disappointing performance. The game in Switzerland was a bit of a problem because we had a lot of the play and we made mistakes – Kenny Sansom was involved in one or two – and it was a bit of a disaster, really, to lose two games like that. We did put it right by beating Hungary in Hungary. It was a big match for me because we'd just been beaten by Switzerland, so everybody was baying for my head. I think the *Sun* ran a 'lovely' headline: 'For God's sake, Ron, go!' You get the best of everything, don't you? For God's sake, Ron, go! Anyway, everybody was keyed up and I've made up my mind what team I'm going to play, and before I announced the team – I won't mention names because that's unkind – I'm looking at them and I know I'm going to play one player in a certain position. I look at him and I can see in his eyes that he doesn't want to play. I'd made up my mind he's going to play and in a second I changed my mind and called out somebody else's name. And that is understanding players. Players are just human beings, and there they were, they knew they were under the cosh. Here was this lad. He didn't want to play. I substituted another name and called out another name and then just read on as if nothing had happened.

Phil Thompson: I played in Norway. Very, very embarrassing. Switzerland. Romania. I can always remember Hungary. We went there under pressure and we beat them 3–1, in their own backyard, and Ron was so thrilled, because he'd loved everything about Hungarian football in the fifties and so on. We were all coming back and of course the door had opened again for England and then it was rock bottom on the plane when Ron said that he was going to pack in.

Bryan Robson: I think before the Hungary game he'd made his decision to retire or resign, and on the plane on the way back – I mean I was just a young lad at that time – I could hear the senior players in the card school talking about Ron going to announce on the plane that he was going to resign from the job. And so a lot of the senior players got together and they went up to Ron Greenwood and thankfully they talked him out of it, because I think he did a really good job in the '82 World Cup Finals.

Ron Greenwood: This *Sun* newspaper article. I mean, they do get to you, don't they, articles? There it was – For God's sake go, Ron. But I was determined that we were going to win in Hungary and we did that. I went into their press conference and I just thanked them for all their hospitality and the fact that it was a delight to play in Hungary, and for me it was ultrasatisfying to have beaten Hungary, the great people that my whole football philosophy was based on. Then, on the way home on the plane, I said to the players that I was going to retire. Having won in Hungary, I felt that I'd given them a platform whereby they could go ahead and qualify for the World Cup. I felt it was nice for the new man to come in now and take them to Spain because I'd done my bit, I'd got them over the Hungarian hurdle. 'Don't be stupid,' they said, and I had great respect for them, Keegan and Brooking and Phil Neal and all of them, and they were genuine in what they said: 'Don't retire, let's see it all out together.' They changed my mind for me.

Phil Thompson: The press were probably just coming into

their own, really, getting their knives out for England managers at the time. Coming back on that plane Ron got hold of Kevin [Keegan] and explained that he was going to pack in, and Kevin then come down, had a meeting with the senior players, and he said, 'Ron's packing in, what do you think?' I said, 'I don't want to go to the World Cup, Kev, without Ron Greenwood. What I've done, I've done for me country and I've done for Ron Greenwood.' A few of us voiced the same opinion. Kevin said, 'Well, I'm glad that's the way you feel about it. I feel very annoyed meself, we know where the pressure's come from. If I know that's the way you feel, I'm going to go back to Ron now and I'm going back to the FA.' And this was all happening on the plane coming back. So Ron changed his mind and it was only when the press got to know about it, about 24 hours later, that everybody heard about it.

The 1982 World Cup Finals

Ron Greenwood: We went to Bilbao and the Bilbao club was brilliant to us because I'd gone over there prior to the World Cup and we'd played a testimonial for José Rojo. It was the first time that England had ever played a testimonial game for a player but we knew we were going to be based in Bilbao and I felt it was good to get the Bilbao public on our side.

Peter Shilton: It was my first World Cup. I remember we got over to Spain and it was very, very hot out there, and we started our opening games in Bilbao, which was obviously Basque country, and there was quite a bit of terrorism around at the time. We had a lot of security guards with machine-guns around the hotel. We went to the training ground on the first day and there was a tank parked in the drive.

Steve Coppell: We felt as if we had a squad that were capable of doing well in that tournament and then during the last couple of weeks we had major problems with Kevin Keegan, who was our top player at the time and a great force within the team, and Trevor Brooking. Both of them had injuries which took the edge off our expectation, but it also brought to the fore Bryan Robson, who took on a major role in that World Cup, Glenn Hoddle, Graham Rix, Ray Wilkins, all these people. Our first game was against France and we won 3–1, and I always remember the feeling after that game – it was almost as if that game was winning the World Cup.

Ron Greenwood: Bryan Robson scored that quick goal, which he's got a gold watch for. We beat France, and France were a good side, and we were feeling confident. And then of course we beat Czechoslovakia and Kuwait. We were full of confidence.

Steve Coppell: We got to the second stage and we were in a group with West Germany and Spain and it was a rush for Kevin and Trevor to get back for those games. We had a 0–0 draw with Germany, and I always remember playing in that game against Hans-Peter Briegel, who was a giant of a man. In the first five minutes I went up to him and tackled him, or tried to tackle him, and he sort of brushed me away and said, 'Get away, little fly,' which always sticks in my mind. Then the Germans beat the Spanish which meant that we had to beat Spain by 2–0. I missed that game – my knee injury finally took its toll – and it was a mad rush to get Kevin and Trevor back and they came back as substitutes in that game. We didn't get through and the feeling in the dressing-room afterwards was just one of devastation.

Ron Greenwood: The sad thing was that Brooking and Keegan, who we thought would be our two leading players, never played. They weren't 100 per cent fit really, but the last quarter of an hour we threw them on and the two of them had opportunities to score, which would have given us two goals, and they would have put us in the semi-final. And not many people realize that when I threw Trevor on in the last quarter of an hour, his injury was so bad and he really tried to help us. The fact is, he didn't play again for six months after that.

Phil Thompson: We didn't lose a game and we only conceded one goal in five games, and we missed out on the semi-finals. France got to the semi-finals and were involved in a tremendous match with West Germany. That could easily have been us getting that far.

A Decline in Skills?

John Cartwright: For a long time, a lot of us, people like Malcolm Allison, Terry Venables and people of that ilk, have been concerned about the problem of young players and how they've developed through this country. The system here is based on competitive football where results are more important than learning the game. Professional football clubs have never been geared to teaching players the game, only smoothing off the rough edges, because young players produce their talent in the streets, and this has always been the development process that youngsters have gone through. As the car took over in the streets, and the young players couldn't practise in the streets and in the school playgrounds, it became a vacuum of learning and so it was thought, by the Football Association, that Centres of Excellence were required to overcome this problem.

Alan Ball: We were still producing players in this country but not in the quantities that were produced in the sixties and seventies. They were hanging off the trees in those days, and I think the quantity of really top players started to dry up at the start of the eighties. I think it was a natural progression in life. Kids weren't quite so hungry as they were in the sixties and seventies. Kids had lots more other things to do. They weren't rushing out from school to play on the rec at the bottom of the street. Kids stopped playing in the street.

Bobby Robson: When I went to school, I played two sports, football in the winter, cricket in the summer. Now they play 14 or 15 sports. I learned *my* football in the backstreets. How do we replace the back streets? We had to do something about it. We had to devise a scheme. We had to come up with a blueprint for the development of football in our country.

Charles Hughes: Bob Robson and I discussed how we should develop a programme for excellence amongst the young children. We examined our continental opponents and concluded that maybe our techniques weren't as good as they ought to be and devised plans to improve that. We brought in the scheme for Centres of Excellence [August 1984] and the National School in September 1984.

John Cartwright: These Centres of Excellence grew from those early beginnings, and the National Football School at Lilleshall took the best players from those centres. The Centres of Excellence started off working with boys at 13 years of age. The Football Association and the ESFA [English Schools' Football Association] got together and they brought the age limit down to 11, which was slightly better, but still there were problems because you were restricted to one hour a week with them, and you can't actually get enough work into a good player with one hour a week. Now the Football Association and the ESFA have got together once again and the time limit has been taken off and professional clubs can now have players as often as they can look after them, which is much better, and hopefully we can see some improvements in the future. The golden age for skill acquisition is seven to 14. If it hasn't been achieved in that period of time, you're very rarely going to achieve high quality later on.

Charles Hughes: The National Football School is established at Lilleshall, which is a major national sports-centre, and the boys come at 14 years of age until 16. The great advantage is not the two hours or so they spend each day on football, it is that they are in a football environment, and their attitudes are developed. I think 14 of the boys have played now for the under-21 team.

John Cartwright: I started [work] at Lilleshall in September 1989 and I left two years later in June 1991, and the reason for leaving was that I failed to see that we could actually achieve what we were after at the National Football School. Working with the best young players in the country, I found that they were still short on the basic skills. Kicking techniques were very poor. Most of them were one-footed. They had no variety in their kicking, and the basic skills such as running with the ball, heading, control and so on all had to be worked on to a great extent, and also importantly their understanding of the game, the actual playing of the game, was very limited and was very staid in terms of their concepts of play. It was basically about knocking the ball forward, scrapping for things in midfield. There was no grace, no art and no imaginative football. I was asked to give an appraisal of the qualities of the boys at Lilleshall, and I gave what I considered to be an honest appraisal, and I fell foul of Charles Hughes, who said that he thought that that was a negative appraisal. I found I couldn't come to terms with the fact that to fulfil his direct-play theory, the boys had to do a certain amount of physical work. I was not involved with this. This was done through the Human Performance Centre. I found that I was losing boys on a regular basis because of overwork, physically, to comply with the requirements of direct play. I said that we could probably do just as much work physically with the ball and not run into the injury problems that we were coming up against.

Jeff Astle: Tony Brown, a big friend of mine, always brings it up. He says, 'When we were playing, we said, "Has he got a lot of skill?" "Has he got a good left foot?" "Has he got a right foot?" ' But nowadays the coaches and the manager say, 'Has he got a good engine? Is he fast?' To me, you don't want fast runners in football, you want people with brains. Years ago, we could use our own brains. We didn't want people to tell us what to do. I think that Linford Christie – I don't know if he's played football in his life – could walk into any Premier Division team, because he'd be such a danger up front with his pace. I think the fast runners nowadays beat the lads with skill.

26

' "Snatch of the day" opened up the market-place'

Televised Football

After various experiments with football coverage, the real breakthrough came with the 1966 World Cup Finals and BBC's regular programme *Match of the Day*. ITV countered with *The Big Match*, launched in 1968. In the late 1970s the Football League struck an exclusive deal with ITV but it was later set aside by the Office of Fair Trading. This led to more competition and, later, interest from satellite television companies.

The Early Days

Kenneth Wolstenholme: The BBC knew that television was going to spread beyond Watford, so they said, 'Let's get a northern commentator', and they got me. Television in those days wasn't black and white, it was grey and grey. Kick-offs were two o'clock on a November day, with no smokeless zones, no floodlights, and by 2.30 you couldn't

316

see a thing. People used to say, 'We can't see the ball.' 'What are you grumbling about, neither can I and I'm supposed to be commentating on it?' And of course it was the old leather ball, brown and black. Then a man went to our producer with an idea. He said, 'The white ball will show up well on television.' The producer said, 'It would get dirty within 60 seconds.' He said, 'Well, drop it in a bucket and clean the mud off it.' 'It'll weigh a ton.' He said, 'No, it's not made of leather, it's a plastic thing.' And they asked the FA and that's how the white ball came about. The first programme was called *Sports Special* [September 1955]. In those days, you could only get film processed and edited in London, and, if you did a match up in Newcastle, for instance, you'd fly the film back, and we had to transmit it in the negative. We had all sorts of terrible mess-ups. I remember doing an international – Wales and England at Cardiff [22 October 1955]. Wales won it 2–1. What used to happen, as the footage was going through the first camera, the assistant would start the second camera to try and get an overlap, and camera number one ran out and camera two jammed. That happened twice and Wales scored both times while it was happening, and yet you got the England goal. Now how do you explain that? You can't. Nobody's going to believe you. Everyone said, 'They wouldn't show the Welsh goals but they'd show the English goals.' We used to have great times. I remember once I was going to cover Charlton Athletic versus Huddersfield and Paul Fox said on the Friday, 'Oh, no, you're going somewhere else. Charlton and Huddersfield is no good.' I went somewhere and it was a goalless draw. I came back and I could see Paul Fox wasn't looking too happy with the world. I said, 'What's the matter?' He said, 'You haven't heard? At full-time it was Charlton 7 Huddersfield 6,' and that was the match we turned down. In 1964 we did the first *Match of the Day* which was on BBC2. It went out at half past six. We did the match at Anfield – Liverpool and Arsenal – and Liverpool fans couldn't see it on BBC2, it was London only. There were more people at

Anfield that day than could see it on *Match of the Day* that night because so few sets had been tuned in to BBC2. Later it became an institution. It used to get about 13 to 15 million people every Saturday night.

John Bromley: I joined ITV in 1964 to produce *World of Sport*, which was a new sports programme they wanted on a Saturday afternoon to compete with *Grandstand*. Eamonn Andrews switched from BBC to ITV so he was an ideal host for that show. We went on the air in January 1965 and it went quite well. My first involvement with football was really the World Cup in 1966, which I have to say on behalf of ITV was a complete disaster, a shambles, on the basis that (1) we hadn't enough experience in production and commentary, and (2) the great moguls of the day decided to run *Coronation Street* at 8 o'clock, which was when the football was starting. They thought the viewers would watch *Coronation Street* then stay on for the football, but clearly everyone went to the BBC to watch the whole football match. We started *The Big Match* in August 1968 with a whole new team. Jimmy Hill, who'd been manager of Coventry City, had come down from the Midlands to join us as Head of Sport, and I was appointed Deputy Head of Sport, and we got Brian Moore, who was BBC Radio's leading sports commentator, and a very good director called Bob Gardem. We had this marvellous blank piece of paper which you'll never get again, and we started *The Big Match*, which was the first programme which really analysed football. We could do that because the managing director at the time, Michael Peacock, invested £60,000 in the first-ever slow-motion machine in this country. Brian Moore was the host, and Jimmy Hill became the first-ever analyst on football in this country. Jimmy Hill was only featured in the London television area and I think two or three other regions, but he wasn't seen nationally and Jim was getting a bit edgy about not being seen in Newcastle, and that's when he joined the BBC. The BBC came to see Jimmy in 1972 and said, 'Look, you should be with us and not with ITV any longer. We'll put you on nationwide,' so he joined *Match of the Day*.

The 1970 World Cup Panel

John Bromley: The panel came about in 1970 for the World Cup in Mexico. We'd sat down two or three months before the World Cup and said, 'We need some people who can actually talk lucidly about football.' We went for Malcolm Allison and a lovely little chap from Manchester United called Paddy Crerand. We went with Derek Dougan, who was then playing at Wolves, an Irishman with all the Irish charm, and at the last moment we drew in Bob McNab. The idea was that we were going to use these chaps individually with Brian Moore, at the end of the show, beginning of the show or whatever. It so happened on the first night they all turned up at the studios and said, 'Well, what am I going to do?' I said, 'I suppose you'd better all sit down,' and they all sat in these chairs and they were there for the whole four weeks. There were two goodies and two baddies. Crerand, the little tough Scot, and Allison, the hard-nosed Cockney boy, were the baddies, and the charming Dougan and the lovely Bob McNab were the goodies. The whole mix was absolutely right, and it took off and they became folk heroes in four weeks.

Derek Dougan: We were the first four people ever invited on television to actually speak about our sport, and now you've got tennis players, badminton players, cricketers, rugby players, all being used to give an opinion about the sport they had been heavily involved with. The chemistry was right, and we used to spark off each other. Not once did we have a rehearsal. Malcolm was the only guy that I have ever worked with who could drink an excess of champagne and go on there and not slur his words. I used to admire him for doing that because I wouldn't try to do it. Bob McNab had flown back from Mexico. He was only going to come on for a couple of days, and he didn't get into the swing of it right away. Bob would sit there and not say a word and someone devised a little flag for Bob. If he wanted to say anything, Bob had to wave his little flag which meant we had to go over to Bob. And then of course the Rabbi was always there – Jimmy Hill. The feuding between him and Brian [Moore], there was something going on between those two fellas which we never could work out, but it was great fun.

John Bromley: They became stars. The Brazilian Embassy rang up and said, 'Come to our party tonight.' I think it was the beginning of showing that footballers could talk and dress properly, but we've never had a panel so exciting and electric as that one ever again.

'Snatch of the Day'

John Bromley: The BBC and ITV in those days went together on football contracts. It started at the request of football, to be very fair to both BBC and ITV (because people said we ran a cartel). We used to meet Hardaker every two years or something and sit down, 'a bit for you, a bit for me' and the deal was on a piece of paper. They had Saturday nights for *Match of the Day*, ITV had Sundays, and that's how it went for year after year. The background to 'Snatch of the Day' was that the President of the Football League at the time was a chap called Jack Dunnett, who was a Member of Parliament. He was a very influential man in football, and he was a friend of Michael Grade, who was Director of Programmes at London Weekend Television. We're now talking about late 1978, and I was sitting in the office one day on the 14th floor at South Bank and I get a call from Michael Grade: 'Brommers, come and see me.' So I go into the office and he said, 'Look, I think there's a chance that we can get the whole of the Football League.' Now this at this stage was a megathought. He said, 'I'm seeing Jack Dunnett in the House of Commons in an hour's time,' and from that meeting between Grade and Dunnett in the House of Commons, and secret meetings, and Hardaker flying down, and people with coats and hats on and scarves round their necks and all this, we came to a situation two months later where Hardaker signed a piece of paper saying, 'ITV have got the exclusive rights to all League football in England,' and the balloon went off. BBC couldn't believe it. Now my understanding is that David Coleman was so incensed at what had gone on he got the top man at the BBC to fight the good fight. Broadcasting House rocked because the BBC had had *Match of the Day* for ever. *Match of the Day* had been the rock around which the BBC had built the whole Saturday evening. It was always *The Generation Game*, a very good hour's theatre, then *Match of the Day*, then Parky [*Parkinson*], and, whatever ITV did, we couldn't break that, so that was the motivation behind getting football. The coup was called 'Snatch of the Day' by the press, which was a great title, and it ran and ran. It got questions in the House and everything, and I think the Office of Fair Trading were involved, and in the end we came across the table with the BBC. We said, 'Okay, we'll let you have some football. We'll alternate Saturday nights and Sundays.' It broke up that cosy relationship that we'd had with the BBC. 'Snatch of the Day' opened up the market-place.

The First Live League Game – October 1983

John Bromley: The Football League were very nervous about live coverage. The first live game we did on ITV was at Tottenham. The gate was brilliant. We'd been running poster campaigns all round the place saying, *'The Big Match*

Live for the first time', and people thought, 'This is an occasion, I'll go.' So the gate was boosted by about 10,000. What's interesting is that live television has not affected gates at all.

The Black-out of 1985–86

John Bromley: We came to this stand-off situation, in '85–86, between us, the football clubs and the BBC. There was this famous meeting at the Café Royal when all the football-club chairmen turned up and we were offering something like £5 million, and Robert Maxwell boomed from the top of his voice at the back of the hall: 'I'm a director of Central Television. I know more about this than anybody else. It's worth £90 million. Don't give in to these mad people from television.' So we walked away and football was off television for three to four months. Nothing.

ITV Beat BSB

John Bromley: At that stage the biggest problem with football was the problem they had with negotiation. None of the chairmen could agree who should negotiate, whereas Jonathan Martin and myself were quite experienced negotiators and we knew what we were talking about and were winning the PR battle. Dear old Ken Bates from Chelsea was running around screaming and shouting, and someone else would run around screaming and shouting, and it was a nightmare. To some extent all this was a fault of football not getting their act together. David Dein from Arsenal and Irving Scholar from Spurs came in as young, bright entrepreneurial-type blokes, and what they did immediately was to take some advice and research the position.

Irving Scholar: It got to the point really where in 1985 we had Heysel, Bradford and Birmingham, and football was on the floor and television wanted too many live games. I became a member of the television committee and we were negotiating with them but it became very clear very quickly that what was operating was a cartel in that ITV and BBC were holding hands under the table, metaphorically, and following each other's lead. These guys were professional negotiators and the people in football probably did not really know what football was worth, and what I asked the committee to consider, which they accepted, was that we went to a professional outsider. We called in Saatchi and Saatchi to advise us on what they believed the value to television of football.

Alex Fynn: When the analysis was first done, in 1985, the television contract was less than £3 million. We showed the clubs, or more precisely the television sub-committee, that the value of the contract was worth at least twice that. They therefore knew and could argue in future from a position of strength. Events conspired that they weren't able to put that knowledge to any use until the television contract came up for renewal, in 1988, when all of a sudden there was competition on the horizon from the then satellite channel BSB. BSB suddenly produced a viable rival for the ITV–BBC cartel and forced the television companies to offer a fairer price for football.

David Dein: There was a comfortable cartel in existence between the BBC and ITV, and when the old BSB came into the picture all of a sudden it introduced a new player. They were the wild card and that's exactly what football needed because we managed to separate the BBC and ITV at that stage, and although negotiations were hot and heavy for several months during 1988, we managed to get a deal which improved football's income from £3 million a year to £44 million over four years, which was the biggest single television deal ever done for soccer.

Greg Dyke: The original BSB proposal would have gone through and been accepted had it not been for one thing, that Coventry City at that time proposed that the compensation paid to football clubs when they were on live was done away with, and that so angered Arsenal, Manchester United and those other clubs that they suddenly became quite interested in talking about an alternative deal. So we [ITV] met with the bigger clubs, five of them, and we said, 'Look, we'll do you a deal. We'll buy your rights. We don't want the rest. We'll take five or six clubs' television rights. We'll try and increase it to 10, but basically we'll buy your home rights. We'll guarantee you £1 million a season, each, and we'll take your rights.' Our legal advice was that the right to televising in a ground belongs to the club and not to the League.

Irving Scholar: I was invited to a dinner at a restaurant in Knightsbridge in London, and representatives of Liverpool, Everton, Manchester United, Arsenal and Tottenham were all there. BSB wanted to buy exclusive League football, live and recorded, and we were very concerned about that. Obviously we preferred either BBC or ITV to have it on terrestrial television where we would have a big audience rather than a marginal audience. Enter Greg Dyke and a host of people, and he started having a little bit of a go at cable and satellite television and I asked him, 'Is there a cartel?' John Bromley, who was the ITV negotiator in all the previous discussions, for many years tried to fluff the answer, and Greg Dyke said, 'I'm going to give a straight answer, yes, there has been a cartel.' We couldn't believe that here was somebody from the very top of ITV negotiating on a straightforward basis and actually admitting there was a cartel. If we could break the cartel we could actually get more of a market price for football. Greg Dyke went out of the room with his entourage and they came back and put a proposal forward, and that was really the beginning of the major breakthrough of football on television.

Greg Dyke: Our intention of doing that deal was to break the Football League's negotiating position with BSB, and it worked perfectly. We then went to five other clubs, which included Newcastle, Nottingham Forest, Aston Villa, and asked them to join so that we could get up to 10, but we would have gone with the five. At the end of that first season [1988–89], as luck would have it, we got one of the great pieces of sports television, which was Arsenal away at Liverpool for the final game. I think it only got about 9½ million because most people thought it was a foregone conclusion. They thought that Liverpool were bound to win and of course Arsenal had to win by two clear goals and they scored the last goal in the last couple of minutes and it was the most wonderful piece of television. I'd taken some criticism for spending £11 million of ITV's money, and I thought it was wonderful.

A Deal for the Premier League

Greg Dyke: Alan Sugar had taken over Tottenham and from that stage onwards it was fairly clear he was going to vote for BSkyB. Alan Sugar had a deal with BSkyB to produce satellite dishes. As it's turned out, there's no evidence at all that the football contract has driven satellite dishes. To be fair to Alan Sugar, he declared a conflict of interest. The others allowed him to vote. As long as you declare it, it seems to me it's legitimate. There are some who would argue that the reason he took over Tottenham was to make sure that at least one of the bigger clubs voted BSkyB's way. There was no doubt that Tottenham wasn't going to sign, but others had come in. Leeds, who had just won the First Division, were very much ITV supporters. We had been told by Rick Parry [chief executive of the Premier League] all along we were in prime position. About a week earlier we suddenly began to realize that he and Quinton [chairman of the Premier League] had been heavily wooed by Murdoch. You wouldn't have expected someone like Parry to get that sort of job, and here he was with Rupert Murdoch. They got won over by Murdoch, who set aside two or three weeks of his life to get the thing, and of course Murdoch used every trick that we know Murdoch can use, and one of them was getting the BBC on his side. In our bid we had gone to the BBC at an earlier stage and said, 'We're happy for you to have *Match of the Day* on Saturday night. We don't think people are very interested in recorded football anyway, but you can have it on Saturday nights and we're quite happy for that to go into our bid as long as you pay this, you know, £3 million or £4 million for it', and that's what they agreed to do. In the week before the contract was awarded, Hussey, the Chairman of the BBC, and Checkland, the Director General of the BBC, both phoned the FA personally to say that the BBC would in no way support a *Match of the Day* if the contract went to ITV and basically overnight it took £20 million out of our five-year deal and that's what lost it. BSkyB increased their bid in the morning when Alan Sugar rang them. Well, first of all, Rick Parry, totally unethically, rang them and said you've got to increase your bid. And the reason that was unethical was because they never gave the same opportunity to us. There's nothing wrong with somebody who's selling a set of rights running an auction, but if you're going to run an auction you've got to allow both sides to bid a number of times, and actually they went into the meeting with Parry still changing the figures. Alan Sugar left the meeting on seeing our new bid and in those immortal words phoned up BSkyB and told them 'to blow us out the water'. He later said he was phoning his girlfriend, and we said at the time, 'We'd like to meet the girlfriend!'

John Bromley: ITV have suffered dramatically by losing

the deal. I mean, that's the way the world goes. You win some, you lose some. It was the clubs outside the big five who swung the vote to BSkyB. They got miffed. No one massaged their egos. No one went round saying, 'Don't worry, lads, in the new system with ITV we'll look after you, Mr Southampton and Mr Coventry.' They got very browned off under the old ITV deal, but the top five were creaming off everything, and then when it came to the vote, hands up lads, 14–6 or whatever for the BSkyB deal. That's the reality of that deal.

Sir Bert Millichip: We are receiving great criticism now for playing certain matches on Sunday, certain matches on a Monday night. The criticism is coming from many areas and these are certainly matters which will have to receive a consideration when existing contracts finish, but nothing can happen until those contracts have finished. We're not going to allow this to happen again. It might mean that less rather than more money will be considered in the future. I don't think it matters what subject you bring me to discuss, eventually we'll get down to the fact that money is the trouble, the root of the evil.

27

'In Gascoigne we had a rare talent'

England Under Bobby Robson, 1982–90

Bobby Robson took over as England manager in 1982 and, despite media criticism to the contrary, proved very successful, taking England to the World Cup quarter-finals in 1986 and the semi-finals in 1990. He stayed in the job for eight years.

A Management System

Don Howe: Ron Greenwood gave me and Bobby Robson the 'B' team, and we were fairly successful. He put Dave Sexton and Terry Venables with the under-21 team and he put Brian Clough and Peter Taylor with the youth team. The continuity was there and, when Ron left the job after '82 in Spain, Bobby Robson took over. I'd moved up anyway with Ron, so I was the coach with Bobby Robson. When Bobby took the job on, he was the England team manager plus the director of coaching. He wanted me full-time and he wanted

Harold Wilkinson full-time, and the FA wouldn't allow him to do it.

Bobby Robson: It's a different feeling to the feeling of a club manager, even if you're the manager of the biggest club in England and you play in front of 50,000 people. It's the responsibility, the enormous importance of that game, that night, and so your hair does curl and you feel a prickly sensation as though you've just come off the dentist's chair. You get used to it, of course, but there are still hairy evenings when an extra important match is looming up, and it can get to you. I remember my first match, England v Denmark in Denmark, and the national anthem. Standing up with an England blazer on, and seeing my team out there play a European Championship qualifying match, believe me, the hair bristled up the back of my neck.

Systems of Play

Bobby Robson: I wanted England to play football the way I wanted to see it. There has to be a balance between direct football and possession of the ball. If you play overdirect football, the first thing you do is lose the ball and then have to chase. I'm saying, 'If you can get there in two passes, get there in two passes, don't take three, you might lose possession.' I always say P P P – Patience, Penetration, Possession – and I brought that into the England scene, but I also know that the Hoddle pass, the direct pass over the top, the long pass at the right moment, is the finest pass in football, because it puts four defenders out of the game with one pass, but you can't play that pass too many times.

Gary Lineker: By and large most of the players in the international team are the most technically gifted players that we've got and are capable of playing that way, as we proved in Italy. We played a game that the continentals played. We were as good as Germany and Belgium and all those very strong sides and we've shown that we can play that way. The players that play at the top level are the ones that can pass the ball to each other. The thing about international football is that you cannot give the ball away. You must have players that can keep the ball because the other teams are so strong when they get it that it takes you 10 minutes to win it back. People throw statistics at you, very high people in the FA, about how it's only three or four passes that make a goal and it's very rare that it's more than that, but what these people don't realize is that teams that have the majority of possession don't have to work as hard and don't have to chase the ball as much as the teams that don't have possession. People bend statistics to suit themselves, and the true fact is that, by and large, the best teams, the best technical teams, the teams that have the most possession in games, generally win.

v Brazil (1984)

Bobby Robson: I can remember the match very vividly. It was the first time we'd ever beaten Brazil in Brazil. We lost to Russia eight days before that, 2–0 at Wembley. I worked with a very young team and it was a summer tour. I have it on file that I had 19 senior players who couldn't make that trip, so we went to Uruguay and Brazil with a young team. We played Brazil and we had four experienced players. I had Sansom, Peter Shilton, Bryan Robson and Ray Wilkins, and the rest were young players. We played in the Maracanà against Brazil and I played a 4-2-4 formation with young Chamberlain at outside-right, John Barnes, Mark Hateley, and we won 2–0. An incredible performance. We were under great siege the first 20 minutes but held firm, and went on to win the game. It was one of the turning points in my life. The goal by John Barnes was the best goal for me. There was immense quality about the goal, the way he scored it, the great individualism that he portrayed during that 45- to 50-yard surge. A wonderful goal. The best goal for me.

Mexico 1986

Bobby Robson: I appreciate Martin Edwards and Ron Atkinson's point of view [at Manchester United]. They had paid £1.5 million for Bryan Robson, he was their player, they were paying him a huge salary to play, and they had a chance that year of winning the League. Bryan Robson was very important to them, and he had this injury of the shoulder-joint and the more it comes out the more vulnerable it is to being put out again. I hear this, and we wanted Manchester United to take him out of football for two months – this is only February – and get his shoulder right. It was a two-month job, so he'd be ready for England for the World Cup in that summer of '86. They had a difficult decision to make, and their decision was, 'No'. They felt they could keep him going and get a high number of matches from him to help them win the League. As a result of that, when it came to the World Cup we took him but he was a gamble, a risk which came unstuck, because the shoulder came out twice in three games. So we played the World Cup without our best player. Now, Manchester could have solved that, and at the end of the day nobody won, because Manchester United didn't win and England didn't win.

Bryan Robson: Yeah, a lot of things were said about me shoulder. It was just an unfortunate predicament I was in at that time because people were saying I should have had the operation before I went, but I'd spoken at length with a surgeon and the surgeon said I needed 12 weeks to recover. Now, there were only 10 weeks leading up to the World Cup Finals so it meant I could have the operation and go in cold into the World Cup Finals. I'd have had no training, no match practice, going into the World Cup Finals, which wasn't the right preparation. I'd spoken to a few people, like John Francome, the jump jockey, who'd dislocated his shoulders a lot, and they said to me, 'You can build your shoulder up really well without the operation and if you can build up the muscles around it you should get through the games okay.' That was the gamble I took. Unfortunately, the shoulder came out in the second game, so I wasn't fit enough to play after that. A lot of people said I should never have gone. Maybe they're right, but they're only right after the event.

Peter Shilton: The World Cup Finals were in Mexico. We went to Monterey and played Portugal in the first match. It wasn't a great stadium, and the pitch was awful. The grass was very long and it was very bumpy underneath. There was hardly any atmosphere. We knew we were in front of millions of people, but I think there was only a few thousand in the ground. It was very tough to get motivated because it was about 90 or 100 degrees, and we ended up losing the first match, 1–0, when we should probably have won it. Then we had to play Morocco.

Bryan Robson: We were playing against Morocco and I went in for a sliding tackle with a lad. I jarred the elbow and the shoulder just jumped out. At that time I couldn't have done any more, because I was up to something like 200 press-ups a day, but it still wasn't enough to keep the shoulder in.

Gary Lineker: Against Morocco Ray Wilkins got sent off, so we were up against it straight away and we managed to get a draw. Obviously there was a lot of pressure on the team, as there always is. The manager and everybody were probably being ridiculed at home, but we escaped a little bit from that. We knew what we had to do and then we turned it round against Poland.

Viv Anderson: It was just a general meeting. Peter Reid mentioned that we were playing 4-3-3 at the time and he said, 'Why don't we go to a 4-4-2?' And we went on from there. We did quite well after that. We brought little Hodgey into midfield with Trevor Steven. Peter Beardsley came in. That's where they started the combination of Peter Beardsley and Gary Lineker up front. So it was just a chat amongst the players and the staff were there at the time.

Bryan Robson: I think that's a good sign of a good manager, one who'll sit and listen to the players. He doesn't have to do what the players say or what they think is right. The manager always makes his own decision, but I think Bobby Robson always used to take the opinions of the players and, if he thought it was right, he was man enough to say, 'Right then, let's try it that way and let's see if it works.'

Gary Lineker: I think I'd not scored for England for about six games. If we'd gone out of the World Cup that might have been the end of my England career. Who knows what would have happened? But I finished up scoring three in that game against Poland. I went on to be the top scorer [in the 1986 World Cup Finals] and I moved to Barcelona, so things changed a little bit because of that, and obviously I became a famous footballer throughout the world rather than just on one side of Merseyside.

Peter Shilton: I remember the game [against Argentina] for a couple of reasons obviously. I was made captain in the quarter-finals of the World Cup. The atmosphere in the Aztec Stadium was fantastic. Brilliant stadium. The pitch wasn't particularly good but the atmosphere was great. It wasn't a great game but we contained what was quite a good Argentinian side. And we felt we were still right in the game. We said at half-time that if we could keep it going, the first goal could be vital. And we didn't feel under any pressure defensively. And obviously we had the Maradona handball incident, and I felt that was a crucial point in the game. A lot of things have been said about the goal. All I've ever said is that if the referee wasn't in a good position to see it, the linesman certainly was. I looked straight across that way, knew what had happened, and the linesman looked at me ... and then ran off up the pitch. I started running after the referee and one or two of the players did, but you learn over the years that it's not going to do any good. It was a sickly feeling. A lot of people said to me, 'Why didn't you go and crunch him?' but it wasn't like that. He actually played the ball into the box and started running for a one-two. I think he would have been offside, but I think it came off one of our players. He was running into the box at full pelt. I suddenly realized what was happening and I felt that I could go and get it. Something tells you that you can just get to the ball if you go for it. And I think I would have maybe got a fist to it. And that's why he probably handled it. Because he knew that I was going to beat him to it. Straight after that, Maradona scored a very good goal. I still feel that we lost our concentration a little bit because of the incident and he was allowed to run through us a bit too easily but credit to him, he took his goal well.

Bobby Robson: I blame the referee, I don't blame the players. Players will try some things, saying they're legitimate, a little nudge or whatever, but his was a blatant handball. I don't think for one moment Maradona thought he would ever get away with it. It's up to the referee, and the linesman, who was in a good position, to see that. That is their job.

Coping with the Media

Nigel Clarke: I suppose it all started really in the European Championships of 1988 when we'd gone there hopeful of doing very well – we hadn't lost a qualifying match – and our first match was against the Irish and we thought we would beat them but we got beaten 1–0. The next game was against Holland. We lost that 3-1 and then we lost to Russia, also 3–1, and I remember to this day the boos rising up to the terraces in Frankfurt and [Bobby] Robson sitting there with his frozen face, shifting round uncomfortably.

Sir Bert Millichip: The public and the media were really bringing great pressure upon me and upon the Football Association to get rid of the manager, but the pressure not only came from the media. We were getting pressure from the government upon withdrawing the team from Germany because of crowd misconduct. The sports minister, Colin Moynihan, was certainly trying to pressurize me to say that the team should come home before we finished the competition.

Nigel Clarke: The headlines said then that Robson should go and he didn't go, and they started to get personal at the start of the World Cup campaign. That year we were at home to Sweden and we drew 0–0 and afterwards, in the dressing-room, I asked him a question and he said, 'Well, a draw, nil–nil, against Denmark is quite a good result.' I filed this, that he'd got the wrong team, and the headlines next day, 'Go, in the name of God, go, because you can't do the job, you don't even know who you're playing against.' That really started the fury, and then we had a friendly against Saudi Arabia in Riyadh. We drew 1–1, and afterwards I was talking to the Saudi Arabian manager and he said, 'Mr Robson is not a good manager, he should be a train-driver,' so, bang, that went in as well, followed by the big headline, 'Go, in the name of Allah, go.'

Peter Shilton: Deep down, I don't think any of the players were very happy about the criticism. It's happened to nearly every England manager over the years, but it got personal with Bobby Robson. I remember there was a photograph of Bobby Robson looking down the beach. They brought the wives over to keep us company for a week, which was a good idea because we'd been out there a little while. And there was a picture of Bobby Robson looking down the beach and it said Bobby Robson was eyeing the wives up. It was scandalous thing for the press to do. We thought Bobby Robson took everything really well, and he came out of it with a lot of credit, at the end of the day.

Bobby Robson: It's very difficult, because I am as human as you are. I have feelings, I have a family, I can read, and I couldn't stop it, I couldn't change it. I just had to ignore it and get on with things. I had vitriolic attacks. They got very personal. They got over the top. Unfortunately, it sells papers and most people in the country buy those sort of papers. The England job was about getting results. If you get results you'll get a good press. If you don't get results you'll get a bad press and you've got to get out of the job because it'll go on.

Gary Lineker: You couldn't help but like Bobby [Robson]. I mean Bobby's a really nice guy who's incredibly enthusiastic about the game. He's very loyal to his players. He proved, with his fair amount of success, that sticking by the players that you can trust at that level works, and I think they were his great strengths. I don't think tactically he was the greatest coach in the world. He got names wrong and things like that, but that added to the way the players were fond of him, and he was good to work for.

Heavy Programmes

Steve Coppell: There is a long-held theory that there were too many games and all the important international tournaments came at the end of the season in June. I always remember my first trip abroad with England – with Don Revie to South America – and Emlyn Hughes was complaining almost non-stop during that tour that 'This is 67 games,' or 70 or whatever. He had played a lot of games and to go on tour at the end of it was a real effort for the likes of him and the Liverpool players, the more successful club players. There was a priority without doubt towards club football, and international football was an afterthought. That was why the England national team was not successful during my time.

Viv Anderson: At Forest, I think we ended up playing maybe nearly 80 games one season and then at the end of the season we went on tour. We went to Sweden for an international [June 1979]. I think we drew, Emlyn Hughes hit the bar. And I remember meself and Tony Woodcock being in the bath after the game. You wouldn't believe how tired we were. We didn't play anyway near as we should do for our country, and that's solely because we'd played so many games.

Bryan Robson: I can remember a perfect example because I don't think I ever felt as tired in an England game. We had just beaten Everton 1–0 in the FA Cup Final [in 1985] and on the Sunday I had to fly out with England to play a game in Finland, and it was a really hard game for us. I felt shattered. We were only halfway through the game and I was feeling as if it was the last 10 minutes.

Steve Coppell: I think the England team is handicapped. Whenever we enter a world or a European competition we start behind everybody else because our preparation is so poor because of the number of games we play. I still go back to the World Cup in Italy which I think was our most successful campaign and that was as a result of not being in Europe. We didn't play European games in 1990 and we didn't have 22 clubs in the First Division, we had 20 clubs, so the players during that season played 38 competitive games, no European games and Cup competitions. I'm one of the few people who felt that our time out of Europe was a bonus.

The 1990 World Cup Finals

Bobby Robson: I knew that in Gascoigne we had a rare talent. A lot of people were asking me to put him in the team before I did. You've got to ignore what people say. You have to do what you think is right. I saw Gascoigne developing, and he was a kid learning the game. He did silly things. He was indisciplined. He cost Tottenham points once or twice. That's all right at Tottenham, but you can't do that in international football. I didn't play him until I felt he was ready. Of course, I used to make him angry when I didn't pick him and I wanted to make him angry: 'You're not ready, I've watched you play, I've seen you do daft things. When you learn how to play correctly and don't abuse other people, I'll pick you.' He accepted it because he's a lovable character, great to work with, and when I put him in I thought he was just about ready. He was young, raw, but full of talent, and he did reasonably well. I think he probably played a little bit better than I thought. I knew that we had in him a different player, someone who could make a difference, provided he could control himself and keep his head.

Peter Shilton: The first game was against Eire, just for a change. I mean, we always played against Eire. But I remember that we came out in Cagliari, and I stood there and just before the kick-off I looked up the pitch and there was a wind blowing directly down the pitch straight into my face. And it was like a First Division match on a Saturday afternoon in England, and here we are in the World Cup in Italy, and I'm seeing all the players that I play against on a

Saturday, in opposition. And it was a real tough battle in that first half. The ball was being pumped forward and we were having to win it, and the wind was against us. And what an opening to the World Cup in Italy.

Bryan Robson: We played the first game against the Republic of Ireland and then we felt that a sweeper system would definitely suit the players that we had available at that time. It makes you a lot stronger at the back and you don't give anything away. Myself, Gary Lineker and Chris Waddle had a chat to Bobby Robson and we said that we felt a sweeper system would suit the team, and he agreed because he had Mark Wright, Terry Butcher and Des Walker, who were three really good centre-halves at the time. The three of them weren't afraid to go into a sweeper system and it was the right choice. I mean, it nearly won us the World Cup. A little bit more luck in the penalty shoot-out in the semi-final and we could have gone on to win it.

Don Howe: Tactically, in the modern game, I think you've got to be more adaptable. There's no doubt about that. We sometimes get accused of having players that can't adapt. I think they can. I think Bobby Robson proved in Italy that you can adapt our players to different systems. We played the Republic of Ireland in the first game and we drew 1–1, and then we got to play Holland in the second game. And Bobby had discussed it at length with the staff and he'd decided he wanted to play a sweeper. One of the things that influenced Bobby and myself was that we'd played Holland in the European Championships two years ahead of that in Germany and we got walloped and van Basten and Gullit ran wild and we couldn't cope with them. And that's what influenced Bob to play with Mark Wright as a sweeper. Terry Butcher went in at right-back, and we got on with the job. We got a creditable draw out of the game and we coped with all the problems that the Dutch had thrown at us two years earlier, and the players liked it very much. In fact, they were convinced about it. We went into the third game against Egypt, and Bobby went back to 4-2-4. I wouldn't say the players were moaning, but they were saying, 'Well, we like the sweeper.' He brought it out again when we played Belgium. The players were so convinced about it, and so keen on it, that they wanted to keep it going all the way through. And it got us a fair amount of success and then we had that semi-final against Germany where we played with the sweeper, and the game could have gone either way on the day, and we lost the semi-final on penalties.

Bobby Robson: Because we got confident, the team liked it, and it was right. There was a spare player. If we got into trouble, we could always play the ball back, not forward, and use Wright to keep the movement continuous. Walker tackled, marked and dispossessed, Butcher did the same, and Wright became the elegant player. It suited Walker, it suited Butcher and it suited Wright. But every time I got a goal behind I took the sweeper off. I dispensed with the sweeper against Cameroon. I started with a sweeper but found we were 2–1 down and had to take him off. I did it with the semi-final. I started with a sweeper, we were trailing, I took him off.

Peter Shilton: I think the England manager's job is something that every person should aim for, if he goes into management, because it is the ultimate job. I'll never forget when I came back from the World Cup in Italy and we went through the streets of Luton; the response we got from the public who turned out to cheer us home just showed how much it actually means to the nation to do really well. I would say to anybody that gets the England job, 'Grab it with both hands and you've got an opportunity of a lifetime. You've got to be thick-skinned and strong enough to be able to cope with it.'

28

'Graham Taylor had the pedigree'

The Graham Taylor Era, 1990–94

Graham Taylor took over from Bobby Robson as England manager after the 1990 World Cup Finals. England lost only one of Taylor's first 21 internationals, and they qualified for the 1992 European Championships. However, they finished bottom of Group One after goalless draws against Denmark and France, and a 2–1 defeat to hosts Sweden, a game in which England captain Gary Lineker was substituted. The 1994 World Cup campaign fell away with defeats in Norway and Holland, and England didn't qualify for the Finals. Taylor and his assistant, Lawrie McMenemy, resigned in November 1993 and, in January 1994, Terry Venables was appointed England coach.

Taylor Appointed

Charles Hughes: Graham Taylor came as a student on our courses, and I got to know him as a young coach. A very good coach, and a great enthusiast. I think he was at Lincoln at the time I got to know him and then he went to Watford.

They were in the Fourth Division when he went there and they got to second position in the First Division. I watched the club play several times during that period and sometimes the football was really outstanding.

Steve Coppell: I think he was given the international job more because of his success at Aston Villa when he didn't play long-ball football. He played with a very innovative five-man defence with three centre-halves. They were the only team in the country who did it and they finished second in the League and you could argue that with a little bit more luck with injuries they could have won the League. But the 'long-ball type', the direct style of play, is a tag you just do not shake off. There's always somebody in the press who'll ram it down the readers' throats. Or, people don't remember Graham Taylor for his passing Aston Villa side, they remember the Watford side.

Gary Lineker: I think it's certainly difficult for someone who's no international experience whatsoever to take over the England team. He was a very good club manager and probably will be again. He's a great organizer and a good coach, but he'd never been a player at international level. Well, there's no way else to get experience until you get the job, so it was difficult for him to appreciate the game and the differences that there are.

Players

Graham Taylor: Taking over in 1990, I was taking over a side that had reached the World Cup semi-finals and probably I'm the only England manager that's taken over what has seemed to be a successful side. I took over and Shilton retired. Along with Banks, he was arguably our best-ever goalkeeper. He played 125 times, a great goalkeeper. Butcher, 70-odd caps, retired. A leader in his own right. He would get people to play not only by how he performed but how he told them. And then Bryan Robson was injured and ultimately he retired. A leader. Ninety caps. A team had peaked, but I'd got to come in and change that *and* qualify for the European Championships. It didn't go well for me because we didn't qualify for the World Cup. Our record, not just under my managership, shows that we're pretty good at winning our friendly games but we tend not to win the vital games.

Charles Hughes: I think he worked hard enough to deserve success but the gods decreed otherwise. One example was the game in Holland. That game could have gone the other way. There were two home games when we could – and I think should – have won but we didn't. Now those games were beyond the control of the manager. He'd done everything he could to prepare the team, but on the day they didn't get the result.

Graham Taylor: I had 38 games in charge and Gascoigne only played in 11. He could have played in 12 but I made him substitute in Dublin. Once he'd come back from injury, and I'd picked him, I decided that his talent was such that he should be given licence to go and play. I'm probably one of the few England managers who said, 'Look, I recognize him as a gifted player, let's give him a platform.' In eight World Cup qualifying games, Paul Gascoigne scored four goals. In a couple of those games he'd be the first to say that he probably didn't play as well as he should have done, but he did score goals and of course his presence on the pitch lifted everybody. I'm only too sorry that Paul was suffering first of all from a hernia injury and then got this [knee] injury. The other person that I still find most interesting was Barnes. Liverpool withdrew him from the tour to New Zealand and Australia, as Manchester United and Arsenal did with their players, which they had a right to do. Barnes then got injured and you can't play players if they're injured. My disappointment was that the two players that I thought had great talent were not available for a long period of time.

Gary Lineker: I think the first couple of games he stuck by the team that had done so well in the World Cup and they did well in those two games. Then obviously he wanted to change it and play his team and he got rid of a lot of the experienced players, like Beardsley and Waddle and Robson, players that had proved they could do it at international level. I would think now if he had his time back he might rethink a little bit. In the European Championships admittedly Barnes and Gascoigne were injured, but we still left Waddle and Beardsley at home, the other two that can create something. There was hardly a chance in those tournaments for the strikers. Nothing really fell to me so I could certainly sense the difference on the field.

Graham Taylor: Chris Waddle was in the first six or seven squads I named. He was selected to play against the Republic of Ireland in Dublin and pulled out a couple of hours before the game with an ankle injury, but all of that was lost in the fact that I'd made Gascoigne a substitute. Chris was also selected to play against the Republic of Ireland in the return game, in March, but pulled out through an injury. He had suffered a concussion when he played for Marseille. If I made any mistake with Chris it was because at the start of my campaign I told him and John Barnes that I couldn't see myself playing them as two wide players, I could see myself playing one up front and one wide. I'd have been better saying nothing because once I'd said that I then selected John Barnes and I know in Chris's position I'd think, 'Well, that means I'm out.' We went to Turkey and I saw that as a solid 4-4-2 game. Facing reality, Chris isn't always the best selection for what is going to be a scrappy, hard game. We won the game 1–0 with a scrambled goal, but I think that was a starting point where certain sections of the media decided that you can always be flogged if you leave out what is seen as a skilful player. I did bring Chris back, at home against Turkey, when we beat them 1–0, when Bryan Robson played as well, and he got heavily criticized for his performance.

Systems

Bryan Robson: I think he felt that putting a lot of good players together they would naturally play, and I still think good players need a formation and a team pattern to go to. Now whether he actually acquired that in the latter part of his career with England as manager, I'm not sure because I wasn't involved, but that's what I sensed in the first couple of years.

Graham Taylor: I wanted the ball to be passed. If we were going to keep possession, which of course you have to do, I wanted it to be passed earlier, even if we kept it at the back. That's what I mean by 'keeping the tempo'. I'm probably a member of the Hansen and Lawrenson fan club. If they kept the ball between them it was never sloppy passing, it wasn't a pass that went behind them, it wasn't a pass that was dying, it was the right pass. When you come on to the international scene you have to keep the ball. It's harder to get flank men going because they're man-marked. You've almost invariably got a sweeper against you so you can't actually push the ball in space.

Bryan Robson: I think the difference between the continental teams and the British players is that in general their defenders are a lot more comfortable on the ball than a lot of our defenders. If you give the ball away a lot at international level they will punish you and they'll make it a very hard game for you because you're forever chasing. Over the last 10 or 15 years we've looked towards the hard-work, commitment side, and we're talking a lot about 'the long ball', whereas in Holland and Germany and Italy, they all work on the technique of the players, and the touch on the ball, to be comfortable in any area that the ball comes to you. People keep saying to me that we should play the British way and play flat out, but people want to go to places like Monterey, where it's 110 degrees and high altitude, and try to run about like you do in England. You'd probably have a few heart attacks about the place. You'd end up with not enough players for a team. It's important that we do change our methods in England and play a passing game. We've got to educate our players on how to slow a game down to the pace they want to go and then quicken the pace of the game when they want to quicken the pace.

Ian Wright: It's difficult, especially for the first five or six games. The opposing defenders get the forwards to keep running across and trying to close them down, and the emphasis is more on not giving the ball away. No matter how many runs I might make as a forward, the emphasis on the midfielders is not to put that ball through if they don't feel it's 100 per cent on. My first games for England, I found I could hardly walk when I was coming off the pitch. I was doing so much running, and I had touched the ball maybe two or three times in each half. Towards the end of the World Cup run, I found that I was trying to stay more in the last third and not worrying so much about closing the defenders down and I think the players got more confidence in me when they was laying it in to me, but at the start I was so eager to do well I was losing the ball and I was trying to get it back and I was just digging a deeper rut for myself.

David Miller: Instead of making the player fit the system, the England managers have been trying to adapt the system to suit the player, or players, and therefore you've had constant change and it's not surprising that the players are often bemused. It's history now, but the daftest thing you've ever seen was the tactical system that Taylor came up with to play against Norway, in Oslo, in the World Cup qualifying match. It was bizarre. There was no possible way it could work. It baffled the players. It had failed before it had even got on the field.

Coping with the Media

Sir Bert Millichip: Graham Taylor had the pedigree of being a successful manager, a son of a journalist, a man of great dignity, a man who we thought could control the media. He was a gentleman and I have to say that I was very sorry that he did not succeed, or that the team did not achieve the results that allowed him to continue as manager.

Nigel Clarke: Graham Taylor wanted to be liked. He wanted journalists on his side. He gave his number out so he could be contacted in an emergency but he didn't do one basic thing – he didn't win important matches. Whether you like a person or not, whether they're a friend or not, you have to report the truth, see only what your eyes tell you and hear what you hear. You could sit in press conferences with Graham Taylor and begin to wonder what he was saying. You could look at the team he fielded and begin to wonder what you were watching. Now, you owe it to your newspaper and to yourself to be honest. You have to write what you see is the truth. You have to write this because you're not writing for Graham Taylor, you're not writing for the Football Association, you're writing for the people who buy the *Daily Mirror* every day, and you can't treat them as fools.

Graham Taylor: It's like taking any job. Until you've done it the first time, you think about what it's like and then you suddenly find out what it is like. I went into the 13th game before we were defeated. We went the whole year without a defeat, but as soon as you lose a game, or don't perform in a way that people think you should, or in fact leave somebody out and don't pick somebody else, you're always going to be hounded. People say it goes with the job; a lot of it does go with the job and you've got to be prepared to accept that. I think there's a difference between constructive criticism and personal criticism and I think all England managers, not just myself, have suffered far too much personal criticism.

Peter Swales: Nobody in the world could have taken the type of pressure that Graham Taylor took. He took some real stick and that's bound to get you on edge and bound to get you rocking a bit, and must mean that you're not thinking about the right move every time. You tend to take gambles that you wouldn't have taken if things had been going okay. I'll always maintain that under different circumstances Graham could have been a good England manager. Newspapers today aren't *news*papers because they can be beaten to the punch by television and by radio, so they've become more critical. I think papers have changed their roles and they're either for somebody or against somebody and, if they get their knife into you, you've had your chips. I can think back to some of the situations – when we lost an odd game with Graham Taylor, or Holland equalized at Wembley, or Norway equalized at Wembley, or we didn't play as well as we should have done in Poland – and they can be mightily destructive and very personal really.

Nigel Clarke: We went to the European Championships under Graham Taylor [in 1992] and we didn't play very well in all three matches. The last match, against Sweden, we were winning 1–0, then Graham Taylor completely and utterly blew it. The Swedes equalized, 1–1, and then brought on Johnny Ekstrom as an extra forward and Taylor didn't seem to know what to do and how to combat a straightforward substitution like that. He could have reinforced his defence or pulled somebody out of midfield, or anything. We lost 2–1 and it was an appalling performance, culminating, of course, in him pulling off Gary Lineker, the only person who was likely to get a goal, with 20 minutes to go.

Gary Lineker: Obviously I wasn't particularly happy about it but it happened. There's been a lot spoken about it, whether it was right or whether it was wrong, but the manager did it. I was choked at the time, of course I was. A striker always fancies scoring and I still fancied that if the chance came along I might get that goal that would get us through but that didn't happen and that ended up being my last game. But I don't lose any sleep about it now, that's for sure.

Nigel Clarke: I think the *Sun* called Graham Taylor 'the turnip' and we did a back-page picture of him standing on his head, because we felt he didn't know what he was talking about, always blaming other people. Other newspapers wanted to get in on the act and the headline was unbelievable, 'Swedes 2 Turnips 1', which was a classic, and a picture of Taylor's face as a turnip on the back. We got after him and the *Sun* got after him and of course he became nationally known as 'Taylor the turnip' and I suppose he took it very well. He must have hurt inside an awful lot but he still spoke to us and acknowledged us. From there it became very personal. In some ways that was wrong and in some ways it was right. The tabloid press knew, and we said it, that he wasn't good enough and I suppose the papers had had enough of him and they felt that it was fair game to have a go at him personally. In the end the headlines got as bad as you'll ever get: 'Go Now Taylor,' 'It's Time to Quit,' 'You've Fallen' and all that and piles of horse-manure on the back. After we'd lost to Norway, which was a dreadful result, the headline was 'Norse Manure'. He hung on and hung on and he made it worse for himself and I think the last headline was the San Marino one when the *Daily Mirror* used the whole back page as an open letter to the Football Association written in Graham's hand – 'Dear Sir Bert Millichip, here's my letter of resignation' – and left a place blank at the bottom for him to sign it.

Jack Charlton: Who do we let select the England team? Do you let the manager do it or do you let the media do it? If you pick a team, some paper would disagree with three of them, and another paper would disagree with three others, because they've all got their individual choices and selection has always been and always will be a matter of opinion. Now the opinion of the manager is the only one that counts. He's got people round him if he wants to float an idea: 'I'm not sure, what do you think?' The pressure put on England team managers by the press to do what they say is enormous, and if you don't do what they tell you, you finish up 'a turnip'. They're the turnips.

Graham Taylor: If people want to act the way that they act, if people want to say that, they must live with themselves. I remember one of the most difficult things was when we were in the States. We'd gone out there on the back of this draw with Poland, defeat in Norway, and then we'd lost to the States 2–0, and my wife was being chased up back at home. She's at home with her mother, my mother-in-law, who's 84 or 85, in a wheelchair, and she's looking after her at home. She comes back one day and she can't get into the drive because the media's there, people wanting interviews. She's no responsibility to do interviews. As the England manager I think I've a responsibility to face the press but my wife doesn't have to do them. She can't actually get into the garage, and a gentleman, if there is such a thing, from the press, says, 'Do an interview,' and she said, 'No, I don't do them,' to which he politely tells her that it's about ******* time she started then. I know the paper he works for and that's something the public doesn't read about. But they'll read about Graham Taylor with a turnip on his head. When I resigned from the FA I couldn't get into my house for two days. My parents had a knock on their door, opened their door and a television camera is already working, asking them questions. They are in their mid-seventies. I'm saying, 'Well, hold on a minute, come on, getting the story beats everything, does it? It doesn't matter what you do, it doesn't matter who you upset, it doesn't matter who you hurt?' And yet you people will criticize *my* language. I've seen these people behave. I've seen them on England trips. I don't do myself any favours by saying this to you because some of them will think, 'Oh, right, we'll have him,' but there's so much I could say about their behaviour, about their conduct, when they are representing England. We represent England playing, they representing England as England's journalists. I've seen their behaviour but our public don't read about them because it's not a story, is it?

Bryan Robson: I always think it's been wrong, the amount of criticism that the England manager goes through, because, no matter what happens, that man is put into a job and he's trying to do the job to the best of his ability. It is a sport. We all want to do well for our country. Nobody wants England to fail, but you've got to appreciate that there are going to be pitfalls and people are going to fall down somewhere, and I don't think they deserve the amount of criticism that they actually take on.

Terry Venables: It's a game that we will never agree on, and that is what is wonderful about the game. I can guarantee that you and I and a couple of friends can go to different corners of the stadium – we've done this before as an exercise – and when we come back we'll all have different opinions about how players have played. We will never pick the same team. We always think someone's better or someone's worse, and really it's what people think that is important. The barometer is in the pub, or in the cafe, where the guys are chatting about their teams and their players, and this is where I believe newspapers have a terrific responsibility to their readers because fans can't come up to me, or anybody else in the game, and ask about what's happening; they have to rely on newspapers to give them credible information, because with the wrong information they're going to have the wrong arguments in the pub, and people can be taken down the wrong road.

Terry Venables – England coach

Terry Venables: The first thing was to look at two or three systems of play fairly quickly to see what was suited, and then maybe have two very simple systems so you could actually change during the game. It's like cricket; sometimes teams get their eye in, and they've got you, and I think if you can make a change without any complications it can throw them again. Now, I don't have the players for a long period of time, so I had to see if I could get intelligent players, players who could understand what I wanted. I had to get players together who could sacrifice the way they played at their club for this England team. I want the star of the team to be 'the team'. I talked about 'Christmas trees' and 'oak trees' to give a visual idea of what I was doing. The Christmas tree expression came after I'd written a formation down and it looked like a Christmas tree, so I just mentioned that, and of course that became the vogue. But it's a system which I can change to another system with the same players, and they have to know exactly what their jobs are. At the very highest level, you have to have plans, short-term and long-term, so my first thing was to try and get results straight away because we hadn't been getting them. We wanted everybody to start feeling good about themselves again, and people thinking, 'We can win at this level'. I feel quite confident about it, but you've got to have the breaks, there's no doubt about that.

29

'Players' wages have risen'

Into the 1990s

Through the 1980s, and in the early 1990s, changes came thick and fast: innovative financial schemes such as stock-market flotations, debentures, mergers and ground-sharing; the long-term effects of 'freedom of contract' on players' wages; an increasing awareness of supporters' opinions through fanzines and organizations like the Football Supporters' Association; new safety regulations after the Hillsborough Disaster and the subsequent Taylor Report; schemes to link clubs with the community and families; and the launch of a Premier League.

Going Public

Irving Scholar: When I first became involved, about 1982, Spurs had the biggest debt in football. At the time it was certainly very substantial. It was between 5 and 6 million pounds. The bottom had fallen out of the transfer market. The 1-million-pound players had come, failed and gone. I think the biggest single transfer following that period was around £500,000, when we bought Alan Brazil [in March 1983]. It was clear that we needed to raise a substantial sum of capital. I wasn't in favour of selling players, so we had discussions with a number of City advisers who finally said they thought it was possible. We went in to float the company, which we did in October 1983. At the time we raised about £1.1 million from the existing shareholders and then from the City we raised another about £3.8 million, which didn't clear our debt but went a very long way to doing so. We were the first club in Europe to do it. We had a lot of inquiries, funnily enough, from European clubs, very few, if any, from other English clubs. Manchester United seemed at the time to be most intrigued by it but it was many years later that they did their flotation and at the time I think it was about four times oversubscribed so it proved it could be done. I was always concerned that there would be some Football League or Football Association regulation that was going to prohibit it but the call didn't come and everything was fine.

Bernie Kingsley: I had an objection, and a number of people did at the time, to the whole concept. I don't particularly like the stock exchange anyway. I don't think it's a good thing, floating the club on the stock exchange. There is this club which you really care about, and you care about its stability, and suddenly you're part of this massive international casino, this big gambling game.

Freedom of Contract

Phil Thompson: I don't think you'll be seeing too many testimonials in the forthcoming years for players who gave their all for 10 or more years. The loyalty side of it is not as much. They don't see it as 'I'm going to a football club, I'm going to be there for 10 years.' I think it's four at the most, and moving on again. It's a sad side of football, but it's the way that it's gone, and the way it will go.

Alan Ball: If I buy somebody and give him a two-year contract, and at the end of the second year we get relegated, he and other people have failed, as indeed the manager has, and, at the end of his two years, I've got to give him the same money, or something a little bit more, or he gets a free transfer. Now he's failed, he hasn't done his job for two years, but he's still going to get the same money or more. Or, if I'd have bought him for £100,000, I lose £100,000 and he gets a free transfer. So I lose, everybody loses, but he gains. And he's been a failure. Now that puts it in a nutshell for me.

John Giles: I think it's a great thing that there are now players who had the benefit of the freedom of contract actually coming into management, the likes of Kenny Dalglish, Hoddle, Kevin Keegan, who are financially independent of the game, which is a big change to years ago where players made very little money from the game and, to stay in the game, management was the next step.

Jon Holmes: If we take a situation where a player's coming up to the end of his contract. He's maybe got 18 months to run. We would have a meeting and I would say to him, 'How do you see your career going? Where do you want to be, professionally, in five years' time?' That doesn't mean just geographically. It means in what situation do you want to put your life, and so on, and I would try to get them to elaborate on where they actually think they want to go. Now it may be that they are able to achieve that with the current club. It may be, on the other hand, that they feel they've got to move on, for whatever reason, and in consequence we would devise a plan of action. Should you go in and see the manager now or should you wait for the manager to call you in and say, 'Look, we want you to sign a new contract?' In general my advice would be to wait and let the other side take the action, because the nearer to the end of your contract you get, the more powerful you get. I do remember talking to Gary Lineker about going to Barcelona. I did outline to him an alternative scenario whereby he stayed at Everton and didn't take the [Barcelona] opportunity. I think he's glad now that he took that opportunity but you have to see both sides of it and someone has to be talking to you objectively about the big decisions you're taking in your life.

Players' Wages

Peter Hill-Wood: It's always surprised me that there are clubs who are prepared to pay quite a lot more than we are for individual players. I think the players generally are very well paid. Our players are very well paid. I don't think it has got totally out of control yet, but in the end the spectators and the commercial side have to provide enough money to pay the wages and maintain the stadium and buy new players.

Tommy Lawton: I don't begrudge the player at all. If I'd have been in the same position I would have done the same, and I think any normal, sensible person would turn round and say, 'So would I.' I blame the system. The system is wrong whereby a player can earn £10,000 a week plus his perks. I mean, £10,000 a week!

Jon Holmes: The clubs still do hold the upper hand. They have the players under contract and while they're under contract they're not allowed to talk to anyone else, unless the club says so, and they do get compensation in the form of transfer fees whether they move in contract or out of contract. Now, it's my opinion that the transfer fee is, in fact, a restraint of trade, and there are moves in the European Parliament to get it to be declared a restraint of trade but it's a fairly common system throughout the world. Interestingly, when I dealt with Gary Lineker's move to Japan, the concept of transfer fees was completely alien to them. They couldn't understand why the player, if he was at the end of his contract, couldn't just move for nothing. That was the system they were using in business.

Peter Swales: The sooner we get licensed agents in Great Britain, certainly in England, the better. I probably would like to see all players handled through the PFA. I think we could have one central agency.

Gordon Taylor: The PFA have tried to develop a much more hands-on approach as a union at the time of players signing contracts and transfers, so we've been handling some of the younger stars, such as your David Battys and your Roy Keanes, in order to avoid many of the problems we've had with some of the old established ones where we've had to settle rows between their agents and lawyers, their accountants and the Revenue.

Ian Wright: I think a lot of the time it is a very well-paid profession, I'm not trying to hide that fact, but when they write how much people are earning they do exaggerate a lot. It's a short profession and you have to try and get as much as you can.

Jon Holmes: Players' wages have risen. I think what's happened is that most clubs have realized now that they've got to compete with the top clubs. Therefore they've all started paying bigger and bigger wages. Funnily enough one or two of the bigger clubs don't pay as big wages as one or two of the smaller clubs. Blackburn will be popularly perceived as the biggest payers currently in football, amongst the clubs, and they're not one of the bigger clubs. You might say they're exceptional, but then you could say the same about Derby, who've been taken over by Lionel Pickering, a gentleman with a great deal of money, and

Wolves, taken over by Sir Jack Hayward. Neither Derby nor Wolves would be perceived as one of the big clubs, but they're now perceived as big payers. At the same time, a lot of the money has gone on stadiums. I don't think it's fair to say that all that money has gone to players. They now pay directors and chief executives. They now have larger staffs, commercial staffs and so on. They pay managers a lot more money now.

The Hillsborough Disaster

Trevor Hicks: I'm chairman of the Hillsborough family support group. I had the misfortune to travel to Hillsborough on 15 April 1989 with my family – my ex-wife Jenny and our two daughters. We set off as a family in the morning, and by the evening of that same day there was only Jenny and I. Our two daughters were dead. I think we saw all the ills of 60 years of neglect coming together all on one day and unfortunately 96 people died. We saw the FA as totally insensitive to representations of fans from Liverpool Football Club regarding the choice of venue. We had a police operation which was totally geared up to running a police state, confining people, locking them up like animals behind fences. We had a ground which was totally inadequate in terms of its technical merits. We had supporters who, to some extent, did come late, but sadly the ones at the front in many ways were the ones who died. There was a club without a safety certificate, trying to bring far too many people through too few turnstiles.

Sir Bert Millichip: What happened at Hillsborough was something which, quite frankly, could have happened years before. It is surprising that it hadn't happened before. It's surprising the complacency that there was even after it had happened. I do believe, now, since Mr Justice Taylor's report and the considerable amount of money that is being poured into the game – some of it by relaxation in taxation by the government, some of it under the goodwill of the Football Trust and the remainder of it found by the clubs themselves – that clubs are now far better equipped with far better facilities for spectators and greater safety.

Ground Changes

Peter Hill-Wood: As a result of the Taylor Report you have to put seats in a ground. People can't stand. Inevitably, to sit at a football match costs more than to stand, because you have to pay money to buy the seat to put there, and therefore the prices of entry have gone up, and it is an expensive pastime and therefore it is a worry that the less fortunate, less well-off people cannot afford to come to football as often as they used to. Here at Arsenal we try and provide seats for local schoolboys which we give them for nothing when we have a match that isn't going to sell out. We try to get them used to the idea of coming to football, but it is much more expensive than it used to be.

Irving Scholar: Whoever chose Lord Justice Taylor really deserves an enormous pat on the back. If you'd have left it to football, football would have hoped that the problem would go away. It would have been 'heads in the sand'. I don't mean that in a nasty way but I don't think that they wanted to face up to the facts that football grounds in the UK needed an enormous amount of money. They were fortunate that when the legislation came out it coincided with probably the deepest recession since the 1930s, so building costs had reduced substantially.

David Dein: At Highbury we had a difficult problem because we had 28,000 standing positions and something like 16,000 seats. We had to find something like £22 million, which was found from a cocktail of sources. We funded it from a debenture bond, from our own resources and from the Football Trust.

Peter Hill-Wood: We devised this debenture scheme which wasn't universally popular. It was a debenture that cost you either £1,500 in the centre and top or £1,100 in the lower tier, which didn't entitle you to a great deal. It entitled you to apply for a cheap season ticket and it enabled you to have access to all the facilities in the new North Bank.

Ken Chaplin: There was no way that we could spend the money to bring the Plough Lane ground [Wimbledon] up to the standard required by the Taylor Report. We had only 2,000 seats available at the start and the council actually declared that the seating accommodation would have to be reduced by 10 per cent each year. The move to Selhurst was a necessity. It's not home at Selhurst, it's just a temporary lodging as far as I'm concerned.

Alec Lodge: There's nobody more disappointed than myself that we've got to leave here [Leeds Road, Huddersfield], but, when you think of all the ramifications of the Taylor Report, you've only got to walk round this field and you can see it's just not a proposition to keep it going. I hate moving, because in all honesty there isn't a better playing field in the whole of England. I don't think anybody wants to leave. It's just the financial aspect of it. I don't know how to describe it. It's like a chap who goes into a new house and makes a garden and he absolutely dotes on the garden and if somebody comes to plough it up he'll feel disturbed about it, just as people feel disturbed about having this place ploughed up. It's a personal thing.

Launch of a Premier League, 1992–93

Irving Scholar: I think the Premier League was first

discussed about '85 or '86. I'd actually had a discussion with Ted Croker, who was then the secretary of the Football Association, and I said to him, 'If we were to set up our own League, would you back us?' He said they'd be very, very interested. It had to be in tandem with the FA because, at the end of it all, it's the Football Association that grants the right for the League to exist, and it actually happened around 1990. We were all invited one evening to ITV to have a dinner and it was discussed then, and it was agreed that David Dein and Noel White, who was then chairman of Liverpool, would go to the Football Association and have a chat with them and see what their reaction would be if we were to approach them and it was very warm, very, very warm indeed.

Alex Fynn: When the ITV contract happened in 1988 and ITV showed that all they were interested in were the big clubs, the clubs themselves realized that they were the only clubs that mattered, but they were locked in this archaic structure of a 92-club League. How were they going to get out of it? They had won the advantage of keeping 100 per cent of their home gate receipts. They had won a television contract which would show them at the expense of the smaller clubs. And the next step was to try and be successful in Europe. The next step was to play within a League that benefited just them. The only way this League was going to happen was if it also matched the FA's agenda. The FA wished the England team to do well. That is almost their sole prerogative in life. At the same time as David Dein and Noel White were empowered by the big clubs to talk to the FA about the prospects of a breakaway Premier League, the FA – and I suggest this humbly – were told by me that if there was a smaller First Division then they would be placing the England team at the top of the pyramid alongside the big clubs for the first time. The FA suddenly realized that there were big clubs willing to do their dirty work for them. To break away and create a League, all they had to do was to support the big clubs. And, at the same time, they would be rid of this bugbear of the Football League, who were demanding equal power-sharing for the professional game. And that is how the Premier League came into being.

Gordon Taylor: Three-quarters of our membership was outside the top division, and we weren't convinced that the Premier League was in the best interests of the game as a whole. It was really trying to thwart the interests of the big owners and big business, who were determined to have a League if they could – Arsenal and Arsenal Reserves. Perhaps that's not fair on David Dein but I think of Arsenal because they were one of the big five, along with Manchester United, Everton, Liverpool and Tottenham. There were others who were willing to join, such as Aston Villa, but they were the main motivators. I believe Greg Dyke would have almost had a League of the big five clubs, with ITV just paying the money to them.

David Dein: In the end it took a handful of clubs to approach the FA – I have to say that we were in that group – to say, 'Look, we believe that the time is right now to set up a Premier League, a Super League, whatever, still with relegation and promotion.' I think the FA took it on board. We only ever went there with the idea that it was for the benefit of the English game as a whole. It certainly wasn't to destroy it at grassroots level and I don't think it has.

Alex Fynn: The Premier League has a lot to answer for because it has created a line of demarcation between the 'haves' and the 'have nots'. And it has created really the fear of failure, the fear of falling off the gravy-train. The clubs have spent beyond their resources. They have paid players' wages, and experimented in the transfer market, to an extent that they can't afford. Television has paid for part of these excesses but not all of it. When you add on the requirements of the Taylor Report the clubs need money so where are they going to get it from? Eureka, the fan. The fan is not a customer, he can't take his business to another shop, he is emotionally tied to that particular club.

Football in the Community

Denis Howell: Football in the community, in my view, was a very important subject which we hadn't given much thought to. One or two clubs had, but I suddenly discovered one day that there was some money going begging in the Department of the Environment. So I said to my boss at the time, the Secretary of State, 'I can spend some of this money on football in the community.' I think I got about £6 million so I sent out a message saying, 'We want schemes for football in the community and the government will give a very substantial grant towards them, provided you've spent the money by 31 March.' A lot's been done now. I mean, the Professional Footballers' Association and Gordon Taylor have been magnificent in this area and they've tried to send footballers into schools, which is another thing I feel very strongly about, bringing players into schools, bringing youngsters into clubs to enjoy the magic of the club. I don't think people in this country sufficiently realize the vital importance of the club in the community. I'm very reluctant to say there should be ground-sharing because the football ground is the cathedral church of a local community, if I can use that expression, and if the football club has that role in its community then it should be exercising that role. Football can make a great contribution if they come to see their social responsibility as well as their football responsibility.

Eddie Plumley: We [Watford] were having to renew certain players' contracts and we wanted to be absolutely sure of the community link with this football club, and the family link. We wanted to tie it down so that there was no comeback from the players' union or from the players themselves and we devised a simple phrase that we inserted into all our contracts which said that the players had to perform [in the community] for the club out of football hours on certain days of the week for a given length of time. Just a few hours a week. That grew with Graham [Taylor] and Bertie [Mee] and myself and Elton [John] back in the late seventies.

Football and the Family

Eddie Plumley: We made it so that to get in our family enclosure you had to have a child with you, a person under 16 years of age. It sold out the first year. The 500 seats were gone. There was never any·trouble because they were all Watford fans, and gradually we spread it from a seated enclosure which held the 500 to a terrace which held 1,500. As we all know it's gone on and it's spread right throughout the game. I'm going back to '78, '79, '80, when it first started.

Jack Curtis: My initial employment at Leicester City Football Club was, when I retired as a principal, to start a family enclosure. An area of the ground was given to me to develop as a family enclosure, to encourage parents and children to come back. Here was an area in which people said they were safe: 'All I've got to be is a member, buy a ticket and I know nobody else will go into that section other than a member.' So parents then allowed their youngsters to go down on their own. The last five years we've sold 6,000 membership tickets for our family enclosure, which is tremendous. And other areas of the ground, too, have developed along the same lines. The old main stand and this new one we built, everybody who goes in there will have to be a member, and you won't be allowed to get in there unless you are.

Supporter Power

Alex Fynn: Unfortunately the clubs didn't see the fan as a customer. If they saw the fan as a customer, they might actually be bothered to find what the customer wants, but the fan was a very loyal adherent who was there to be exploited.

Bernie Kingsley: Fans weren't really involved with the club at all, and never had been in the 70 years that football had been a big industry. We just went along and that was it. I think there was a view that things needed to change.

Irving Scholar: When the Spurs' West Stand was built, in the early eighties, there was no consultation [with supporters], no discussion. There was a decision taken by the board and no one seemed to be too bothered by it. By the time the East Stand was proposed, supporters viewed themselves differently, so that when there was an announcement, they said, 'Well, hold on a sec, no one's asked us,' so it was the beginning of supporter demonstrations, and that has escalated ever since, but I don't blame them, mistakes were made in terms of non-consultation and so forth.

Bernie Kingsley: The question of getting organized and trying to find out exactly what was going on at the club then came up. The real turning-point was the Shelf and the whole East Stand project. That was what for the first time really in the Scholar regime started to turn the mass of supporters against the still relatively new board. It was the idea of putting executive boxes on the best bit of terrace that we had. That really turned people against the club and against the regime at the top. It also coincided with the start of the fanzine movement. So there was a mouthpiece, if you like, for supporters to express their view.

Irving Scholar: If Tesco, for instance, decide that they're going to change something on one of their counters, they don't have all their customers standing up outside, queuing up and complaining and protesting. If they don't like it, they'll go somewhere else, but football's completely different.

Martin Cloak: I think at the time of the Shelf redevelopment it personalized the differences between Scholar and the supporters. Scholar, I think, was quite surprised that supporters had organized and that the Football Supporters' Association existed. I think the FSA actually gave us a lot of help at the start of that campaign.

Bernie Kingsley: The victory that was achieved through the 'Left on the Shelf' campaign, which was started at that time, was to retain the front part of the Shelf as a standing terrace until, obviously, everything had to go all-seater in 1994. The campaign had to be organized very, very quickly because the club released the news at the end of the season. So there was a demonstration at the last home game of the '87–88 season, which was the last game that the Shelf was in its old form.

Martin Cloak: *The Spur* was the fanzine that came out at the end of that season when they were redeveloping the Shelf. It was a new thing. I think the main reason that people liked it was that one of the many things that people have been really fed up about the club over the years was the state of the programme. They thought it was overpriced and like some sort of kids' magazine. Fans wanted something that looked as if it could try and find information. *The Spur* built up quite a sizeable sales base, and that was just people in their spare time pitching in, contributing to the magazine and selling it outside the ground. It was something that came together at around the same time as the supporters' organizations, obviously for a lot of similar reasons. The following season saw the appearance of another couple of fanzines – *My Eyes Have Seen the Glory* and *Off the Shelf.*

Peter Swales: I always think that when Howard Kendall left Manchester City the supporters appointed Peter Reid, which was probably a good choice for City. The supporters had decided that he was the man and they weren't going to accept anybody else, so if I'd come up with George Graham they wouldn't have accepted him. It was Peter Reid they wanted. From then on they were always going to have a say in any major decision, whether that was a player coming in or a player going out, a manager going out or a manager coming in, a chairman going out or a chairman coming in.

Alex Fynn: Yes, supporters are being invited on to committees, supporters are actually being invited on to boards. At Bristol City there is now almost a co-operative situation whereby the club is being run. Leeds United have an associate board, which doesn't have real power, because real power is still in the hands of the chairman and maybe one or two other colleagues, but it does have a supporter on that associate board. Charlton has got back a lot of its pride, because it went back to its roots.

Bernie Kingsley: Most of the organized voice of supporters has been born out of things which are really very negative or very unfortunate – disasters, financial crises and attempts like the bond schemes at West Ham and Arsenal. The clubs have suddenly realized that they can't just carry on taking the supporters for granted, and if supporters are going to get organized then they have to at least listen to them and talk with them.

Football in England

Peter Hill-Wood: There's no evidence that the people that go to football nowadays are less passionate than they used to be. I think it's a popular sport and I don't think the income that you have determines whether you are interested in football or not. I think the passion is still there.

Sir Stanley Matthews: Oh, I think it's fantastic, even today. You can't criticize the players or the game today. I still enjoy watching it. I envy the players today because I know very well that one or two will be nervous in the dressing-room and you're never sure you're going to win. It's a great game. I think I've been very fortunate. I'm very lucky to have been born in Stoke-on-Trent, where the people are wonderful, and, when you're a sportsman, you train outdoors, they pay you to keep fit, and you see the world for free and meet wonderful people. It's been marvellous for me.

List of Interviewees

Players, Managers and Coaches

Malcolm Allison
Eddie Baily
Alice Barlow
George Best
Noel Cantwell
Sir Bobby Charlton
Denis Compton
Pat Crerand
Joe Devlin
Ted Drake
Tom Finney
Neil Franklin
Gyula Grosics
Johnny Haynes
Jimmy Hill
Charles Hughes
Ian Hutchinson
Denis Law
Francis Lee
Nat Lofthouse
Zilwood March
Charlie Mitten
Jimmy O'Neill
George Petherbridge
George Robb
Bryan Robson
Jackie Sewell
Reg Smith

Viv Anderson
Tommy Baldwin
Dave Bassett
Billy Bremner
John Cartwright
Jack Charlton
Steve Coppell
Stan Cullis
Tommy Docherty
Billy Elliott
Trevor Ford
John Giles
Alan Hansen
Nándor Hidegkúti
Eric Houghton
Norman Hunter
TG Jones
Tommy Lawton
Gary Lineker
George Male
Peter Marinello
Alan Mullery
Peter Osgood
Ted Phillips
John Robertson
Ian St John
Len Shackleton
Tommy Smith

Jeff Astle
Alan Ball
Brendon Batson
Jenö Buzánszky
John Charles
Brian Clough
Ray Crawford
Ray Daniel
Derek Dougan
Mike Ferguson
Bill Foulkes
Ron Greenwood
George Hardwick
Alan Hill
Don Howe
Geoff Hurst
Bobby Keetch
Jimmy Leadbetter
Larry Lloyd
Wilf Mannion
Sir Stanley Matthews
Bill Nicholson
Syd Owen
Ferenc Puskás
Bobby Robson
Tom Saunders
Peter Shilton
Nobby Stiles

369

Gordon Taylor Graham Taylor Phil Thompson
Bert Trautmann Terry Venables Joe Walter
David Webb Sir Walter Winterbottom
Billy Wright Ian Wright

Supporters

Norah Ball David Barr Harry Beattie
Brian Belton Frank Bishop Peter Blake
Dale Campbell Ruth Chadwick Richard Chapman
Martin Cloak Dora Cobbin Harold Corns
Jack Curtis Barrie Fay John Fitt
Maud Gascoyne Bert Gregory John Haddon
Jim Hamill Percy Harwood Trevor Hicks
George Hudson Rose Jales Jim King
Geoff Kingscott Bernie Kingsley John Lee
Frank Leigh Alec Lodge George Mansell
Jack Mellor Audrey Nicholls Rita Petherbridge
Shirley Pilkington Harold Riley Mark Sambrook
Anne Savage Ken Sheehan Rev Peter Smith
Cyril Wilds Dr Sydney Woodhouse Percy Young

Officials, Administrators and Others

Sandor Barcs John Bromley Frank Butler
Philip Cassettari Ken Chaplin Nigel Clarke
David Dein Jack Ditchburn
Chief Inspector
  Bryan Drew Greg Dyke Alex Fynn
Barrie Gill Brian Glanville Michael Gliksten
Sir Philip Goodhart Edward Grayson Charles Harrold
Peter Hill-Wood Jon Holmes Denis Howell
Harry Jacobs Glyn Lynch Alvaro Maccioni
Brian Mears David Miller Sir Bert Millichip
Terry O'Neill Eddie Plumley Charles Reep
Vidal Sassoon Irving Scholar Ken Stanley
Peter Swales Georges Szepesi Greg Tesser
Clive Thomas Kenneth Wolstenholme Arthur Would